An Artists' Village

An Artists' Village

G.F. Watts and Mary Watts at Compton

Mark Bills

with contributions by
Hilary Underwood
Veronica Franklin Gould
Desna Greenhow
Perdita Hunt
Catherine Hilary

WATTS GALLERY
COMPTON ~ SURREY

Philip Wilson Publishers

First published in 2011 by Philip Wilson Publishers Ltd.
109 Drysdale Street
The Timber Yard
London N1 6ND
www.philip-wilson.co.uk

ISBN 978-0-85667-696-3

Distributed throughout the world (excluding North America) by:
I.B.Tauris & Co. Ltd., 6 Salem Road, London W2 4BU

Distributed in North America by:
Palgrave Macmillan, a division of St Martin's Press,
175 Fifth Avenue, New York NY 10010

Copyedited by Colin Grant
For PWP: David Hawkins

Designed by Webb & Webb Design
Printed in China by Everbest

All modern photographs are by Anne Purkiss, and all historical black-and-white photographs are from the Watts Gallery, unless stated otherwise.

Watts Gallery Registered Charity No. 313612

Cover photograph: The Watts Gallery, 1906

Endpapers: Early twentieth-century map showing the outlines of Limnerslease and Watts Gallery off Down Lane

Contents

6 Acknowledgements

7 Foreword
Simon Thurley Chief Executive, English Heritage

9 **'Two artists who are of just the same mind concerning their ideals of art':**
George Frederic Watts (1817–1904) and Mary Seton Watts (1849–1938)
Mark Bills

25 **Limnerslease: 'Only a great artist can make a house look like this'**
Mark Bills

47 **Mary Watts, the Home Arts and Industries Association and Compton**
Hilary Underwood

67 **Mary Watts and the Creation of Watts Chapel**
Veronica Franklin Gould

87 **The Symbolism of Watts Chapel**
Desna Greenhow

103 **Compton Pottery**
Hilary Underwood

121 **The Watts Picture Gallery**
Mark Bills

137 **The Future of Watts Village in Compton**
Perdita Hunt

157 Appendix: **Mary Watts's Ceiling Decoration at Limnerslease**
Catherine Hilary

162 Chronology
164 Bibliography
166 Index

Acknowledgements

Watts Gallery is deeply grateful to all its generous donors and benefactors including:

Heritage Lottery Fund
The Deborah Loeb Brice Foundation
The Isabel Goldsmith Patino Foundation
The George John & Sheilah Livanos Charitable Trust
Garfield Weston Foundation
Richard Ormond CBE
Esmée Fairbairn Foundation
Sir Siegmund Warburg's Voluntary Settlement
English Heritage
An Anonymous Donor
Christopher Forbes
J Paul Getty Jnr Charitable Trust
The Ingram Trust
The Foyle Foundation
Professor Rob Dickins CBE
The Linbury Trust
Art Fund
David Pike
Guildford Borough Council
The Robert Gavron Charitable Trust
Hamish Dewar Ltd
Peter Harrison Foundation
The John Ellerman Foundation
The Finnis Scott Foundation
Restoration Fund
The Wolfson Foundation
Surrey County Council
The Mercers' Company
KPMG Foundation
The Pilgrim Trust
Surrey Hills LEADER
Oxford Exhibition Services
The Billmeir Charitable Trust
The Monument Trust
The Wates Foundation
Man Group plc Charitable Trust
The Henry Moore Foundation
Rothschild Foundation
Michael Marks Charitable Trust
Foundation for Sport and the Arts
John Lewis

Watts Gallery is very grateful to the Paul Mellon Centre and to Hilary Bachelier-Carasco for their support of this publication.

Supported by The National Lottery® through the Heritage Lottery Fund

heritage lottery fund

ArtFund

Foreword

Until recently I knew Compton for its extraordinary parish church with its unique double-storey chancel and Norman balustrade. But, since being introduced to the home, studio, gallery and chapel of G.F. Watts, I have realized that Compton is important for another reason, too. Here in the Surrey countryside is a unique collection of buildings, now a memorial, to one of the most famous and successful men of his age: a painter who was a legend in his own time, a man who prefigured the modern cult of celebrity artists like Damien Hurst and Mark Quinn.

People have been rude about the achievements of G.F. Watts and his wife Mary Seton Watts at Compton. Ian Nairn writing in the Pevsner volume for Surrey called their house big and dull and the interior of the chapel 'one of the most soporific rooms in England' due to the 'intolerable torpor and weariness of the motifs'. This judgement would not be held by many today, for both the charm and interest of the house and studio and the originality of the Art Nouveau chapel are now widely recognized.

The fact is that Compton is an extraordinarily English place. It was created not by big-name London architects, but by little-known practitioners and amateurs, much of it overseen by Watts's wife. Over the years, since her death, nature has begun to reclaim it. Trees have grown up, moss has invaded Mrs Watts's terracotta gravestones and visitors now can feel they are discovering a place lost in nature. But at the same time the whole ensemble is profoundly un-English. I can't think of anywhere else in England with a mortuary chapel as at Compton. Such things do exist, but in countries like Russia. So in an English context not only is this building one of extraordinary charm and strong emotion, it is possibly unique. Built in Watts's lifetime, by his wife, the chapel must have been a constant reminder of his mortality. Yet the pharaohs, as they built their pyramids, and Tudor noblemen, as they had their alabaster effigies carved, looked on at their final resting place with interest and perhaps even a little expectation. Perhaps this memento mori was likewise admired by the great man. Whatever he thought of it, this 'catafalque', built as the final resting place of a Victorian celebrity, takes its place in the history of the architecture of the afterlife.

The Watts Gallery Trust that now cares for the gallery has preserved this unique complex largely for its original purpose. So these are no dry monuments. The gallery is a living place with a living programme devoted to the memory of Watts, yes, but also to preserving, deep in the Surrey countryside, a slice of English eccentricity for the enjoyment of future generations.

Simon Thurley
Chief Executive, English Heritage

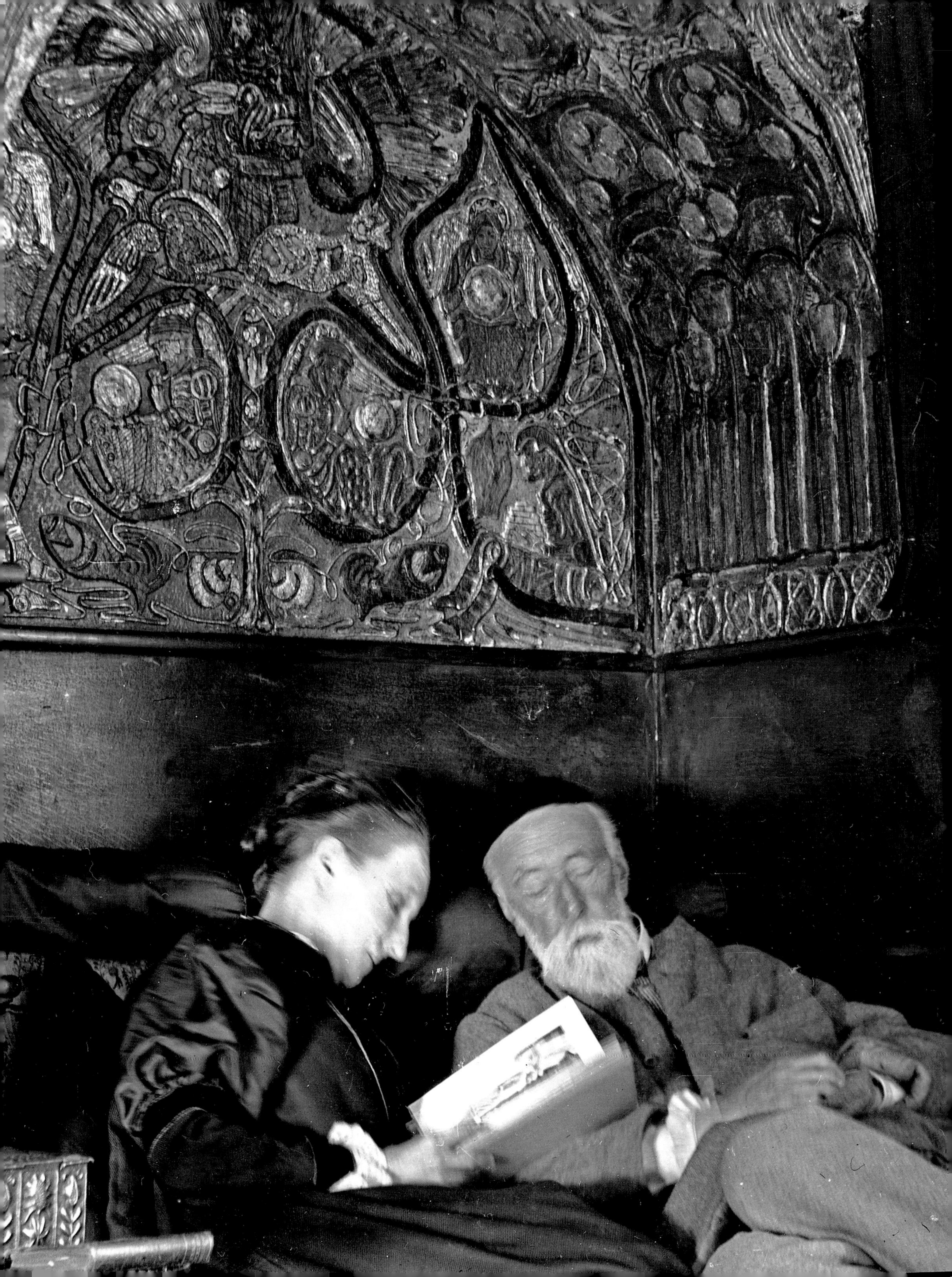

'Two artists who are of just the same mind concerning their ideals of art':[1] George Frederic Watts (1817–1904) and Mary Seton Watts (1849–1938)

Mark Bills

When George and Mary Watts built Limnerslease, their Surrey home, between 1890 and 1891, they created not only an autumn and winter retreat, where they could escape the weather and the 'strife of tongues' of their London home, but also an Arts and Crafts project that was to transform the village of Compton.[2] Surrey gave both George and Mary a new lease of life, freedom for George to work in peace and freedom for Mary to develop her art beyond the walls of a gallery and create, together with her husband, a home and centre for arts and crafts. What began as a retreat and half-yearly studio became in the first years of the twentieth century a more definite base that included the Watts Gallery for the permanent display of Watts's paintings, the Compton Pottery with accompanying accommodation for potters in the gallery and village, and the extraordinary cemetery chapel, as well as the Wattses' great house and home, Limnerslease, designed by Sir Ernest George (1839–1922).

Undoubtedly, the Compton project was always regarded as a partnership of 'like minds', but it was also widely considered one of unequal prestige and talents. The developments in Compton clearly followed an Arts and Crafts ethos, but they were also created as a living memorial to George Frederic Watts, whom many considered the age's greatest painter. Indeed, for the first decade after G.F. Watts's death in 1904 it was a much visited place, where everything was viewed within the great man's shadow. 'And now let us contemplate the beauty of this village that is immortalised as the country home of our poet-painter',[3] wrote a visiting journalist in an article entitled, 'The Shrine of George Frederick [*sic*] Watts, RA'. Subsequently, Mary's role was downplayed not only because of the shadow cast by George but also because of her own very self-conscious role as devoted acolyte and her self-effacing attitude: 'Some future day,' a journalist wrote after visiting Limnerslease, 'I hope to be able to tell you more about the part which Mrs. Watts is taking in it (she will not allow me, for all my asking, to do so now).'[4] One thing that is clear about the remarkably rich legacy that the Wattses left in Compton is that it is indelibly imbued with the spirit of the two very distinct individuals who created it. To understand this idiosyncratic and exceptional heritage requires knowing something of its creators and the complex partnership they forged through the development of Compton.

G.F. WATTS

By the 1880s George Frederic Watts had attained unprecedented renown as an artist. In this decade, when he was in his sixties and early seventies, the very substantial achievements of his lifetime were being celebrated through a series of retrospective shows beginning with an exhibition at the Grosvenor Gallery between 1881 and

Opposite: George and Mary Watts reading in the niche in the Red Room at Limnerslease, c.1894–95

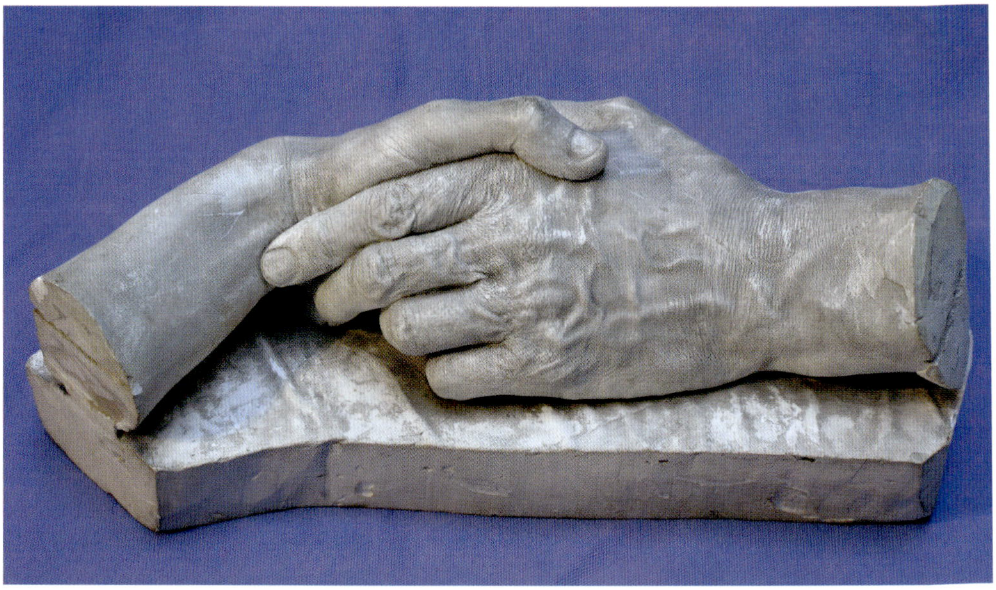

Plaster cast of the left hands of Mary and G.F. Watts, 1889, Watts Gallery

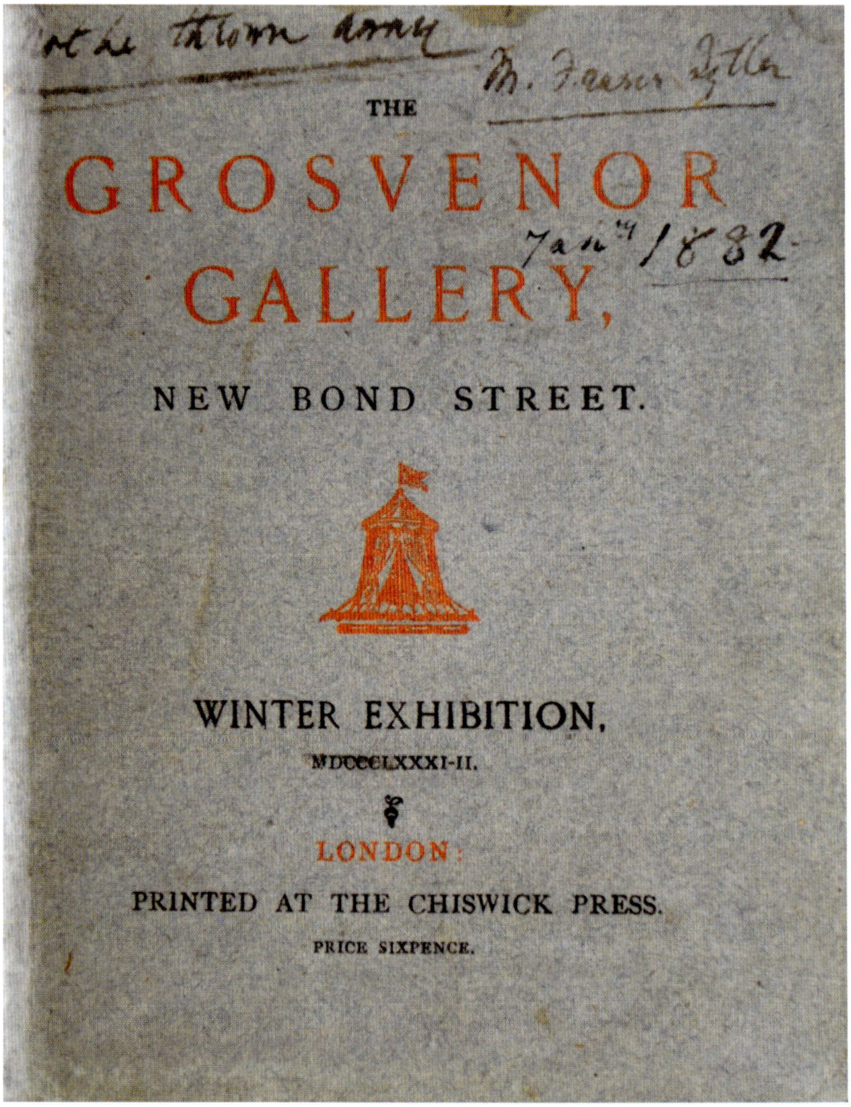

M. Fraser Tytler

THE

GROSVENOR

Jan'y 1882

GALLERY,

NEW BOND STREET.

WINTER EXHIBITION.

MDCCCLXXXI-II.

LONDON:

PRINTED AT THE CHISWICK PRESS.

PRICE SIXPENCE.

Cover of the Grosvenor Gallery Winter Exhibition catalogue, 1881, Watts Gallery Archive

1882 and then a solo exhibition at the Metropolitan Museum of Art, New York, in 1885. He was also honoured with a Doctor of Laws (LLD) from Cambridge and a Doctor of Civil Law (DCL) from Oxford, and he often wore the robes in later life. Importantly, he was financially secure and his reputation was such that he was able to explore grand themes in his allegorical paintings or, as he described them, 'poems painted on canvas'. In the early 1880s Oscar Wilde sent a copy of his own poem, 'Ave Imperatrix', to Watts, 'whose pictures are great poems'.[5]

Watts held a unique position where he was critically respected, admired by his fellow artists and popularly adored, allowing him the platform to explore his idea of a poet-painter who could preach eternal truths and provoke social reform. During this period he painted some of his most memorable and iconic images, including *Hope* (*c.*1885–86; private collection), which inspired and continues to inspire artists and thinkers internationally,[6] and *Mammon* (*c.*1885; Tate), his great protest against the destructive motivating force of greed. A passage from a book on Watts by Hugh Macmillan, written at the twilight of the artist's life, gives an indication of the reverence with which these paintings were treated:

> All who visit the Tate Gallery know the marvellous series of allegorical paintings, by which as a prophet and teacher of eternal truth, he has left his mark on the minds and hearts of the people of these realms. When you enter the gallery, and find yourself gazing upon these masterpieces, the great sordid world of trade and commerce is shut out, and you feel yourself in a sanctuary. You are at once ushered into a visionary world, in which the hard facts of experience are transfigured into noble imaginings, and life and death and love glorified with a radiancy of light and colour which seem to belong to a heavenly sphere.[7]

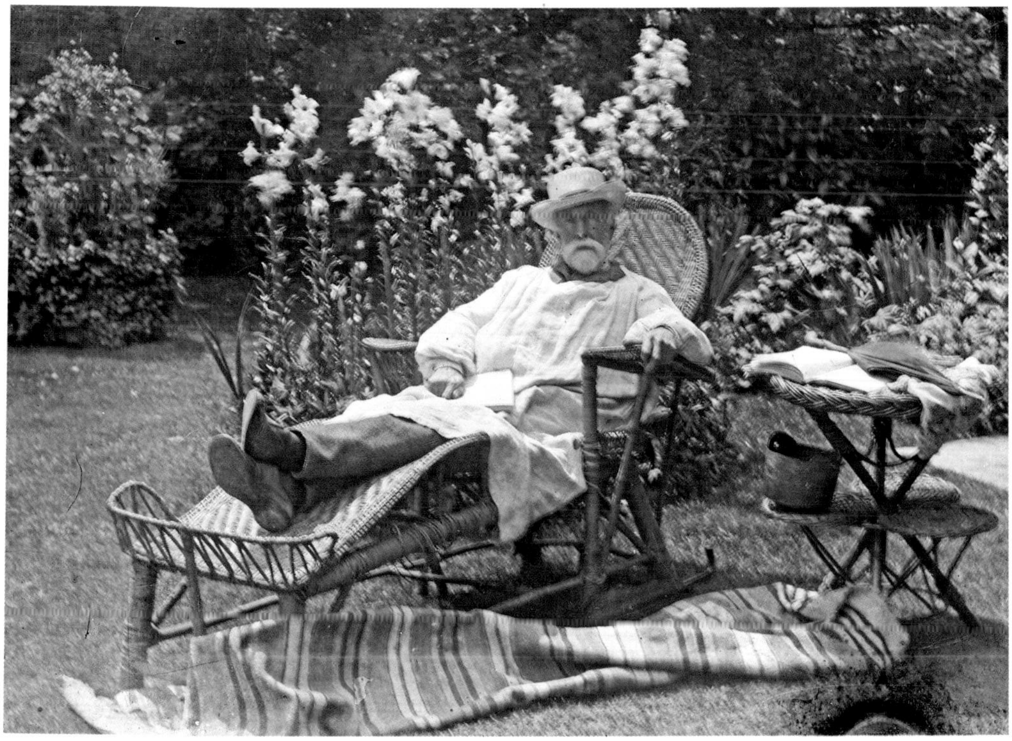

G.F. Watts in the garden at Little Holland House, c.*1890s*

Watts was always conscious of his wider public and sought for his paintings to reach every level of society. This he did through the mass reproduction of his work and through building art galleries, as well as supporting the construction of those that showed his work.[8] He built a gallery extension onto his studio home at Little Holland House in Kensington and opened it to the public from 2pm to 6pm every weekend. He promoted and encouraged the view that he was a servant of the nation and that his works should be in the public realm for all time. He was a very public figure in the 1880s, a distinguished artist in his sixties, and he surprised many in 1886 when he made the decision to marry a second time. He had married the actress Ellen Terry (1847–1928) in February 1864, but the union was short-lived and they were separated soon afterwards. The headstrong teenage muse and the retiring artist in his mid-forties were an incompatible pair. His second marriage to Mary Fraser Tytler was to be very different.

MARY FRASER TYTLER

In the 1880s Mary was in her thirties, a painter and sculptor of little renown who worshipped the art of G.F. Watts. She was born in India in 1849, the daughter of Charles Edward Fraser Tytler, a civil servant there, and Ethelreda (née St Barbe). Before she reached the age of two her parents brought her back to the family

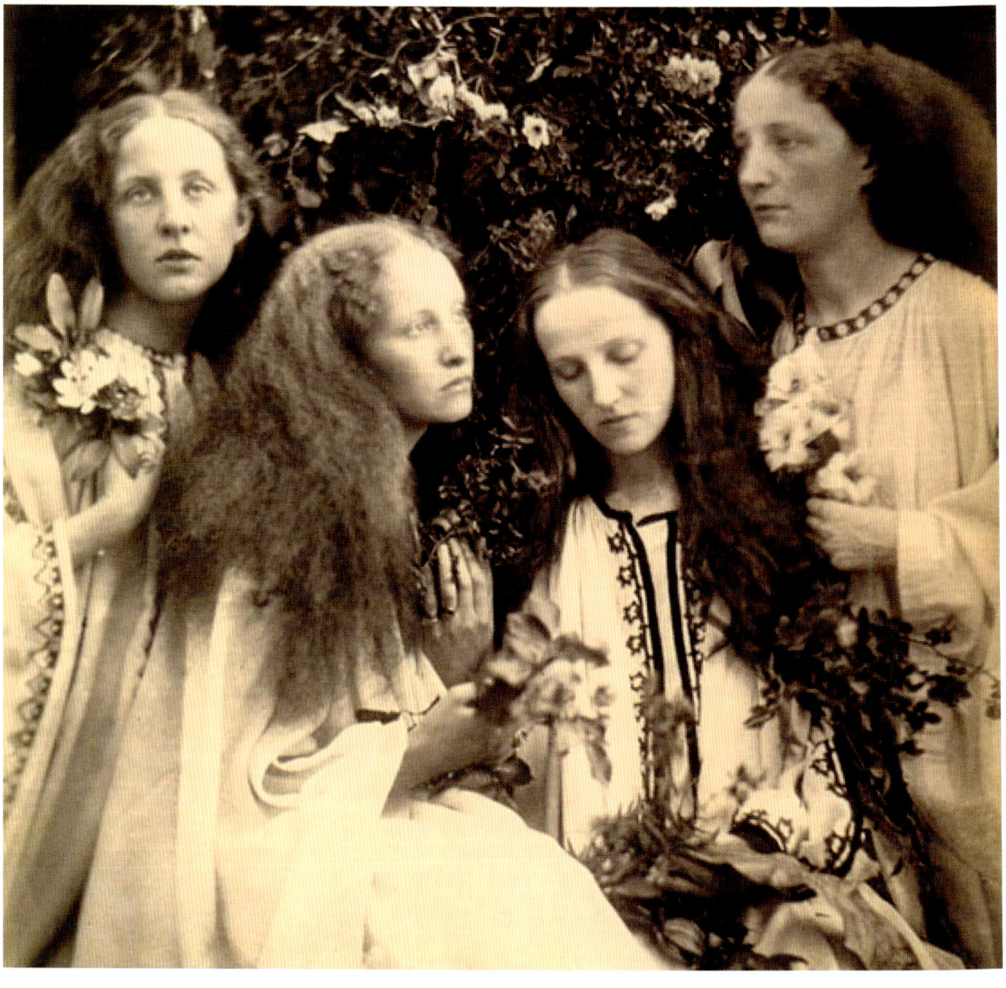

Julia Margaret Cameron, The Rosebud Garden of Girls *(Eleanor, Christina, Mary and Ethel Fraser Tytler), June 1868, albumen print, 35 x 29.2 cm, National Media Museum, Bradford/SSPL*

seat at Aldourie, her grandparents' estate in Inverness-shire. When her father retired, her family moved close by to Sanquhar, Forres, in 1861. Visits to the Isle of Wight in the late 1860s are evident from both Mary's photographic album and her appearance with her sisters in photographs by Julia Margaret Cameron in 1868, indicating a familiarity with the circles with which Watts had long been involved.[9] Studying art briefly in Europe, Mary returned to Britain and entered the South Kensington Art Training Schools in 1870 and the Slade School of Art in 1872. She also trained during this period with the French sculptor Aimé-Jules Dalou (1838–1902), an exile from France due to his involvement with the Paris Commune of 1871.[10] His fascination with images of motherhood worked in terracotta had a strong influence on Mary, as can be seen in her *Mother and Child* (1873–79; Watts Gallery). In 1884 Mary took her skills in clay modelling to the poor of London by holding classes for bootblacks, an undertaking that perhaps reflected Dalou's beliefs as well as the philanthropic art initiatives that Watts supported.[11]

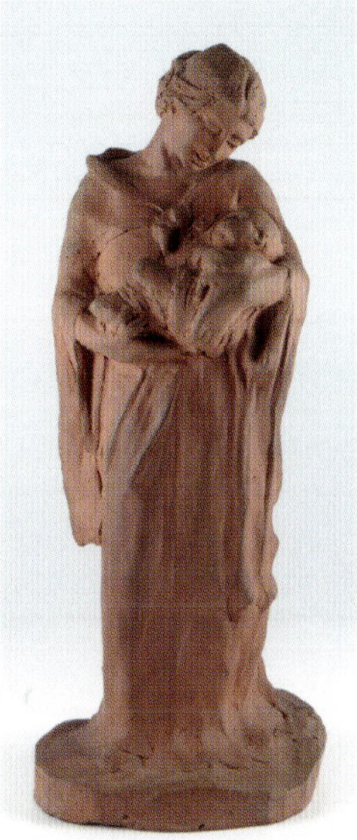

Mary Seton Watts, Mother and Child, *c.1873–79, terracotta, 31 x 12.5 x 12 cm, Watts Gallery*

Mary revered Watts. Her own painting at this time, which was predominantly portraiture, shows the influence of the eminent artist, although her work is a little stiff, fairly conventional and unreflective of the imaginative scope that she was to display at Compton. She looked towards Watts for her development as an artist, approaching him with an unusual awe that was shown in her recollection of her first visit to Little Holland House:

> It was therefore not till 1870 that I first went under its thatched porch, and waited in the room of the blue ceiling till summoned to the studio, to pass with a beating heart through a red baize-covered door. There we read with some feeling of awe a large label – 'I must beg not to be disturbed till after two o'clock' … the studio door opened, and Signor came forward to meet us … In 1870 the beard was only slightly touched with grey, his hair quite brown, very fine in quality, and brushed back from the forehead … I remember the painter much more distinctly than his work; but he nevertheless so distinctly suggested to me the days of chivalry that I believe I should not have been surprised if, on another visit, I had found him all clad in shining armour.[12]

The courtship of George and Mary was gradual and prolonged, punctuated by visits and a prolific correspondence. In her 'Commonplace Book' Mary records the years before her marriage to Watts, writing with a candid pen that reveals both her religious devotion and her admiration of the ageing artist.[13] Her deeply religious nature is often overlooked, but it is evident in most of what she wrote, the art she created and the way she lived her life. On 23 July 1886 she recorded, 'He said "I want you"', and on Sunday 25 July she wrote of her joy at Watts's proposal: 'There are no words for a hour like this – only tears of joy at the fat of God – God & the noblest heart, all mine, all mine – What can I write of this wonderful day?' On 20 November 1886 George Frederic Watts married Mary Seton Fraser Tytler in Epsom, Surrey. 'I give the report with all reserve', wrote *The World* magazine, 'that Mr G F Watts R.A., has once again ventured into matrimony, his bride being a lady of good Scottish family, who has for some time been his pupil.'[14]

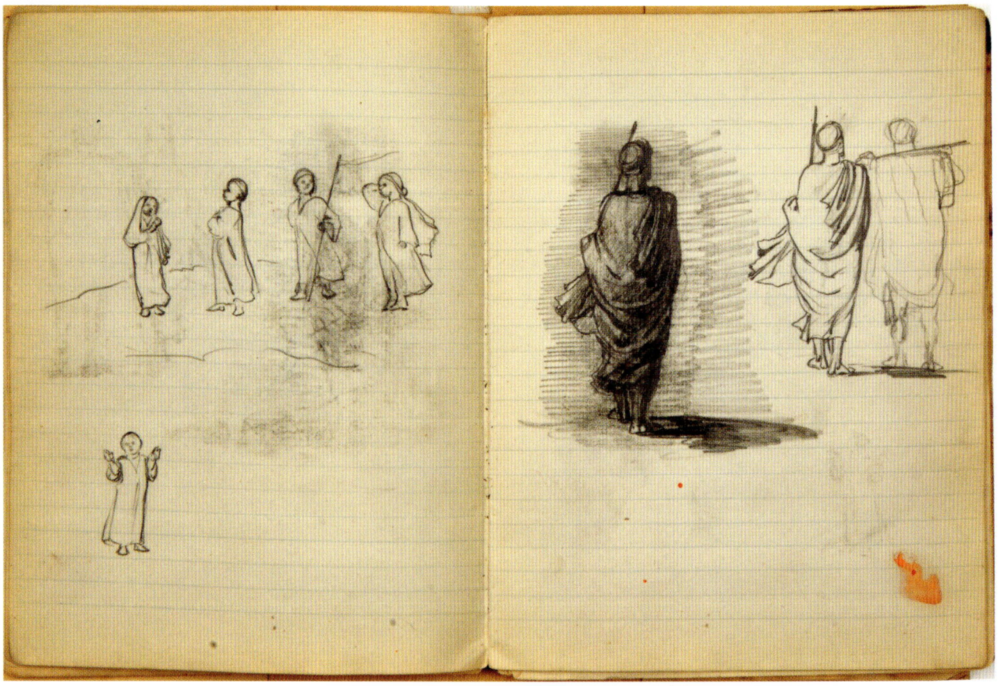

Mary Seton Watts, page of sketches in honeymoon sketchbook, c.*1887, Watts Gallery Archive*

MARRIED LIFE

Married life began with an extended honeymoon between 1886 and 1887 that took them to Egypt, Constantinople, Athens and Messina. Many of Watts's great landscapes, including *A Sea Ghost* (1887; Watts Gallery), were inspired by the visit, and similarly Mary was stimulated by much of what she saw, which she recorded in sketches and notebooks that would later be used in creating her ceilings at Limnerslease and Watts Chapel.[15]

Returning from honeymoon to live with the celebrated artist in the house that he had commissioned at the centre of an artistic community in Kensington must have been daunting for the new wife. Mary's brother had written to her just before she married, commenting on the very public role of being the wife of G.F. Watts: 'Let us know the day, and Ted and I will be there to give you to the Nation.'[16] About five years earlier a public gallery had been added to the house in keeping with Watts's philosophy of his paintings being accessible to a wide audience. Through the creation of his own public gallery he at once had the pulpit for his 'sermons in paint' as well as the possibility of a permanent home secured for posterity.[17] Mary recalled eating in part of the gallery:

> Breakfast was in a room we called the dining-room, but it was in fact the ante-room to the gallery, and … it was open to the public on Saturday and Sunday afternoons. And so we found ourselves breakfasting with some twenty pictures around us, and when I wanted to boast, I could point to my 'dado of Watts portraits'.[18]

Mary was in awe of Watts, overwhelmed by his reputation, and feared that her work would be totally consumed by his influence: 'Instead of my work, I focus [on] him. It will take me a little while yet to get over being under the shadow of his great

G.F. Watts, A Sea Ghost, *1887, oil on canvas, 45.7 x 71.1 cm, Watts Gallery*

work.'[19] Being his wife and living in what was already a monument to the great man surely compounded such a concern. Her description of their new life together, although as devoted and admiring as ever, hints at ennui in her subservient role:

> The next morning the sun rose clear of cloud behind Sir Frederic Leighton's chimneys, and as early as he could, Signor went over there to find his friend. And now the peaceful life in art began for me. From my windows in 'Paradise Row' when I awoke at dawn, I looked out upon the fresh green of the trees of the neighbouring gardens that met round our own, where song-birds and wood-pigeons were common, and the red and white hawthorns were full of flower … we were there till seven; then the real toilet for the day followed, and the real breakfast at eight … If he was well, and the day fine, the working hours were stretched sometimes to sixteen.
>
> With certain friends it had long been arranged with him that their visits should be at particular hours. During many years … Sir Frederic was in Signor's studio by nine o'clock. He never failed unless he was ill, and in that case the note of explanation never failed to come. The two friends were generally alone together, but sometimes Signor sent for me, and then I could enjoy their brisk interchange of thought.[20]

Watts was central to Mary's life, and she devoted so much of her own energies to him, taking on a role that was formed in part by his giant reputation, and in part by her gender, her religion and her belief in service and in the power of art. Mary was, as Wilfrid Blunt (1901–87) put it,

> his companion, his nurse, his slave; his 'guide, philosopher and friend'; his watchdog, and finally, by her biography of him, his advocate and publicity

> agent. She worshipped him blindly. She gave him a new lease of life, and the best years of her own to establishing him as a national monument.[21]

If life had continued solely at Little Holland House, Mary's own art may never have developed to the extent that it did. The troublesome neighbour in the form of Mrs Russell (Emilie) Barrington (1841–1933)[22] and the stifling effect of Little Holland House upon her own art must have stimulated Mary to want to look for another place to live with Watts. Watts himself was also feeling the increasing need to escape the often appalling winter weather of the metropolis, which brought with it poor light and illness. As Watts's first biographer Julia Cartwright was later to write, 'when the days begin to draw in, and the first autumn fogs descend on the London streets, he escapes to the country in his turn, and seeks the purer air and clearer skies of Surrey'.[23] The retreat became much more than that: it was a place where their 'same mind concerning their ideals of art' could be more fully explored.

For Mary a new home brought a new form of art. After the marriage she had effectively stopped her painting, which she must have felt was a pale shadow of what Watts was producing, both imaginatively and technically. Her more natural ability as a clay modeller and her belief in the Arts and Crafts ethos and the importance of the decorative arts led her to an art form where she felt supremely confident and could excel on the national stage.

A PARTNERSHIP

The position of Mary as acolyte and servant to the genius of Watts was constant, but they both shared wider ideals that art could reach all and transform the lives that it touched. 'I can testify after the experience of some years', Watts wrote, 'to the humanizing and even encouraging effects works of art can have upon those whose lives are a round of dulnesses, lacking the ordinary enjoyment known to the more fortunate.'[24] Art was seen as having a role akin to religion, and with an evangelical zeal its priests, the Wattses, spread the word. The move to Compton allowed this philosophy to develop in a rural location rather than the urban metropolis of London. The vision owed much to John Ruskin (1819–1900), to medievalism and to the Arts and Crafts movement, and as a whole it was a vision that they both shared. Art was at its centre, but the belief in the handmade and that beauty could positively affect lives and should be available to all was also fundamental to the wider aestheticism. Watts wrote:

> Your beautiful things are still only for the rich. Is it asking you too much to give this cheer to the cottage, where it is of really far greater importance? Cannot inexpensive things also be of noble design, the beauty of utility, solidity, and simplicity in the commonest cottage furniture, in pots and pans and crockery?[25]

The ennobling effects of art and beauty had been central to Watts's philosophy, but his support of the wider aesthetic mission was greatly influenced by Mary. She had been a committee member of the Home Arts and Industries Association

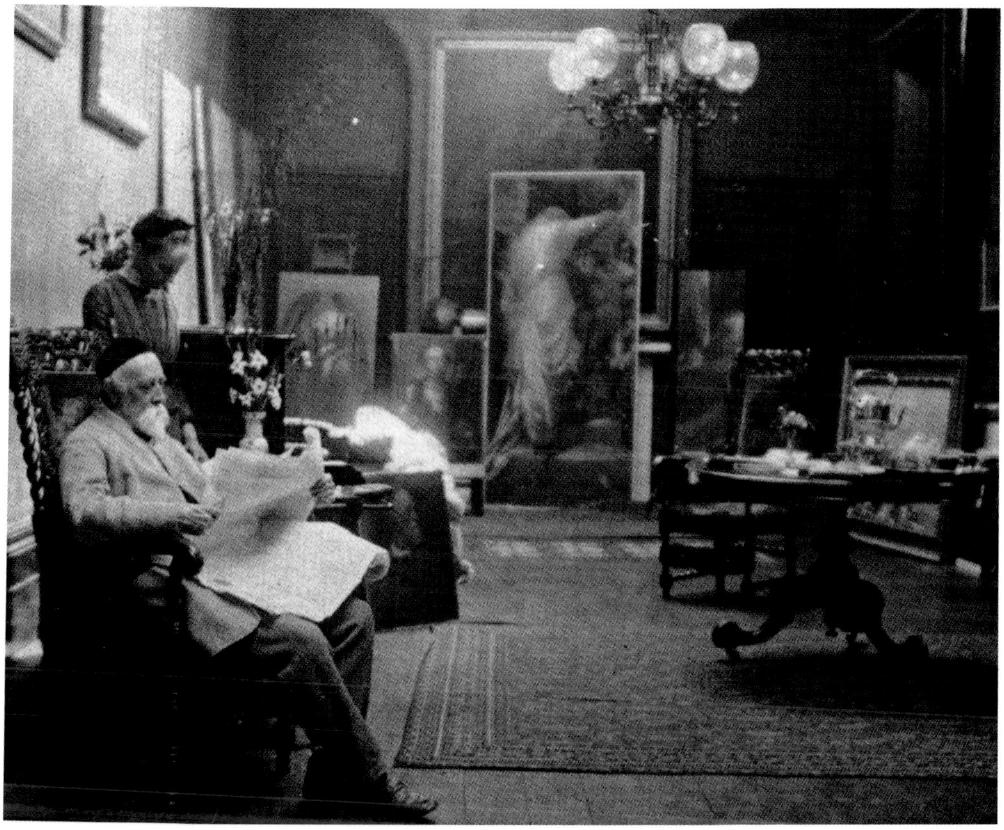

George and Mary Watts at Little Holland House, c.1890

and had given modelling classes before she married Watts. Mary's enthusiastic involvement in the Home Arts and Industries was wholly supported by Watts in both words and actions. He was the biggest financial supporter of the movement and, on the invitation of his fellow artist Briton Riviere, he gave a paper for the National Association for the Advancement of Art and its Application to Industry on 2 October 1889. Watts began:

> It is written that 'Man shall not live by bread alone,' and these words are among the great truths whose widest significance is commonly unperceived ... In addressing the lovers of art, I would beg them to recognise the immense and valuable help they can give by the encouragement of all such work as tends to teach our working classes to love and honour it. In the activity of the Home Arts Association, the Handicrafts Guilds, and our now annual Arts and Crafts Exhibition in London, there is ample scope for their aid in a direction of most vital importance, revivifying the natural artistic instincts of the British people.[26]

This paper was presented just before the Wattses moved to Surrey to spend the winter with their friends Mr and Mrs Andrew Hichens at Monkshatch, Compton. Shortly afterwards Limnerslease was built, and as Shelagh Wilson rightly asserts, 'this vision was realized under Mary's controlling eye at Compton'.[27] To the world at large G.F. Watts was the driving force, the genius at the centre, yet in an article on the Compton Pottery Mrs Steuart Erskine wrote:

> The part Mr Watts plays in this industrious hive of bees, working all day as it were at his feet and under the shadow of his studio, is rather that of an indefinable personal influence; he is the inspirer, the head and centre of the little band ... but he leaves all the practical work of overseeing and designing – and it is pretty hard work, too, though undertaken *con amore* – to his gifted wife.[28]

Mary's greatest achievement as an artist is undoubtedly the cemetery chapel in Compton. As self-effacing as ever, she writes of its construction in 1898 in her biography of Watts:

> A new interest had grown up for us both in the last two years, the building of a chapel for the new village burial-ground, his gift to Compton. He did not design it, but suggested that, if we proposed to hold a class, the people of Compton might like to come to it and be taught to make simple patterns to decorate the walls; so that by this means a special and personal interest in the new graveyard would be acquired by the workers.[29]

This is of course the philosophy, yet Mary did not take such a retiring and facilitating role as she suggests and Watts was always careful to point out that the work was that of his wife. This extraordinary building could not have been achieved without her skill and vision. The modelling and rich symbolism of the decoration are carefully and artfully contrasted, rather than being the 'simple patterns' made by all that she suggests. She also asserts her artistic independence from Watts in both the predominant Christian message and the use of traditional symbolism in the chapel.

It was not until 1903 that an art gallery was built at Compton, just before Watts's death in 1904. The Watts Gallery was the spiritual heart of the complex, where the 'high art' of Signor could be seen by all. The delay in its inclusion at Compton was due to the peripatetic nature of the Wattses' lifestyle, with the gallery at Little Holland House continuing until 1903. The closure of the latter (the paintings were moved in September 1903) marked a more permanent move to Compton in the final months of Watts's life: it completed the whole. The wings of the gallery, which were built as accommodation for apprentice potters, were known as the 'Hostel'. In many ways the Watts Gallery itself is a symbol and metaphor for Mary and Signor's partnership. At its centre the art and genius of G.F. Watts are permanently displayed, while beyond this the wings flank and support the building. The Arts and Crafts vision of Mary realizes and establishes in perpetuity the artistic vision of Signor at the same time as providing a practical manifestation of her philosophy.

THE DEATH OF WATTS

The death of Watts in 1904 effectively ended any new developments in Compton, although the Watts Gallery and the pottery continued to be developed throughout the remaining thirty-four years of Mary's life. The Watts Gallery was expanded further with extra galleries added, and the Compton Pottery thrived. Mary embraced the role of G.F. Watts's main interpreter, the guardian

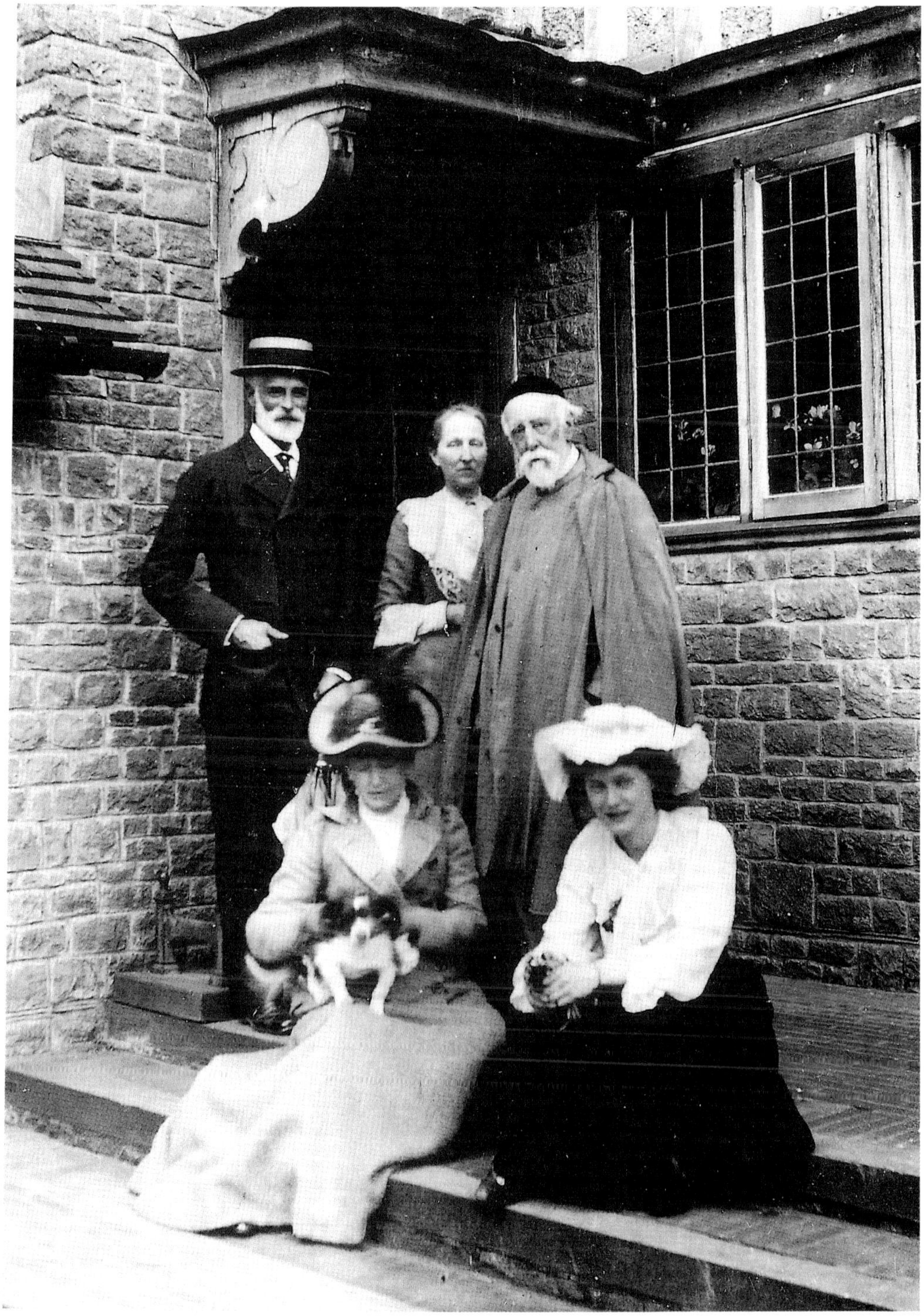

Andrew and May Hichens (left) and the Wattses (including Lilian) on the steps at the front door of Limnerslease, c.*1899*

and advocate of his legacy, and this has had both a positive and negative aspect. According to Wilfrid Blunt, Curator of Watts Gallery between 1959 and 1985, Mary 'was, on occasions not above a deliberate distortion of the truth'.[30] The reverential and adoring portrait of Watts in her biography is at times difficult to read seriously and yet no scholar of Watts is able to get to Watts without entering through the portal of Mary: her catalogue of his paintings and meticulous compiling of his archive ensure this.[31] When Mary died in 1938, Watts's

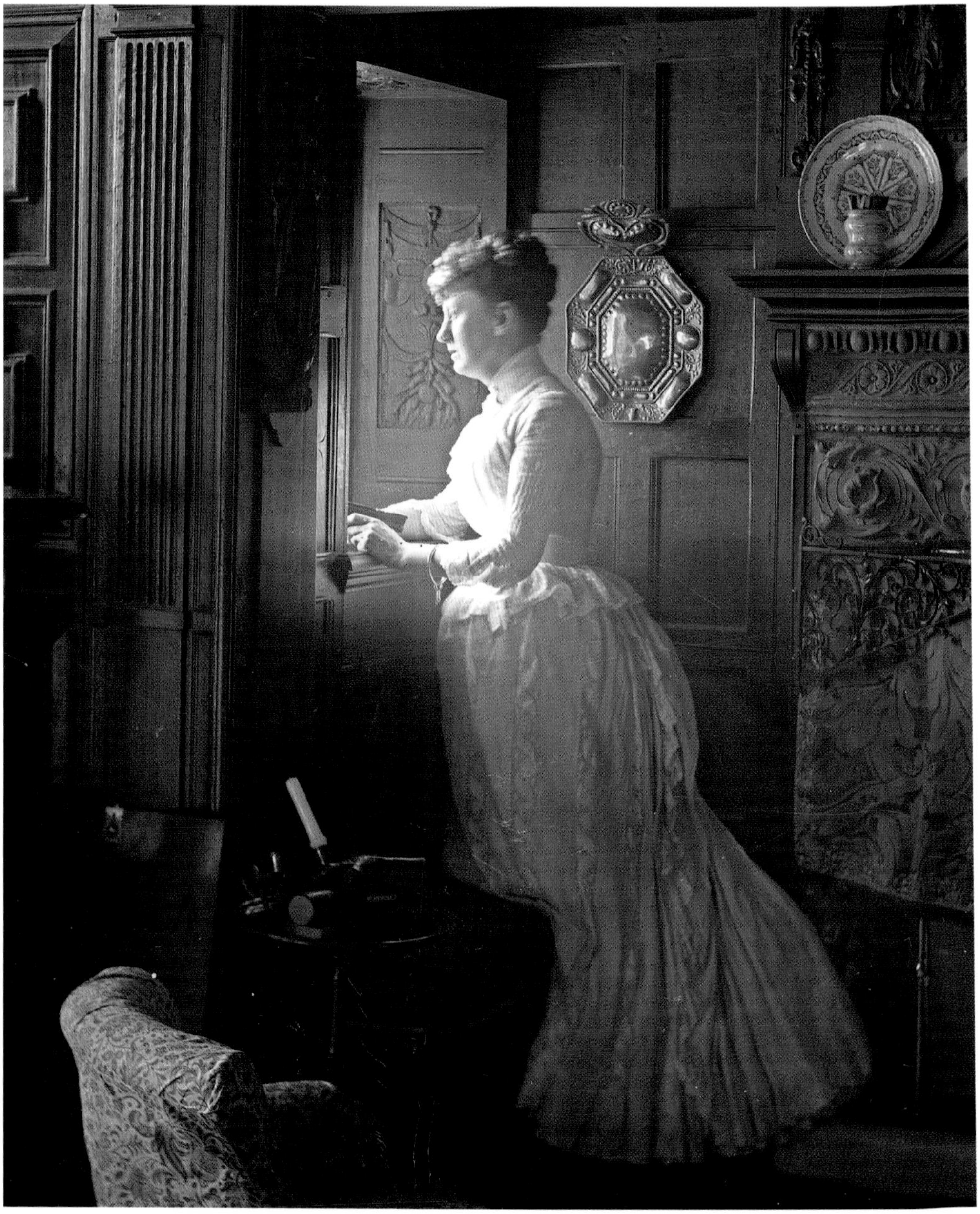

May Hichens in the music room of Monkshatch, c.1890s

reputation was probably at the lowest it had ever been, as was reflected in the derisory valuations given for the contents of Limnerslease (see p.132). It is due to Mary that so much material is still available to researchers today and that so much of his legacy has survived. She doggedly fought for him in an increasingly hostile and unsympathetic climate, ensuring that the permanent room for his work at the Tate remained and that the Watts Gallery was kept as a thriving institution where the vision remained constant. It is telling that in the year of her death the Watts room at the Tate was disassembled and the Watts Gallery was 'modernized' on a shoestring.

The achievement of Compton was undoubtedly one of a partnership, and although this was rich and complex, it is worth finally considering the view that they wished the world to have of their Surrey home:

To share everything with the world was the great master's unceasing intention, to give the best and highest message possible, of aspiration, of hope and love and beauty, to hold up sin and vice and corruption in their true and awful reality to be shunned, and fought against, and conquered. Here, in his country surroundings, might we see him, nearing the end of his earthly pilgrimage, serene in the peace of an intensely happy home, the loveliness of budding flower and tree carrying year by year its message of the Resurrection, in gentle and kind relationship with all his neighbours.[32]

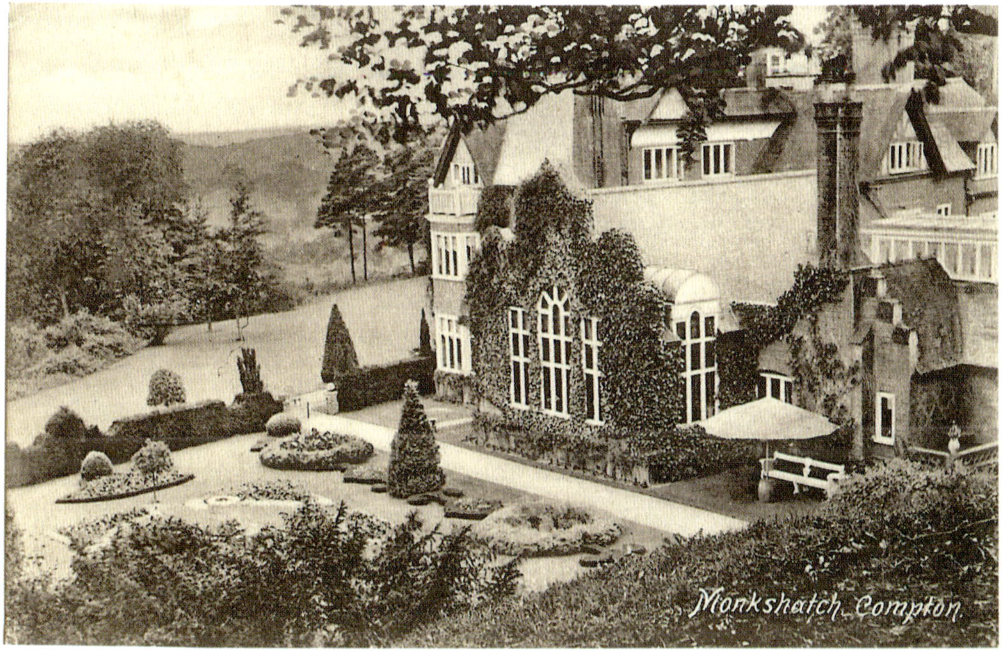

Historic postcard of Monkshatch, c.1900

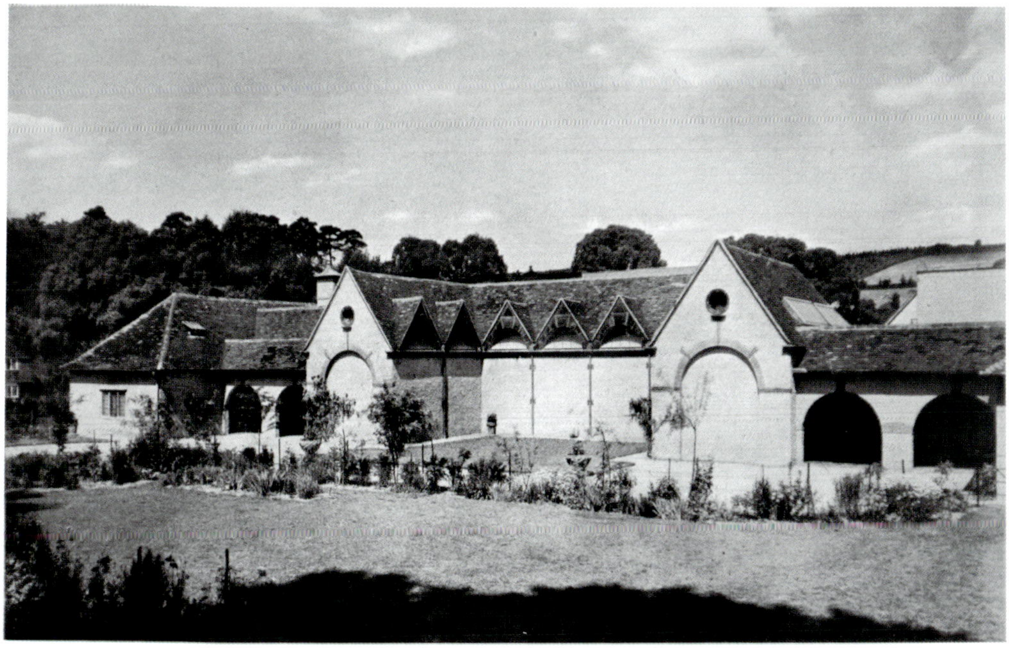

The Watts Gallery, 1906

NOTES

1 Friederichs 1895, p.74.

2 'A modest house, far removed from the strife of tongues, among the fields and woods of Surrey', Revd H.R. Gamble sermon on G.F. Watts, quoted in Haking 1906, p.10.

3 Haking 1906, p.8.

4 Friederichs 1895, p.78.

5 'Dear Mr Watts
Will you accept from me a copy of a poem I have published on England ['Ave Imperatrix'], as a very poor mark of homage to one whose pictures are great poems.
Very truly yours Oscar Wilde'
Oscar Wilde, letter to G.F. Watts, undated, *c.*1881, from Watts Papers (formerly Watts Gallery), unpublished microfiche copies at the National Portrait Gallery (and some originals), Watts Gallery and Tate.

6 As an image, *Hope* has travelled the world. It has inspired, among others, Japanese and Chinese poets, become a stamp for Jordan and most recently made a profound impact on Barack Obama, the President of the United States.

7 Hugh Macmillan, *The Life and Works of George Frederick Watts, RA*, London 1903, pp.41–42.

8 Watts was involved with the creation of the Whitechapel Art Gallery and the South London Gallery, which were built in poor and deprived areas of London in a mission to take art to the people.

9 Julia Margaret Cameron (1815–79), *Rosebud Garden of Girls*, 1868, two photographs that depict Mary and her sisters.

10 Dalou was well received in London and received commissions from the British aristocracy, which he produced alongside his depictions of modern life. See *Dalou in England*, exh. cat., Yale Center for British Art, New Haven, and Henry Moore Institute, Leeds, 2009.

11 See Franklin Gould 1998.

12 Watts 1912, vol.I, pp.288–89.

13 M.S. Watts, 'Commonplace Book', Watts Gallery Archive.

14 Atlas, *The World*, 24 November 1886, reported in Latest London News, *Aberdeen Weekly Journal*, 24 November 1886, issue 9919.

15 M.S. Watts, Notebook, Watts Gallery Archive.

16 Watts 1912, vol.II, p.63.

17 'To the picture gallery at Little Holland House the public are admitted on Saturdays and Sundays, from two till six – a privilege largely taken advantage of by all sorts and conditions of people. It should be remembered that some fine examples of Mr Watts' paintings can here be carefully and quietly studied by the aid of descriptions prepared by the artist.' (Bateman 1901, p.15.) See Barbara Bryant, *Little Holland House and its Gallery*, Studies in the Art of G.F. Watts No.3, Compton 2010.

18 Watts 1912, vol.II, p.84.

19 MSW Diaries, 7 September 1887.

20 Watts 1912, vol.II, pp.83, 84, 85, 96, 97.

21 Blunt 1975, p.xviii.

22 Ronald Chapman, the son of the Wattses' adopted daughter Lilian Mackinosh, writes at length of Mrs Barrington's friendship with Watts and her difficult relationship with Mary in Chapman 1945.

23 Cartwright 1896, p.29.

24 G.F. Watts, letter to *The Times*, 13 April 1897, published 16 April 1897, p.6.

25 G.F. Watts, a paper reprinted from the Transactions of the National Association for the Advancement of Art and its Application to Industry, Edinburgh Meeting, 1889, published in Watts 1912, vol.III, p.266.

26 Watts 1912, vol.III, pp.268–69.
27 Wilson 2004, p.178.
28 Erskine *c.*1901, p.158.
29 Watts 1912, vol.II, p.205.
30 Blunt 1975, p.xviii.
31 Watts *c.*1910.
32 Haking 1906, p.5.

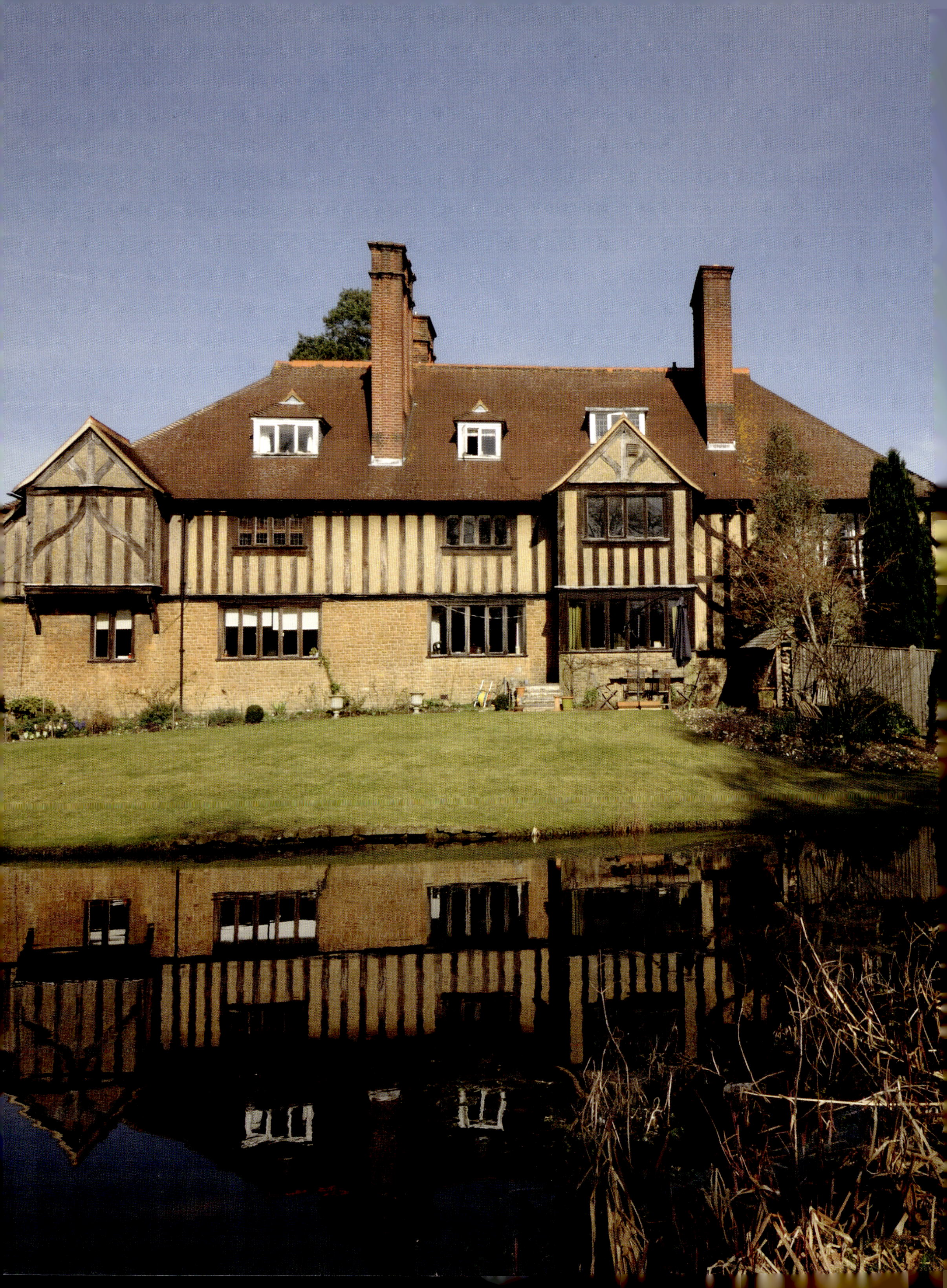

Limnerslease: 'Only a great artist can make a house look like this'[1]

Mark Bills

The creation of Limnerslease grew out of the Wattses' prolonged visit to their friends Andrew (1833–1906) and May (1855–1931) Hichens in Compton in the winter of 1889. Watts had known May Hichens (née Prinsep) since she was a girl at Little Holland House and their strong friendship continued after her marriage to Andrew Hichens. Mary later recalled:

> The only visits Signor was ever induced to pay during these years were to Mr. and Mrs. Andrew Hichens; and when with them for a day or two this autumn it occurred to them to propose that we should try how the climate in Surrey would suit him for the winter, earnestly begging us to make use of their beautiful home during their absence in London … The house, standing high, yet sheltered from the north and east, was a most tempting solution of the question of winter quarters, so anxiously considered by me and his doctor, who rather inclined to Brighton, while Sir Frederic Leighton had urged Italy.[2]

The search for a winter retreat had been motivated in part by Watts's health and the London weather, but also by the need for Mary to find a new home where she was able to play a more significant role. Little Holland House was a grand home, studio, gallery and meeting place at the heart of an artist's community, but it was entirely G.F. Watts and was far from private. The neighbour and admirer of Watts, Mrs Barrington, was an increasing difficulty after the marriage, and according to the son of Watts's adopted daughter, 'Mrs Barrington had met Mary in the hall of 6 Melbury Road [Little Holland House]' just before their honeymoon 'and told her that Watts would die on the voyage'.[3]

The Hichenses' house in Compton was Monkshatch and the Wattses moved there on 21 November 1889, remaining until early April the following year.[4] Monkshatch was a country house on a grand scale, with fourteen bedrooms – a suitable size for the Wattses to stay and work there. During a long, five-month visit Watts of course needed to be able to paint and to do so he required a studio of reasonable scale and rooms for he and Mary to make their own. Mary described their stay:

> 'I always told you I built that studio for you,' Andrew said, delighting in seeing the canvases about in the favourite sitting-room of the house, oak-panelled and lofty, with a fine organ and piano, thus devoted to both arts, and generally called the studio … Sometimes there was music, or they beguiled Signor to play billiards, for which he had a keen eye and steady hand.

Opposite: The back of Limnerslease

> If he wished to be quiet, the library was entirely ours, and our evenings when alone were always spent there. As I write, memories of evenings in that room come back to me vividly – the glow of lamp-light and fire-light thrown upon walls lined with well-chosen books.[5]

It appears that the Wattses found their stay in Compton a happy one. The freedom from London society had a beneficial effect on Watts's depression and the rural setting with its close proximity to London was convenient.

> The winter months as they passed found him so well that the idea of a winter home in the neighbourhood – a cottage, perhaps, to which a studio could be added – was constantly in our minds. One lovely sunny morning Andrew came in from a walk, enthusiastic about a site for a house he had found, and a quarter of an hour later we were standing on a little sandy knoll, well wooded and possessed of some very fine trees.[6]

Mary goes on to describe how this visit became a real project, and it is telling that she appears to be the major instigator, in cahoots with Andrew Hichens, waiting until Signor had retired to discuss the scheme with Andrew.

> After Signor went upstairs Andrew and I talked over the house plan. He refused to allow Signor to make any outlay himself, refused to listen to my representation of the risks he ran in spending time and money on a house which might after all not be found to be permanently suitable, and one which must have expenditure on details which would probably be of no value to future tenants or purchasers. He allowed he would not do it for anyone else, but for 'the beloved little man' (as he and May liked to call him) … And so it came about that, with all the trouble lifted off our shoulders, Andrew bought the coveted bit of land from the squire of Loseley, and asked Mr. Ernest George to make the building plans.[7]

All the expense and initial hassle of the projected building project were taken out of Watts's way. On 24 March Mr More Molyneux, head of the Loseley estate, accepted Hichens's offer of £200 an acre, preparing the way for the construction of the building.[8]

Naturally, Watts wanted a close involvement with the architects over the design and Mary notes that they 'had many consultations'.[9] The model for the house in Watts's mind appears to have been somewhere between the country style and comfort of Monkshatch (the interiors of Limnerslease bearing a close resemblance to those of Monkshatch) and the practical needs of a studio home that he had learnt from Little Holland House. There were no plans for a public gallery or sculpture studio that he had created at Little Holland House. It was to be a winter retreat and at this stage secondary to his London residence.

In her biography of Watts, Mary notes that 'in April [1890] the house was begun'. But in her diary she writes that 20 June was when a roadway was

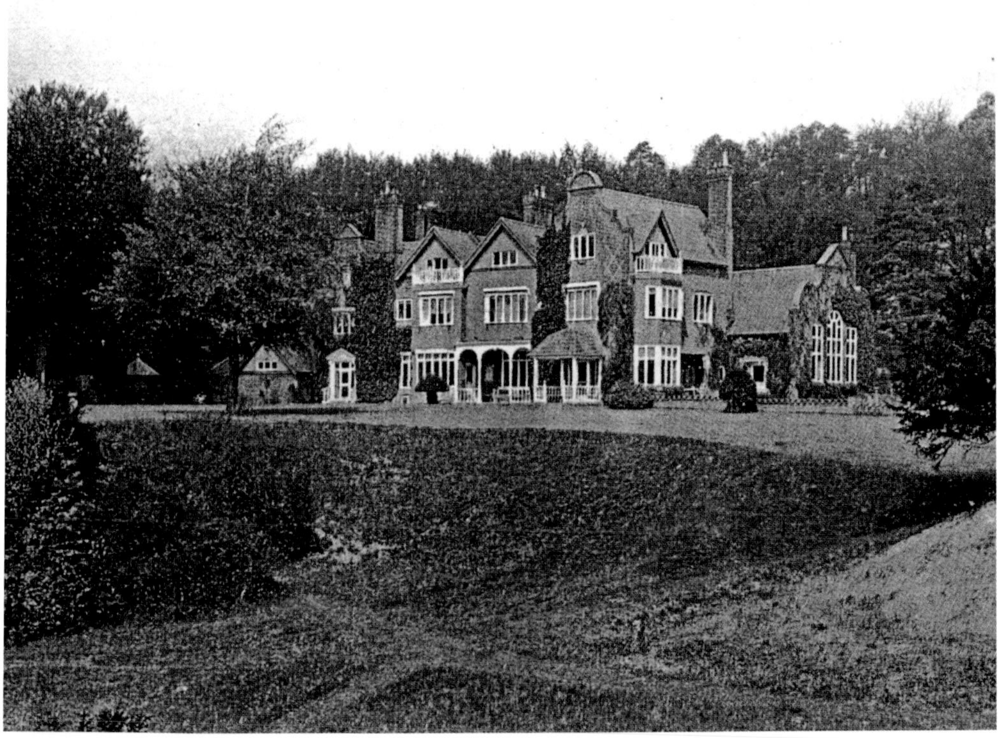

Monkshatch, 1923

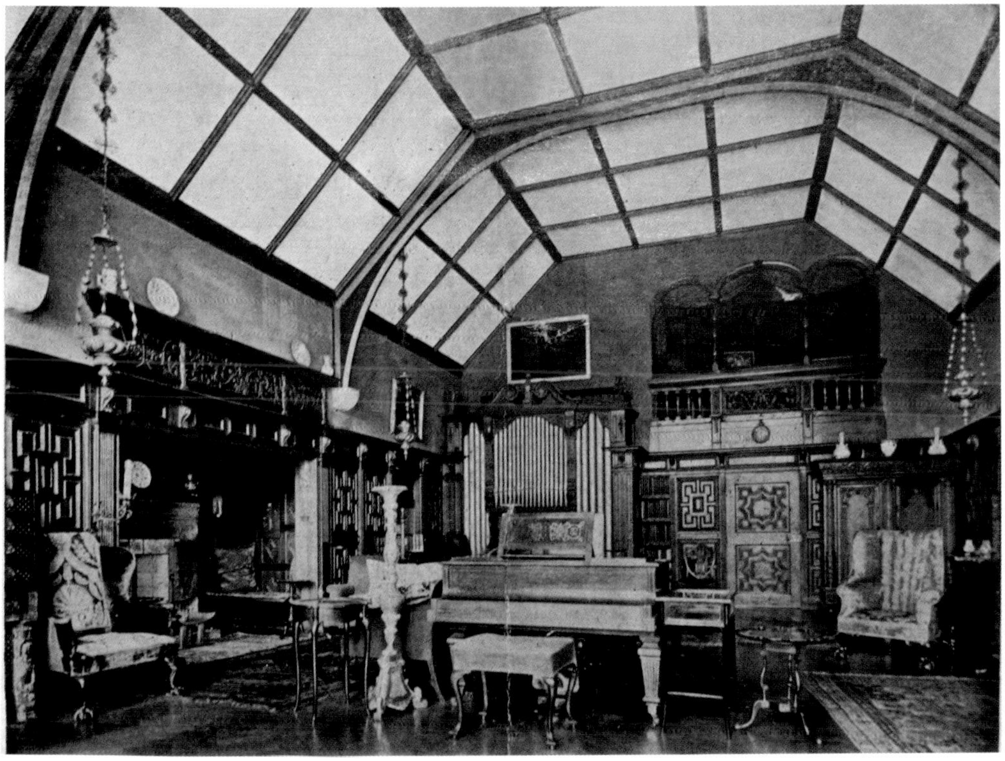

The music room at Monkshatch, 1923, courtesy of Godalming Museum

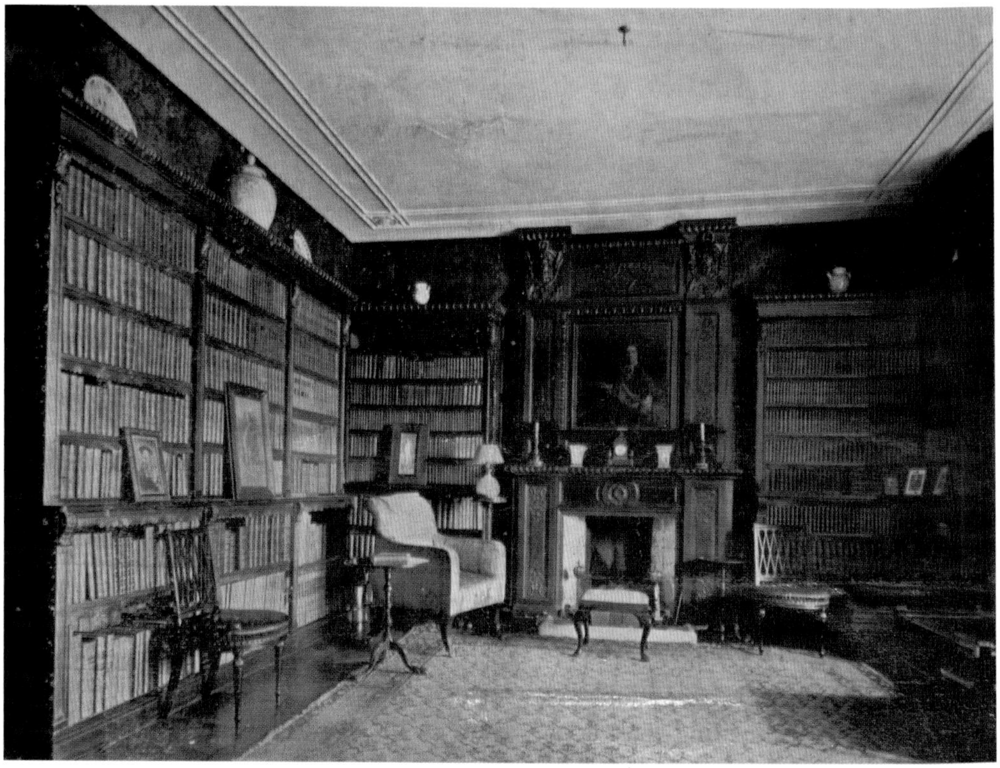

The library at Monkshatch, 1923, courtesy of Godalming Museum

made and the contractors began work.[10] The construction appeared to move very quickly, and from the 'first longings for a Surrey home' that Mary notes in her diary for 3 February 1890 to 4 December when she records 'Limnerslease grown, roofed, floor down', there was less than a year. The building of the property was not without its problems:

> Of course there were the various crises as the building arose, which fussed Watts a great deal, but which in fact did him a lot of good. He grew very cross indeed when the staircase was forgotten … When he saw the naked half-finished structure he decided that the walls which were to have been properly half timbered should have instead mock boards of oak between stucco.[11]

The house was not completed for the winter of 1890–91 and the census of 1891 shows George and Mary resident at Monkshatch. A special meal was shared at Limnerslease to celebrate Andrew Hichens's birthday on 17 June that year and possession was taken of the house on 18 July when Watts was seventy-four. Two days later Mary records that 'Signor's first dabs in his studio were on the Alps at Sunset'. The naming of the house seems to have been decided before it was complete, and the understated 'little house', as it was initially called, became Limnerslease. Mary explains the reason for a poetic name:

> 'Limner,' to keep the remembrance that it was built for an artist, and the word 'lease,' as having a double meaning, for we played a little with the old English word 'to leasen,' which meant to glean, our hope being that there were *golden years* to be gleaned in this new home.[12]

The punning on lease also referred to Hichens's ownership of the property, which continued until 1899 when Watts was able to complete payment to him.[13]

It is clear from Mary's diary entries that Limnerslease was beneficial to them both, and she writes with relish of Signor's joy in the place.[14] The residence was not a permanent home, however, and was built essentially as a winter retreat. Mary and he moved to Compton in October or November and stayed throughout the autumn and winter, returning in June or July to Little Holland House.[15] 'In this ideal home', Julia Cartwright wrote, 'the great painter spends the autumn and winter months, often lingering till the spring is well advanced and the first roses are in bloom.'[16] It was in fact the opposite way round to his artist colleagues and neighbours in Melbury Road, such as Leighton and others, who left London in the summer. 'When the colony of artists living in and about Melbury Road flits for the summer,' a journalist wrote in 1895, 'Mr. Watts remains quietly at home. "It is a good time for working when they are all out of town," he says.'[17] Only in the last years of his life in the first years of the twentieth century did the stays become longer, and the emphasis was put on Compton rather than London.

Limnerslease had originally been referred to as the 'little house', but it was in itself quite an estate that grew in the years that the Wattses owned it. The census of 1901 is revealing in listing all the estate buildings and those who worked there. The estate consisted of four buildings: the main house, the stables and two garden cottages. At the main house the Wattses were supported by five female servants, including a cook, Mary A. Head, who obediently prepared food in line with Signor's dietary whims. Mary recalled:

> He had made a great experiment, and was following the system of the American Doctor Salisbury. Hitherto he had lived much more on farinaceous foods, always very carefully prepared by his devoted and clever cook. Now she put out all her skill to make minced beef as perfectly palatable as might be, and it became the staple of his food, working in time quite wonders for him. After a few weeks he lost all sense of stiffness and pain in the joints, and, what was of the utmost importance, the circulation became good once more.[18]

In the stables were a coachman and his wife; the first of the garden buildings housed George Andrews, estate steward and photographer, and his wife; while in the second garden cottage lived a gardener, his wife, son and daughter. Staff from Monkshatch also assisted Watts, namely the sixteen-year-old Thomas H. Wren, son of the farm's stockman. Wren helped Watts with his sculpture and modelled reduced replicas of both *Tennyson* and *Physical Energy* as well as the monument to Watts in Compton Cemetery.[19] This staff supported George and Mary Watts, their adopted daughter Lilian Mackintosh and their regular stream of guests. At the time of the 1901 census this consisted of George Duckworth and the art student Vanessa Stephen, better known as the artist Vanessa Bell.

Despite its size, Limnerslease was still seen as modest in scale compared to the houses of other successful artists.

> Nearly all the successful artists' homes in London, and, indeed, all over England, are beautiful, and most of them are very much larger, richer, and more luxurious than either Limnerslease or Little Holland House at Kensington. Think of Sir Frederic Leighton's small palace, of which you have recently heard.

Undoubtedly, the less ostentatious nature of the houses was the reason for this widespread opinion, and journalists were keen to use this perception to emphasize the very special nature of Limnerslease:

> I can think of scores of others, all very beautiful, but I do not remember ever having been in a private house so fascinatingly lovely as Mr. and Mrs. Watts' two homes. Only a great artist can make a house look like this.[20]

THE LIVING SPACES

Limnerslease was built to serve as more than just a winter workplace for G.F. Watts. It was a home, and as much care was spent on the domestic arrangements as went into constructing the studio and workplace. The models of Monkshatch and Little Holland House are much in evidence. The entrance hall and sitting room (known as the Red Room) were important spaces that visitors first saw on entering the house. Photographs of the Wattses residing there show Signor at rest in the sitting room with an eclectic clutter of old and new objects around, including wooden screens. These two rooms were central, and their most unique features were created by Mary, with the ceilings and a niche decorated by her in gesso (a mix that has plaster at its base). Julia Cartwright noted:

> But another hand besides the master's own has helped to decorate the home, and at every turn we find signs not only of Mrs. Watts's taste but of her inventive faculties and artistic skill. The gesso reliefs, representing the symbols of ancient religions, which adorn the white-panelled ceilings, are her work ... The same gesso work appears in the arched recess above the master's favourite seat, by the corner of the hearth. Here the richest golds and greens and blues are delicately blended together, and angels and powers bearing appropriate symbols represent the different aspects and meanings of life.[21]

In these two rooms Mary was able to develop her growing interest in ancient symbolism as well as her own personal form and language that were to find their most sublime expression in the cemetery chapel. A sketch for the ceiling (Watts Gallery Archive) shows the ideas that Mary was beginning to express, including the world religions and also more universal symbols. 'Mr. Watts himself, when he points the details of the design out to you, [says], "It is my wife's work. She designed it all, and she did all the actual work."'[22]

Watts's 'favourite seat' was a couch in a niche where he could recline, relax and entertain. The idea of such a space was not new and Mary recalls Watts having one created for him at Little Holland House:

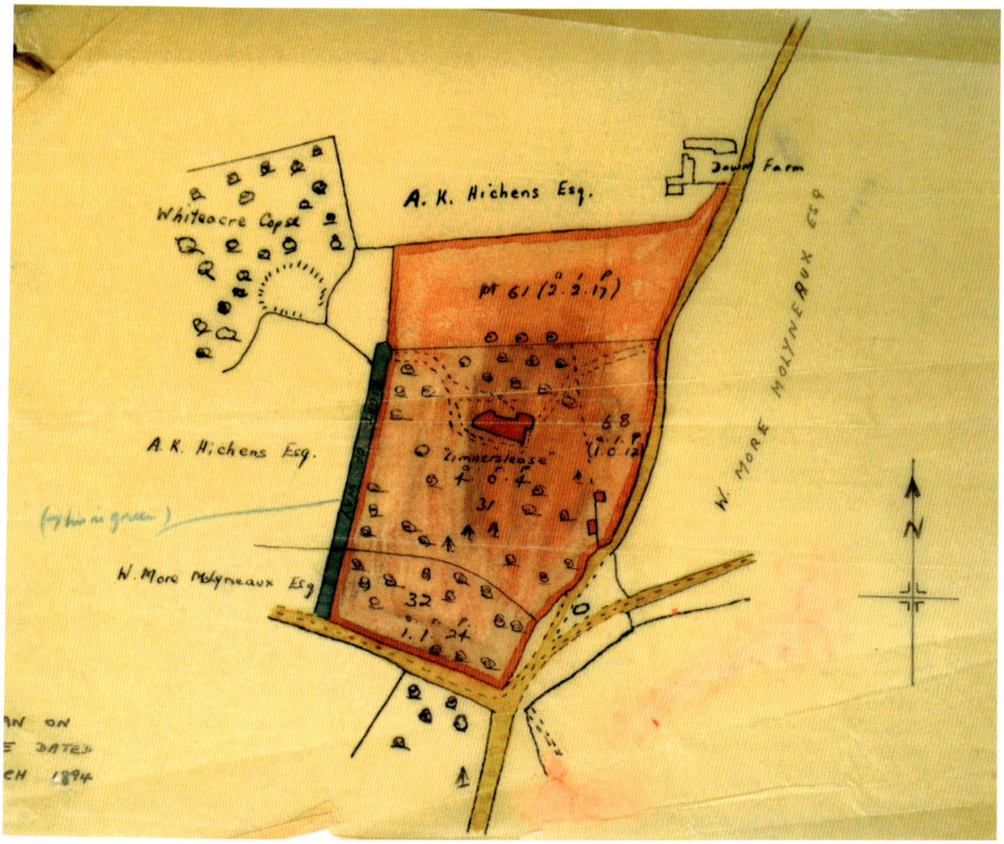

Left: Copy plan on an indenture of Limnerslease, dated 17 March 1894, Watts Gallery Archive

Below: Ernest George's initial design for Limnerslease, published in the Architect, *16 May 1890, Watts Gallery Archive*

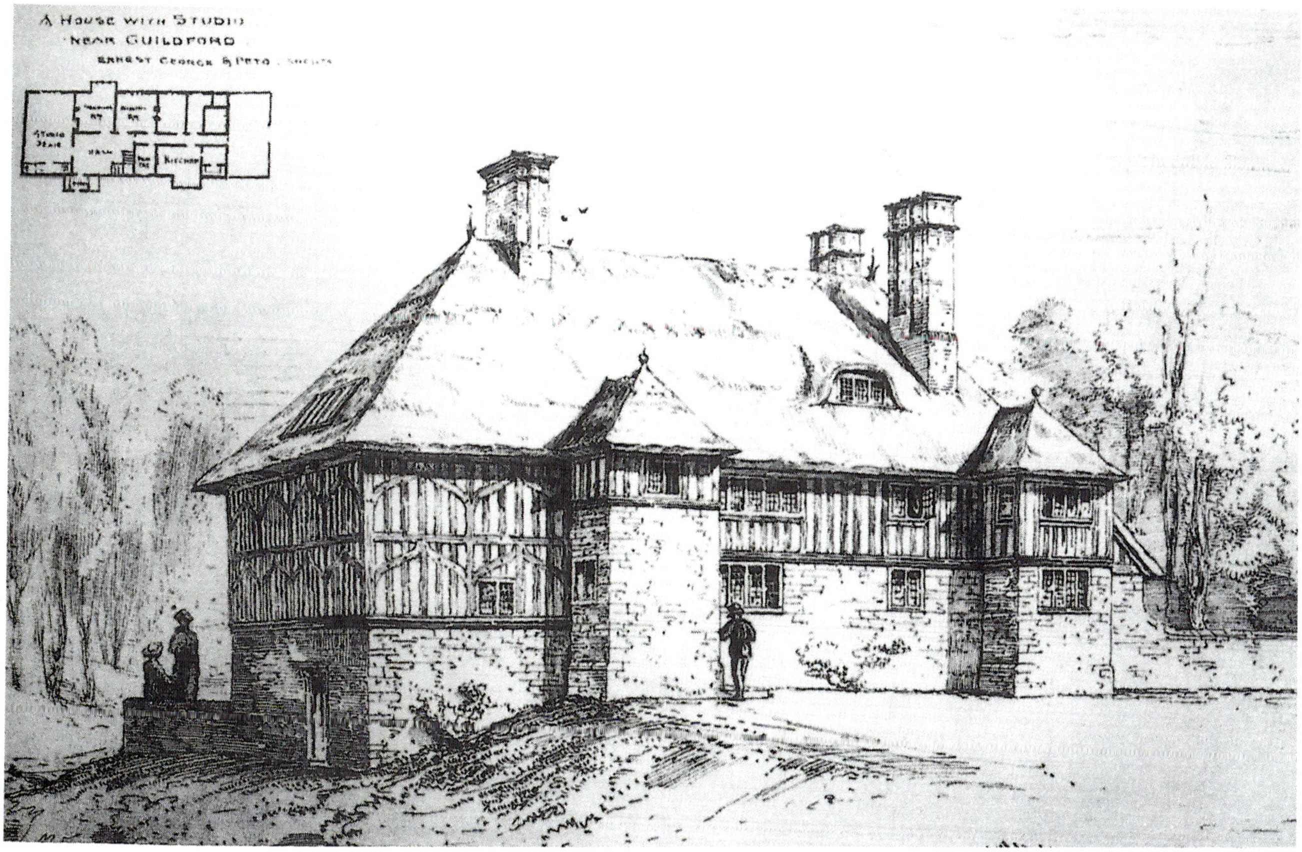

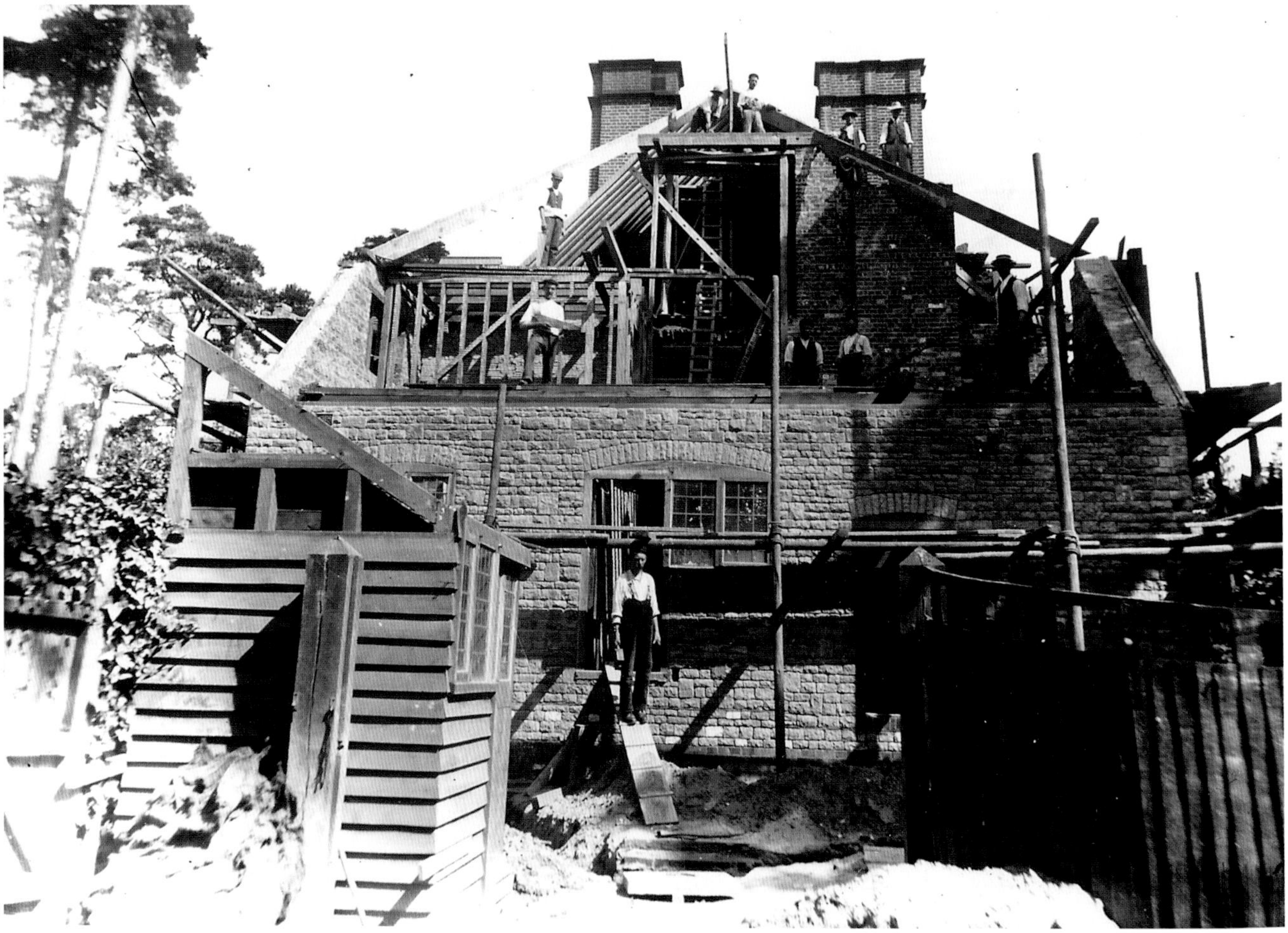

Above: West end extension of Limnerslease under construction, c.1892

Right: Limnerslease, c.1890s

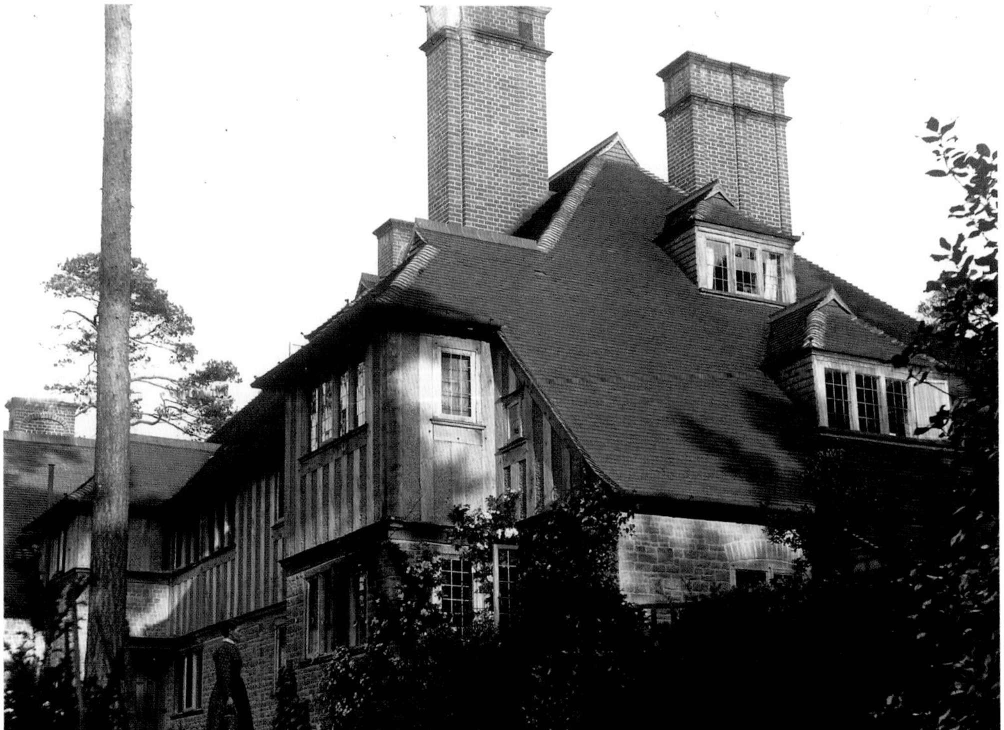

> Mr. Aitchison and he had given the drawing-room a pretty little niche which made the right place for a long divan sort of seat; and it served a double purpose, for, as Signor was slightly deaf, the niche concentrated sound, and he heard better there, and so it became his favourite corner, and he chose to spend his evening lying there, listening to reading.[23]

A photograph (p.8) shows Mary reading to Signor in his niche at Limnerslease, like the niche at his London house, except the one in Surrey was decorated in coloured gesso by Mary. The niche was also employed by Watts when visitors came to the house, and the architect of the Watts Gallery, Christopher Hatton Turnor (1873–1940), remembered Watts using it as a place where he entertained the numerous people who came to meet him.[24]

The living spaces were splendidly decorated and the descriptions of Limnerslease make clear the rich colours that adorned the walls. A plethora of decorative objects, cluttered by modern standards, added to this sense of rich colour, as Cartwright observed:

> The red gleam of copper, the glitter of Algerian and Indian brass-work brightens each dark corner. Persian rugs and Oriental hangings relieve the blackness of old oak chests and cabinets, and the latest specimens of home arts and crafts stand side by side with Damascus pottery or Arab fretwork.[25]

The walls showed works by Watts and reproductions by the artists whom he particularly admired.[26] Watts Gallery still has in its possession autotypes of the works of Michelangelo that the artist used to adorn the main staircase of Limnerslease.[27]

One of the great attractions of their Surrey home was its rural location, which allowed Watts to pursue his outdoor interests of gardening and horse riding. He had stopped riding in Kensington because of the wooden pavements that had been laid as the area became increasingly less rural and the metropolis expanded.[28] He rode again in Surrey along the numerous bridle paths, including the Pilgrims' Way, which ran past Limnerslease. The garden, too, provided an antidote to the heavy moods to which Signor was prone, and numerous examples are cited by Mary of the power of nature to lift his spirits. One of his favourite outside seats was a stone arbour by his studio window, created to install a Della Robbia roundel of a Madonna and Child that was given to him as a gift. Cartwright noted:

> And on the terrace just outside the studio is a Della Robbia roundel, lately brought back from Florence and given to the painter by an old friend. Now the vine-leaves of an English garden trail over the roof that shelters this relic of the Italian Renaissance, and the wild flowers of Surrey blossom before the blue and white Madonna which the Florentine sculptor carved with so delicate a grace.[29]

Probably the most iconic image of Watts in Limnerslease is the artist dressed in his Oxford robes seated in front of the roundel, which was taken by

George Andrews, the estate steward of Limnerslease. This picture was given to the journalists who visited as a definitive image of the master artist. Hulda Friederichs commented that, among the photographs that Mrs Watts had presented to her as illustrations for her article, was this one 'representing the venerable master-artist seated near the beautiful medallion of Luca della Robbia pottery in the little recess under the window of the studio'. She goes on to explain for the sake of Signor's modesty that the photograph 'was not by any means taken to be used as an illustration in any publication, but Mr. Watts donned his studio robes solely to be photographed for a dear old friend who sent him the plaque of Della Robbia pottery'.[30]

The garden and riding served to lighten Watts's mood, but children had an even more peaceful effect on the artist and one gets the distinct impression that in their presence he could truly relax. He allowed the local children to play in Limnerslease, held parties for them and many of his friends visited with their children. Mary observed:

> The children who came occasionally to Limnerslease were a great joy to him. 'I like to have these little lives about,' he said; and the children of his Blanche, Verena and Arthur Somers-Cocks, came sometimes, and my sister's three girls, or my brother's little daughter and son, this little boy being with us when he was only three years old, when Signor became his devoted playfellow.

Indeed, Mary's picture of Watts with children appears very much at odds with the iconic serious and prophetic image that he projected:

> With these little people Signor, when enticed to play wolf or crocodile, became very agile, and ran very fast and lightly. In the evening he often spent half an hour by the little boy's bed, pretending to be a stork that pounced at the white-robed figure dancing about on the bed. If Signor's stork became too vivid for the child's imagination, he would call a truce by saying, 'No storts in dis country!'[31]

Above left: The niche and fireplace in the Red Room in Limnerslease, c.1890s

Above right: Looking towards the hallway from the Red Room in Limnerslease, c.1892

Lower left: The niche in the Red Room in Limnerslease, from the Country Home, *February 1913, Watts Gallery Archive*

Lower right: G.F. Watts sitting next to the Della Robbia roundel at Limnerslease, c.1900

Even though Limnerslease was not in London, it received a steady stream of visitors who came to see the great artist and sometimes stayed. On a typical day work would commence very early in the morning, Watts having retired at 9pm the previous evening, while the afternoon was set aside for seeing people.[32] 'Nearly always one would find some interesting people at Limnerslease after luncheon when he gave up the afternoons to seeing people,' Turnor observed.[33] The spaces used for reception and entertaining were the entrance, the sitting room (the Red Room) with its niche and the drawing room. The last 'had been built for a billiard room', based presumably on the room at Monkshatch where Signor had played the game, but it was 'never used as such'.[34] The space of the room served well for musical performances, and leading musicians flocked to play for Signor and his guests. 'Joachim accompanied by Donald Tovey (piano) played in this room to Mr. Watts and Mr Plunket Greene accompanied by Mrs Maud Valerie White sang

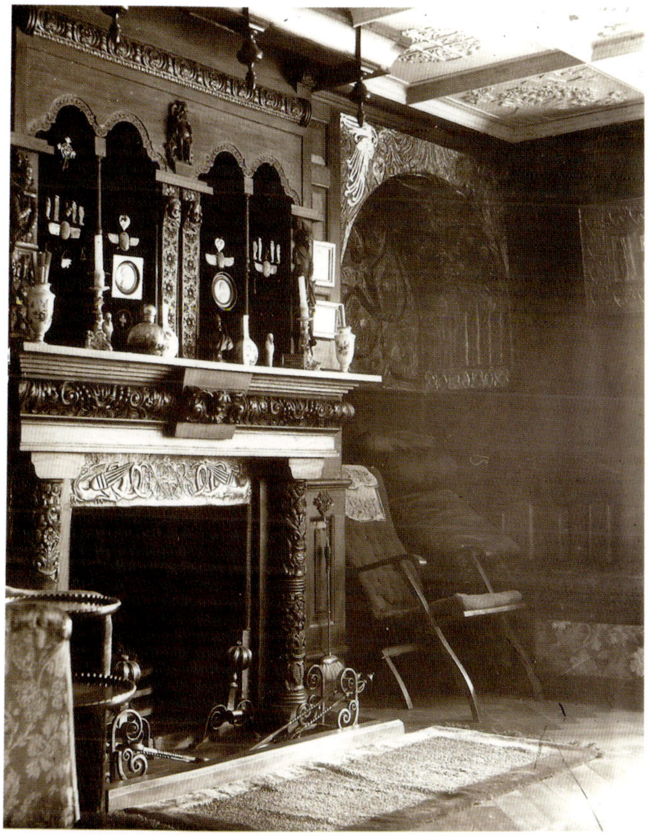

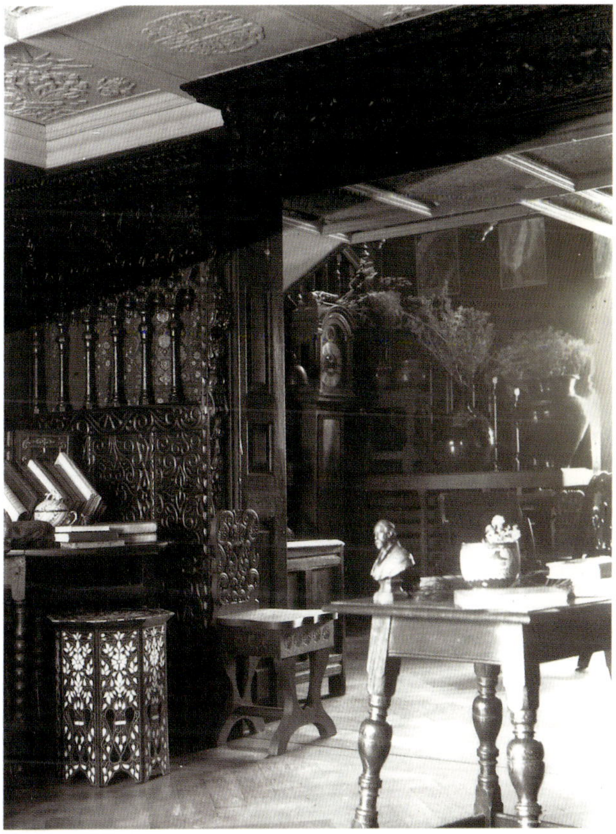

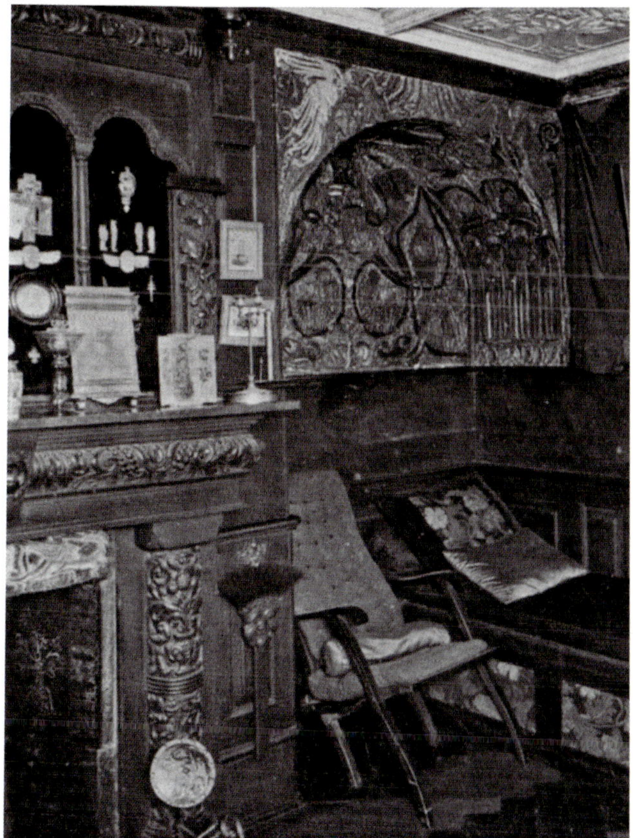

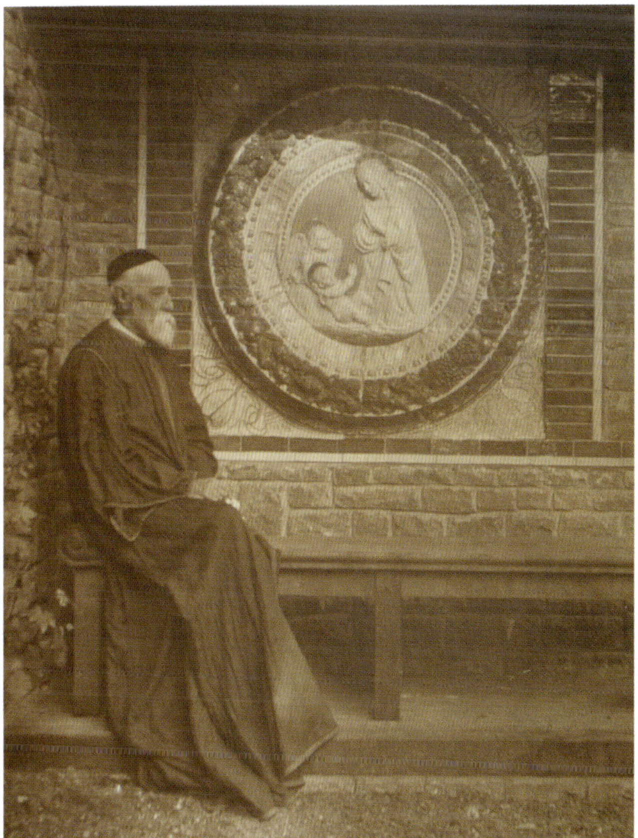

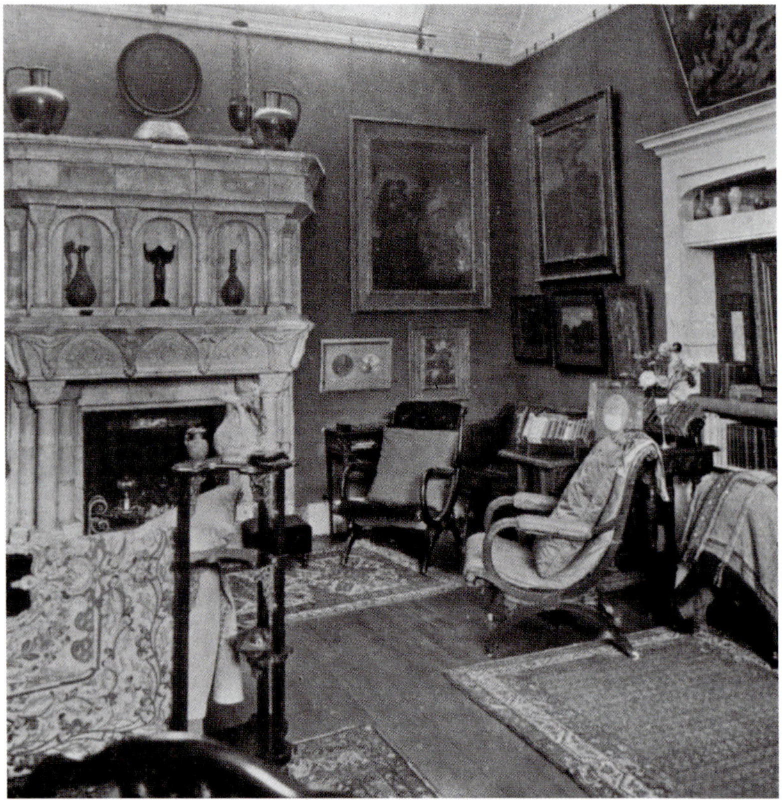

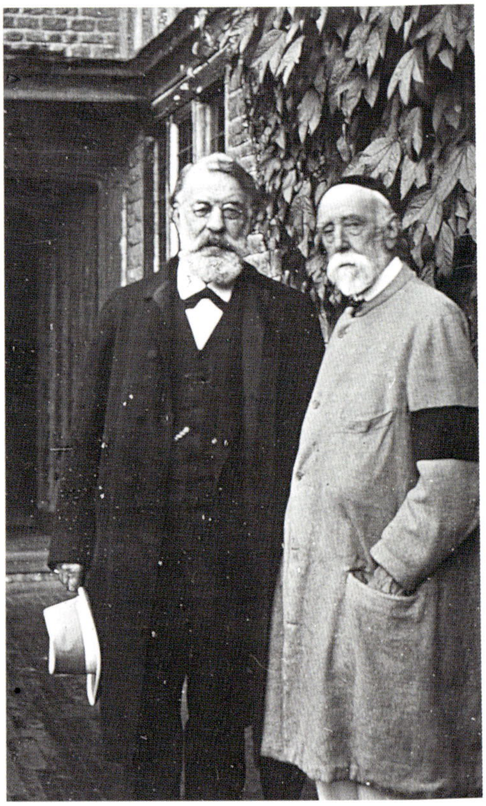

Above left: The drawing room at Limnerslease, from the Country Home*, February 1913, Watts Gallery Archive*

Above right: Joachim and Watts at the entrance to Limnerslease, c.1900

there.' Turnor noted that 'many of the most notable continental musicians came to play to Watts at Limnerslease'.[35] And it was not just musicians, 'authors too visited the shrine',[36] as well as leading figures of the age such as William Gladstone. It was also a place where people stayed to have their portrait painted by one of the most sought-after portraitists of the day. 'Mrs. (Josephine) Butler, for whose heroism he [Watts] had a deep veneration ... was painted ... at Limnerslease, where she came to stay with us.'[37] General Baden-Powell visited to have his portrait painted and declared: 'It has more in it than I know of in myself!' The painting was given to the nearby Charterhouse on Watts's birthday in 1902.[38]

THE STUDIO HOME

At the heart of all of Watts's residences was the studio, the *sanctum sanctorum*, where he could work. There was enormous public interest in artists' studios, the place where the alchemy of creation took place, and those who came to Limnerslease shared that fascination. A steady stream of journalists visited from both the popular and art press and spent much of their resultant articles discussing the studio. It is surprising to learn from these how Watts's studio was seen, particularly with respect to its plainness. 'The studio where Mr. Watts paints is entirely given up to work,' Julia Cartwright wrote; it 'has no ornament saving a few models of Greek statues or casts from the Parthenon frieze.'[39] The fascination came with its workmanlike appearance and large scale. Other studios belonging to artists of Watts's stature were far more richly decorated with studio props and ornament that reflected their owner's art. Watts's studio consisted entirely of the equipment he needed for painting, a large number of paintings in

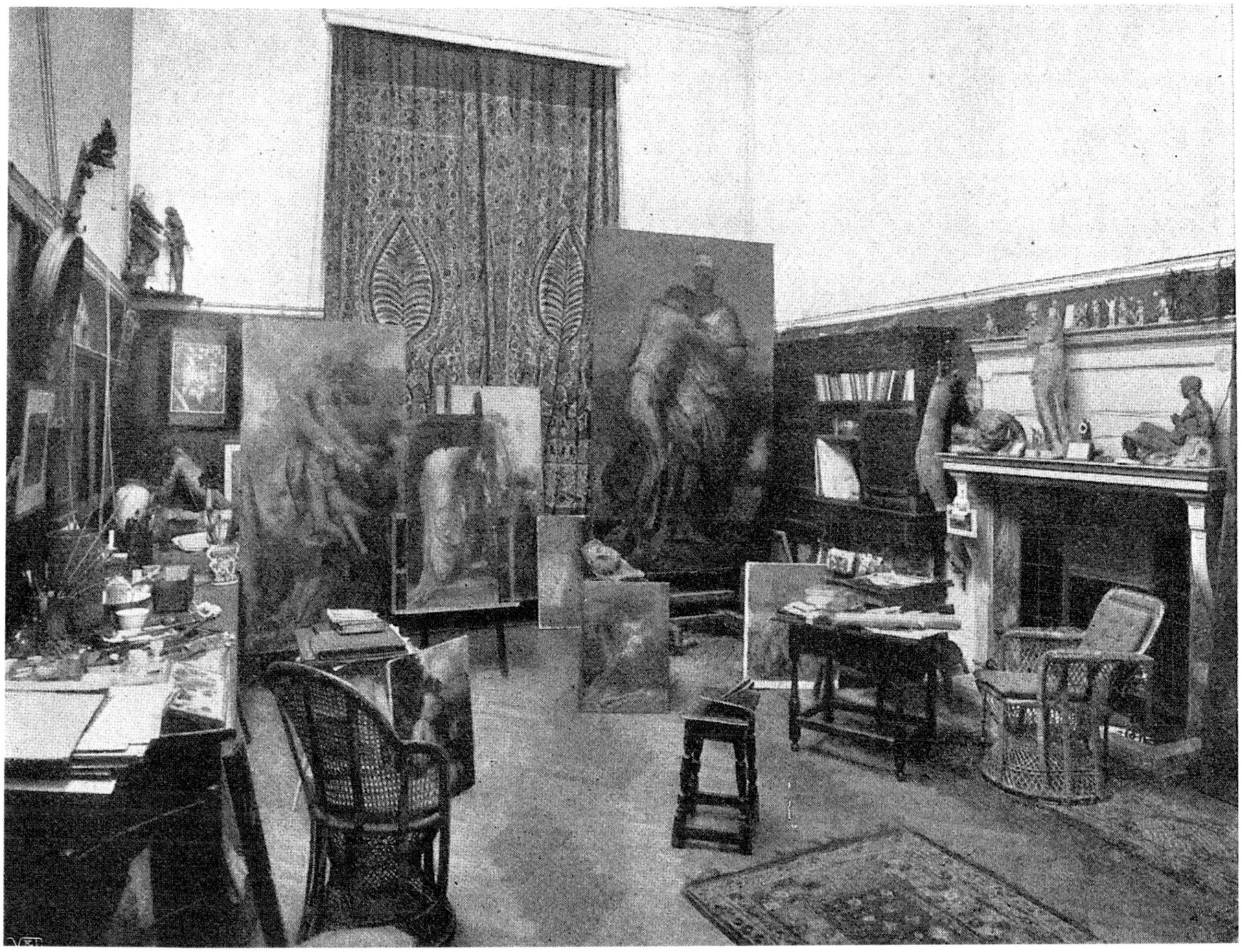

The studio at Limnerslease, c.1900

various states of completion, and some plasters, the last being his own modelling, body casts and antique casts – particularly from those of his beloved Pheidias of the Elgin Marbles. Mary remembered this detail: 'The cast of the Theseus or that of the Ilissus, both of which always stood upon the mantelpiece of his studio.'[40] The unusual quantity of pictures that were being worked on by Watts provided the focus of many conversations. A journalist wrote:

> In other studios, the picture at which the artist is working there and then, and perhaps a few finished specimens of his art, are one of the attractions only. The others are beautiful furniture, stuffs, objects of art, etc. In Mr. Watts' two studios there is absolutely nothing of this sort. Instead, you have any number of pictures, of all shapes and sizes, in various states of incompleteness – which are at least as suggestive as finished pictures can be – and all the artist's own work. Which studios, do you think, are the more interesting?[41]

The studio, which the *Illustrated London News* described as 'lofty and commodious' had to be large enough for him to work on his enormous painting, *The Court of Death* (*c.*1870–1902; Tate), which dominated the space of most of Watts's residence at Limnerslease.[42] He had already begun it prior to building

G.F. Watts, Court of Death *(c.1870–1902), hanging in front of the balcony in the studio at Limnerslease, from the* Illustrated London News, *29 July 1893, Watts Gallery Archive*

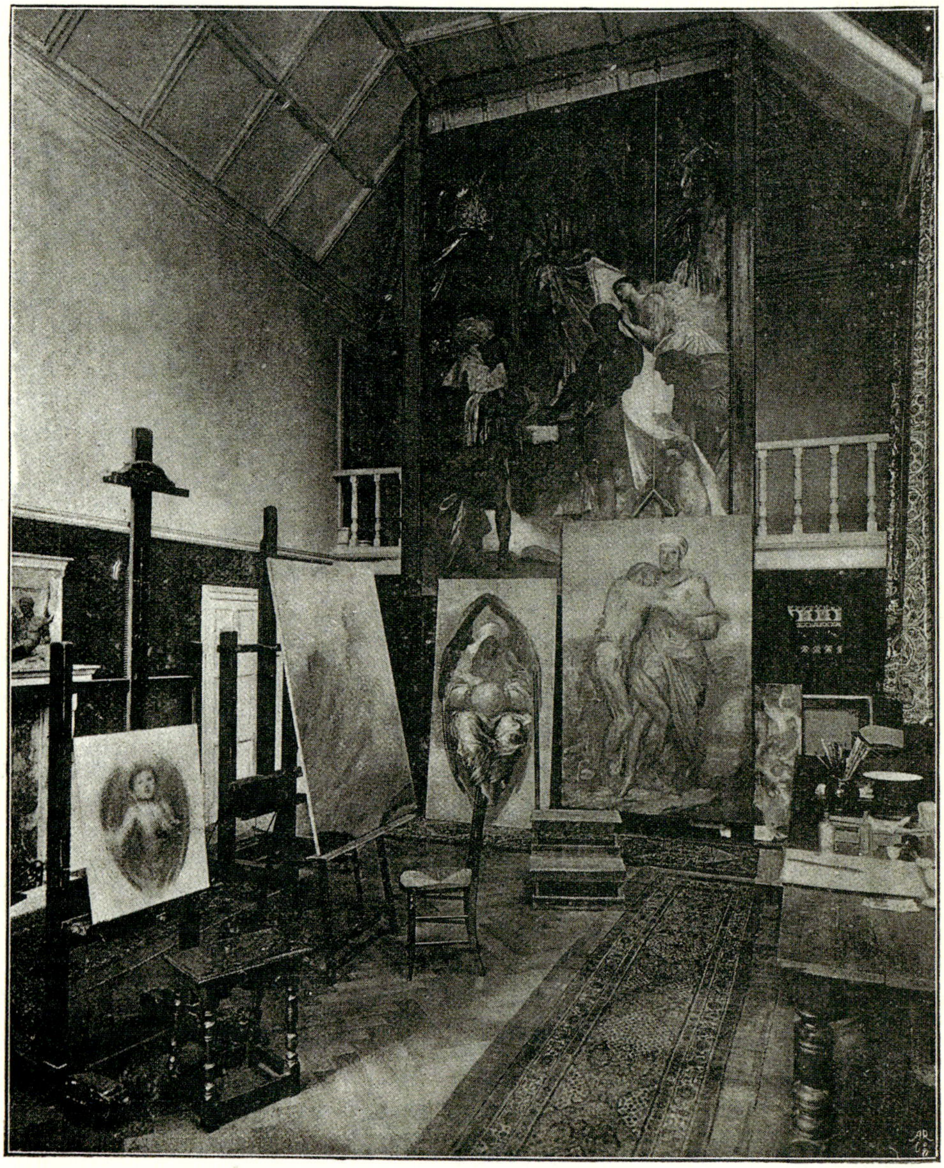

THE STUDIO AT LIMNER'S LEASE.

his Surrey studio and it was moved there by taking the canvas off its stretcher and rolling it up before being transported; letters to George Thompson, his studio assistant, then note its despatch to the Tate in 1902.[43] A photograph taken by the *Illustrated London News* shows it in front of the studio's balcony, a vantage point often used by visitors to Watts's studio. It was held by a purpose-built frame with pulleys, for the 'painting was so large that it had to be lowered through the floor of his studio in order that Mr. Watts may work upon the upper portion of it'.[44]

The orientation of the studio was also atypical, most artists preferring even light throughout the day provided by a north light. The studio at Limnerslease had its main window facing due south and the skylight facing due east. The reasons

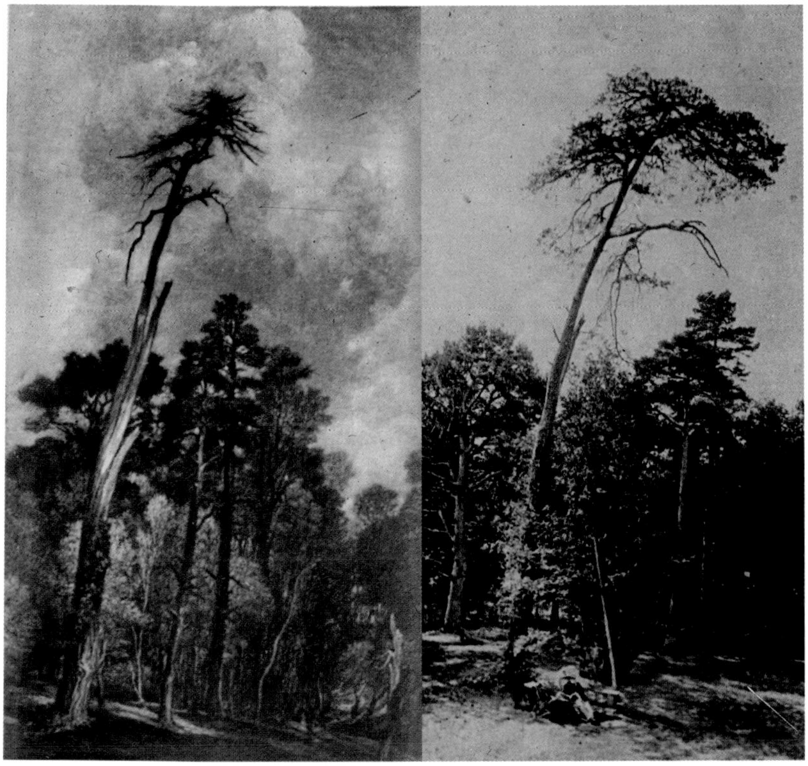

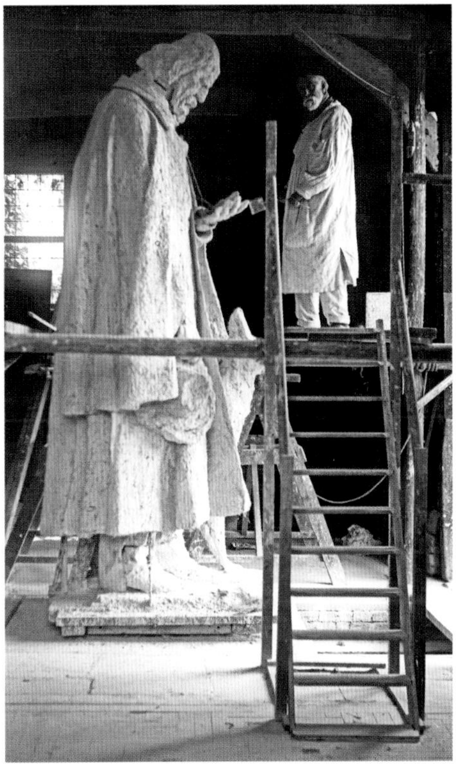

Above left: G.F. Watts, Green Summer, *c.1895–1903, oil on canvas, 168 x 89 cm, Watts Gallery, with a contemporary photograph of the landscape depicted, Watts Gallery Archive*

Above right: Watts working on his sculpture Tennyson *in the Barn Studio, c.1899*

for this are not entirely clear but appear to relate to the times at which Watts worked in the studio, the fact that he wasn't doing traditional observational painting from models and that he liked bright sunshine to view his work. Watts painted mainly in autumn and winter and wanted to maximize the amount of light, which accounts for the large window; he also worked mainly in the mornings, which accounts for the large eastern skylight. Such a studio did have its drawbacks and the amount of sunlight that sometimes flooded in could make it uncomfortably warm. As Mary noted, the drawing room was used 'very occasionally as a studio if the usual studio became too hot, on unusually hot weather'.[45] Common to all the articles on Limnerslease was the information about Watts's working practices: going to bed at 9pm, rising at 5am (in light or dark) and, when not entertaining, working through to the dying of the light.

The impact of the landscape on Watts was not purely recuperative, and the autumns and winters that Watts spent at Limnerslease clearly influenced many of his late paintings. A number of landscapes including *Green Summer* (*c.*1895–1903; Watts Gallery), *End of the Day* (1903; Watts Gallery) and *Surrey Landscape* (1902–3; Watts Gallery) were drawn directly from the landscape surrounding Limnerslease.[46] More subtle and interesting is the autumnal palette that Watts adopted in paintings such as *Can These Bones Live?* (1897–98; Watts Gallery), where the rusty twilight tones evoke a contemplative, haunting and melancholy mood, reflecting the colours of Surrey in autumn, as indicated in this contemporary description:

> The hedges were glorious with signs of 'beautiful decay,' such as orange and coral tinted hips and haws, tufts of feathery wild clematis, rustling leaves of

> every tint of bronze and fawn and brown, and tall grasses turned pale grey and purple ... Can you imagine what this white place looks like, when the orange tints in it are repeated by the red gold of the pine stem which the setting sun brings out? It is a thankless task to try to describe harmonies and symphonies of colour, such as surround you everywhere under Mr. Watts' roof-trees. But think of the colouring of that artist's pictures, of those wonderful mysteries of tints and lights and shades, and you will understand, to some extent, what he has made of his homes.[47]

At Little Holland House Watts had a large sculpture studio where he was able to work on *Physical Energy*. When in the late 1890s he was commissioned to create another sculpture of a similar scale – that of his old friend Alfred, Lord Tennyson (1809–92) for Lincoln Cathedral – he felt the need for a studio in Surrey. 'To enable him to carry this out,' Mary records, 'he arranged with Andrew Hichens for the purchase of a small farm-house close to our gate, where a fine old barn was available for such work.'[48] He bought the buildings of Down Farm, which had both an enclosed cattle yard and barns able to be converted into a sculpture studio and garden. A short rail track and trolley could also be built, just as was done at Little Holland House, so that Watts was able to work outside on *Tennyson* in his favoured method of *gesso grosso* and return the sculpture to the protection of the barn when not in production. Mary recalls in her diary the day, 13 December 1898, when the Barn Studio began to be used: 'When I went up at sunset, a great pair of white legs [of the *Tennyson* plaster model] shone out against the dark background of the barn timbers.' The purchase of the barn 'with its picturesque roofs' also 'gave an opportunity for turning what had been for centuries a cattle-yard into a garden, a very charming cloistered garden; and there Signor often went in the intervals for rest.'[49] This garden was often referred to as one of Signor's favourite places and Mary created a magnificent sundial with Watts's motto, 'The Utmost for the Highest'. The positioning of the studio was important in being at the entrance to the Limnerslease estate and it expanded the Watts presence in the village.

If Limnerslease was predominantly Watts's studio space, it was also used by Mary to hold pottery classes for the villagers.

> The class, begun entirely for pleasure, developed later into a village industry for terra-cotta modelling. The whole was undertaken, and is continued, on account of his great interest in the arts and crafts of the country, and his belief that we must have great craftsmen before we can have a national art.[50]

The industry and modelling rooms became part of the pottery, but initially it was the house and land of Limnerslease that provided both workshop and kiln. In a handwritten note on the back of a Heal & Jackson builder's bill from 1903 she writes of the drawing room at Limnerslease as being 'used as a modelling room for the chapel works'.

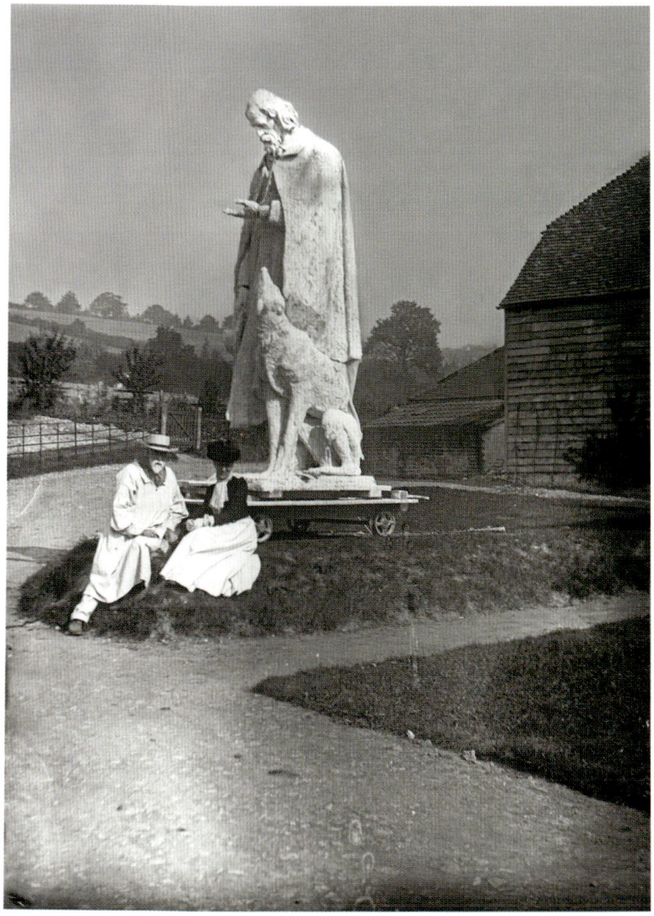

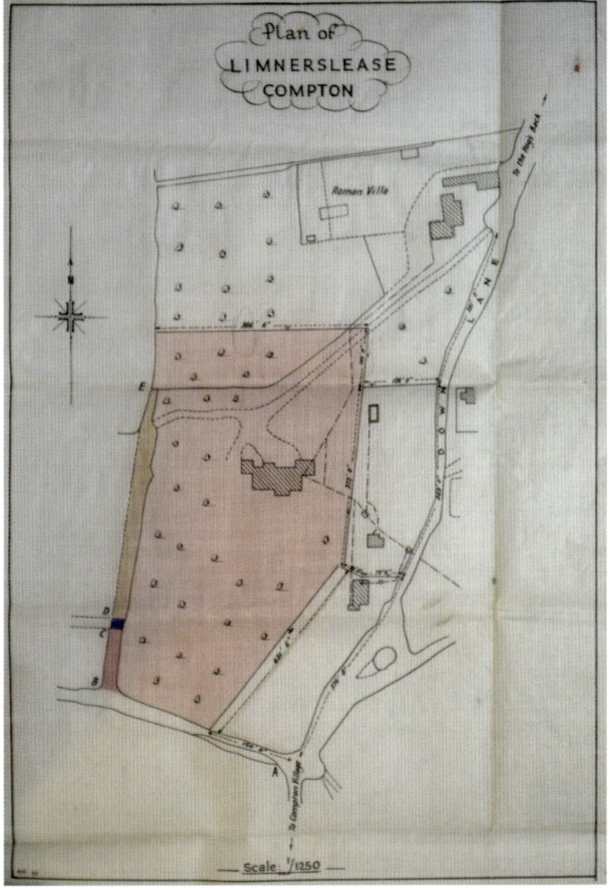

Above left: G.F. and Mary Watts sitting outside the Barn Studio, with Tennyson *behind, c.1899*

Above right: Map of the Wattses' estate in Compton including the Barn Studio (adjacent to the Roman villa), c.1938, private collection

PERMANENCE AND MEMORIALS

On 1 July 1904 George Frederic Watts died at his London home, Little Holland House. Although Watts died there, the focus of his legacy, outside Tate and the National Portrait Gallery, was very much based at Compton. The Little Holland House Gallery had closed in 1903 and works had been moved to Compton, where the Wattses were spending most of their time. After Watts's death it became a place of pilgrimage, a shrine to the great artist. Hilda Haking's article, 'The Shrine of George Frederick [*sic*] Watts, Poet-Painter of the Victorian Age', is typical of several produced by journalists who made their way to Limnerslease in 1905; she wrote:

> Here, the great poet-painter of the Victorian age, George Frederick Watts, dwelt for the greater part of the last years of his life. Here was built, upon the hillside, with the greatest simplicity and charm of design, the house that will be regarded with reverence by the pilgrims of all time, for 'Limnerslease' is indeed a light set on a hill.[51]

With Signor's death Compton became imbued with the sense of being a memorial, as, in part, had been intended. His memory was everywhere; Mary devoted herself to continuing the Compton Pottery and ensuring that the art of G.F. Watts remained in the public eye. Interest in Watts continued throughout the Edwardian period, but the First World War was to fundamentally

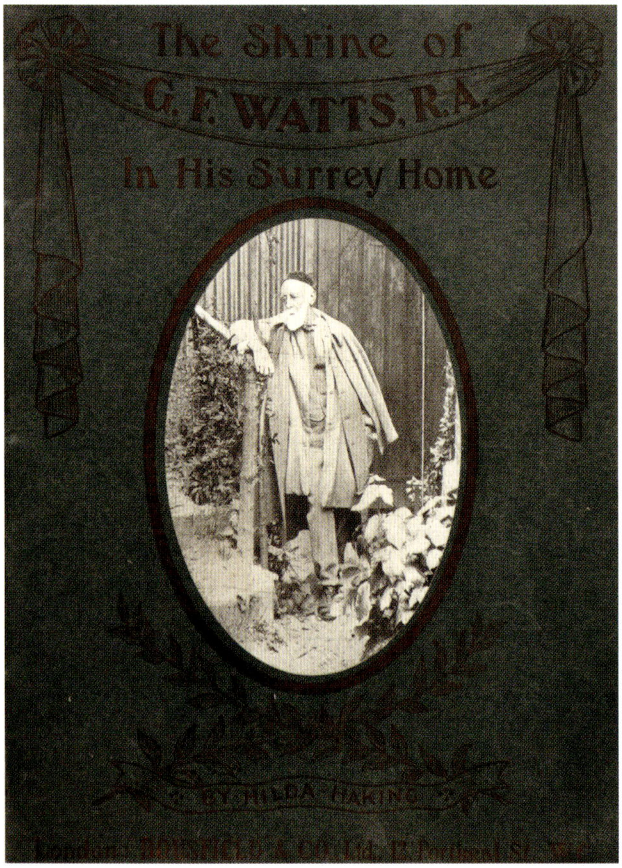

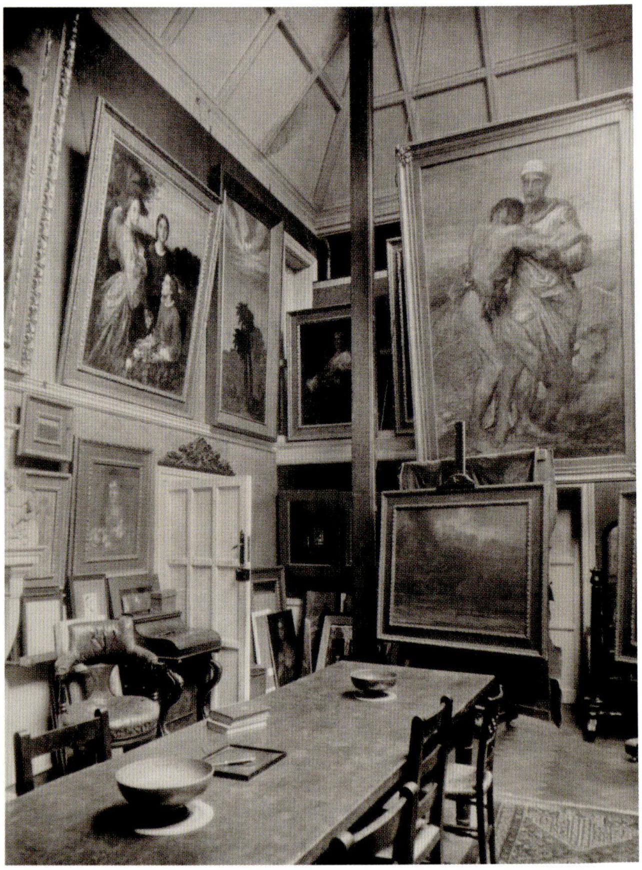

Above left: The front cover of The Shrine of G.F. Watts, R.A., in his Surrey Home *by Hilda Haking, London 1906, Watts Gallery Archive*

Above right: Watts's studio as Mary preserved it, from the Country Home, *February 1913, Watts Gallery Archive*

transform attitudes towards the previous age. The whole feel of the estate is perhaps best summed up in a novel by Ronald Chapman, the son of the Wattses' adopted daughter. The thinly disguised character of Giorgio is Watts, the location Limnerslease:

> Giorgio's shadow pervaded everything. There was no action in the household, if *you* went into it, which did not emanate from some order or other of his. He ruled us from his grave on the hill outside the village. His sad, melancholy, finely modelled features brooded over the place, brooded over it with his greatness and aspirations. He had aspired to greatness and in his lifetime achieved it. Somehow we, and I in particular, as his grandson, were the poorer for it. For what, after all, could we do to emulate him? In the darker paths at the edge of the wood, or when darkness was falling on a winter afternoon, before the lamps had been brought in, his spirit seemed to suck our very life. While he was alive the place had been an object of pilgrimage. Admirers had come to see the grand old man and listen to his views on life. Now that he was dead it was a shrine, still filled with his presence, but without Worshippers. The war had scattered them like dust before an angry wind.[52]

In 1915, when Mary was extending a kitchen garden at the Barn Studio, she discovered a Roman villa in the grounds, which was subsequently excavated.[53]

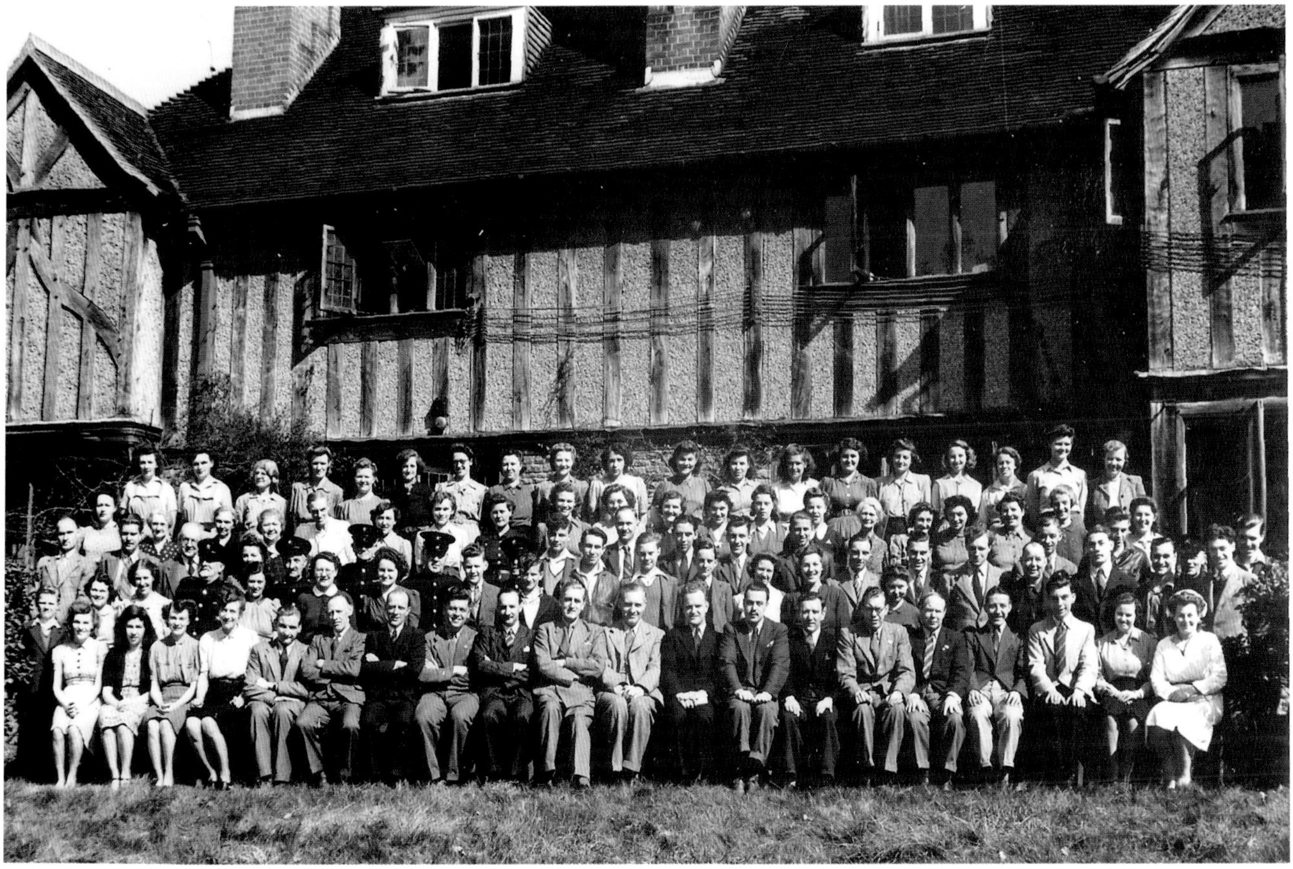

Employees of Ardente gathered outside Limnerslease, early 1940s

The history of Limnerslease continued as part of the Watts Gallery until the death of Mary in 1938. A large part of the collection was then lost, including Signor's library and much of the studio equipment, which had been 'preserved as he had left it the day before his death'.[54] Throughout the Second World War Limnerslease was used by the Ardente company, which produced radar and sonar for the Navy. Subsequently, it had several owners including the sculptor Estcourt James Clack (1906–73), who produced work still on display in Green Park, London, and the Bishop's Palace, Wells. The division of the house and the sale of the Barn Studio, stables and gardeners' houses, together with the De Morgan kiln, have resulted in some fragmentation of the Watts estate, though most of it still survives as a unique enclave with Limnerslease on the hill at its centre.

NOTES

1 Friederichs 1895, p.74.

2 Watts 1912, vol.II, pp.153–54.

3 Chapman 1945, p.127.

4 The dates of the Wattses' residences from 1889 until 1904 are essentially taken from two sources, Mary's diaries (Watts Gallery Archive) and the letters of G.F. Watts, which give the location he is writing from.

5 Watts 1912, vol.II, p.154.

6 Watts 1912, vol.II, p.157.

7 Watts 1912, vol.II, p.158.

8 MSW Diary Notes, 1890: '28 February … Mr. M M has not yet consented to sell (at £200 an acre) … 24 March – Andrew accepts Mr. M. M.s price for Limnerslease land'.

9 Watts 1912, vol.II, p.158.

10 Watts 1912, vol.II, p.158; MSW Diary Notes, 1890: '20 June – Road made to Limnerslease & contracts in'.

11 Chapman 1945, p.133.

12 Watts 1912, vol.II, p.190.

13 'The winter was on the whole dark, and instead of painting, Signor took to using red chalk and made a series of twelve drawings. In May these were exhibited in the Old Bond Street Galleries, a sale being arranged by Sir William Agnew that enabled Signor to purchase the new house from Andrew, which as a matter of business was now convenient to both. For some years Andrew was still the ground landlord, but he permitted Signor to make it freehold by a further purchase in 1899.' Watts 1912, vol.II, p.192.

14 MSW Diary Notes, 1891: '22 January – delight in Limnerslease … 22 October Planting the Yew Hedge. Signor gardening & so happy'; 1893: '2 September Of Limnerslease "We must do something to deserve it" he said.'

15 See note 4.

16 Cartwright 1896, p.30.

17 Friederichs 1895, p.76.

18 Watts 1912, vol.II, p.191.

19 See Stephanie Brown's catalogue entries on bronzes of *Tennyson* and *Physical Energy* in Bills and Bryant 2008, pp.288, 292.

20 Friederichs 1895, p.74.

21 Cartwright 1896, p.30.

22 Friederichs 1895, p.74

23 Watts 1912, vol.II, pp.85–86.

24 'One afternoon a very intense but short-sighted lady sat in the chair – soon she became altogether too intense for poor Signor who succeeded in leaving his nitch [*sic*] over the end of his coach [*sic*] & went off and talked to someone else.' Turnor Memoirs, p.220.

25 Cartwright 1896, pp.29–30.

26 'Many, too, are the paintings by Mr. Watts's own hand, views of the Tuscan Apennines near Careggi, and glimpses of Mediterranean waters, or early versions of well-known pictures, the "Genius of Greek Poetry" and "Olympus on Ida"' (Cartwright 1896, p.30).

27 'Mr. Watts will not suffer any but the most perfect reproductions in his house of the great

Italians, Michael Angelo foremost among them.' (Friederichs 1895, p.74.)

28 'When Signor was once more well we returned to Limnerslease, and during the winter he took to riding again. The wooden pavements over the long distance from park or fields round Kensington had made him give up this pleasure when old Little Holland House ceased to exist.' (Watts 1912, vol.II, p.219.)

29 Cartwright 1896, p.30. There is a question over whether the Della Robbia was original or a nineteenth-century copy. According to an oral tradition, the work was a copy and was given away by Lilian Chapman after Mary's death in 1938.

30 Friederichs 1895, p.81.

31 Watts 1912, vol.II, p.208.

32 Turnor Memoirs, p.220.

33 Turner Memoirs, pp.219–20.

34 M.S. Watts, handwritten note on a Heal and Jackson bill, 1903, Watts Gallery Archive.

35 Donald Tovey (1875–1940), musicologist; Maud Valerie White (1855–1937), composer; and Harry Plunket Green, a distinguished Irish baritone. Turnor Memoirs, p.220.

36 Including figures such as George Meredith: Turnor Memoirs, p.220.

37 Watts 1912, vol.II, p.250. Josephine Butler (1828–1906) was a social reformer and women's activist.

38 Watts 1912, vol.II, p.300.

39 Cartwright 1896, p.30.

40 Watts 1912, vol.I, p.317, now known as Dionysus and Illysus from the Parthenon frieze, the model for many of his works; see my entry on *The Genius of Greek Poetry* in Bills and Bryant 2008, pp.196–98.

41 Friederichs 1895, p.75.

42 *The Court of Death*, *c.*1870–1902, 424.2 x 274.3 cm; D.W. 'The Surrey Home of Mr G F Watts RA', *Illustrated London News*, 29 July, 1893, p.135.

43 G.F. Watts letters to Thompson in Watts Papers (formerly Watts Gallery), unpublished microfiche copies at the National Portrait Gallery (and some originals), Watts Gallery and Tate.

44 D.W. 'The Surrey Home of Mr G F Watts RA', *The Illustrated London News*, 29 July 1893, p.135.

45 M.S. Watts, handwritten note on a Heal and Jackson bill, 1903, Watts Gallery Archive.

46 'He had said, "The desire in me to paint landscape grows, I want to paint landscape more and more"; and from his studio window he painted the picture which he afterwards called "Green Summer". He worked upon it from time to time, for five or six years.' (Watts 1912, vol.II, p.312.) See my entry on *End of the Day* in Bills and Bryant 2008, p.274.

47 Friederichs 1895, p.75.

48 Watts 1912, vol.II, p.283.

49 Watts 1912, vol.II, p.284.

50 Watts 1912, vol.II, p.284.

51 Haking 1906, p.5.

52 Chapman 1969, p.7.

53 Surrey Archaeological Society, Collections XXVIII, 1915. Thanks to Alan Bott for providing a copy of this article.

54 Chapman 1969, p.6.

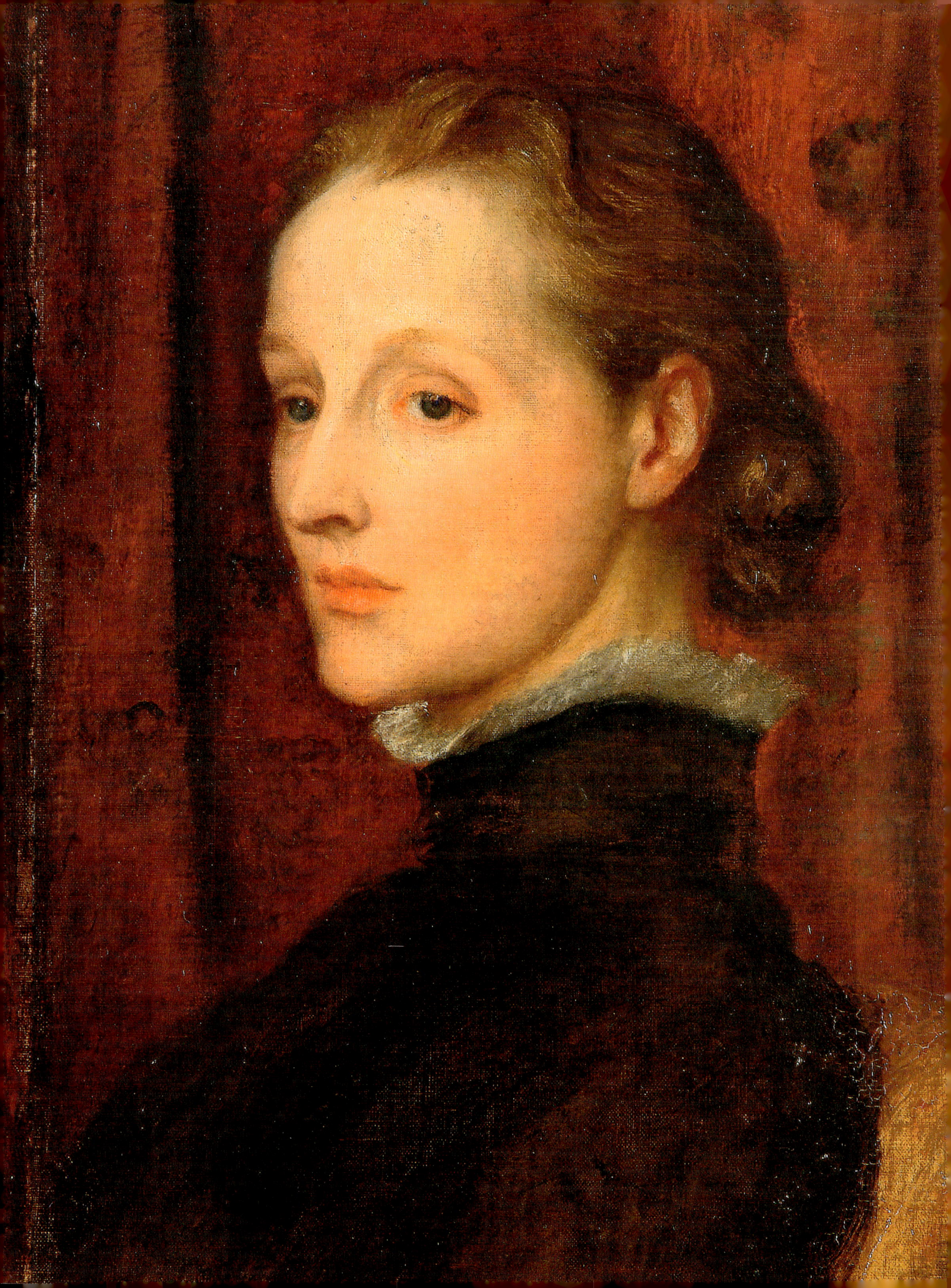

Mary Watts, the Home Arts and Industries Association and Compton

Hilary Underwood

Mary Watts designed and built the chapel at Compton and set up the pottery there under the auspices of the Home Arts and Industries Association, with which she had been involved since the mid-1880s. The history and ideals of the association parallel those of the Arts and Crafts movement, but its scope and impact were limited because of its primary focus on 'cultural philanthropy' rather than professional practice. This chapter examines Mary's relationship to the Home Arts and Industries Association, and the following chapters on the chapel and the pottery show how the scale and ambition of her work transcend it.

The association provided Mary Watts with a vehicle through which she could work publicly in a manner acceptable for a woman of her class and generation. In the nineteenth century middle-class women began to make a slow entry into the fields of professional training and work. Medicine, higher education and art all partially opened to them. Mary Watts, for instance, gained a professional art training at the South Kensington Schools and the Slade between 1870 and 1873. Yet among the wealthier middle classes, from which she came, there was still resistance to women earning money, especially outside the home. On marriage, women were largely debarred from professional work, apart from art and writing. As Mrs Ellis wrote in 1869, 'As society is at present constituted, a Lady may do almost anything from motives of charity or zeal ... but so soon as a woman begins to receive money ... the heroine is transformed into a tradeswoman.'[1] Only charitable work gave a permissible outlet for the energies and skills of leisured women, both married and unmarried. Prominent charities were usually headed by men, but women often provided most of the work and energy. Lord Brownlow (1844–1921) was the President of the Home Arts and Industries Association, but the majority of classes were organized or run by middle-class women. Mary Watts was exceptional in turning her class into a successful business. She benefited from the support and the capital of her husband, and a well-chosen manager, but she controlled the business and was a significant designer in its early days. However, it was the label of philanthropy that made the enterprise possible.

The Home Arts and Industries Association developed from woodcarving classes for agricultural labourers and servants that Eglantyne Louisa Jebb (1845–1925) had started in 1877 on her husband's estate at The Lyth, Ellesmere, Shropshire.[2] The scheme expanded, encouraged by the American industrialist Charles Leland (1824–1903), who supported similar projects in Philadelphia, Pennsylvania. Under the name of the Cottage Arts Association it ran around forty classes by the mid-1880s. In 1884 it was renamed the Home Arts and Industries Association and Lord Brownlow was appointed President. In 1885

Opposite: G.F. Watts, Mary Seton Watts, *1887, oil on canvas, 48 x 36 cm, Watts Gallery*

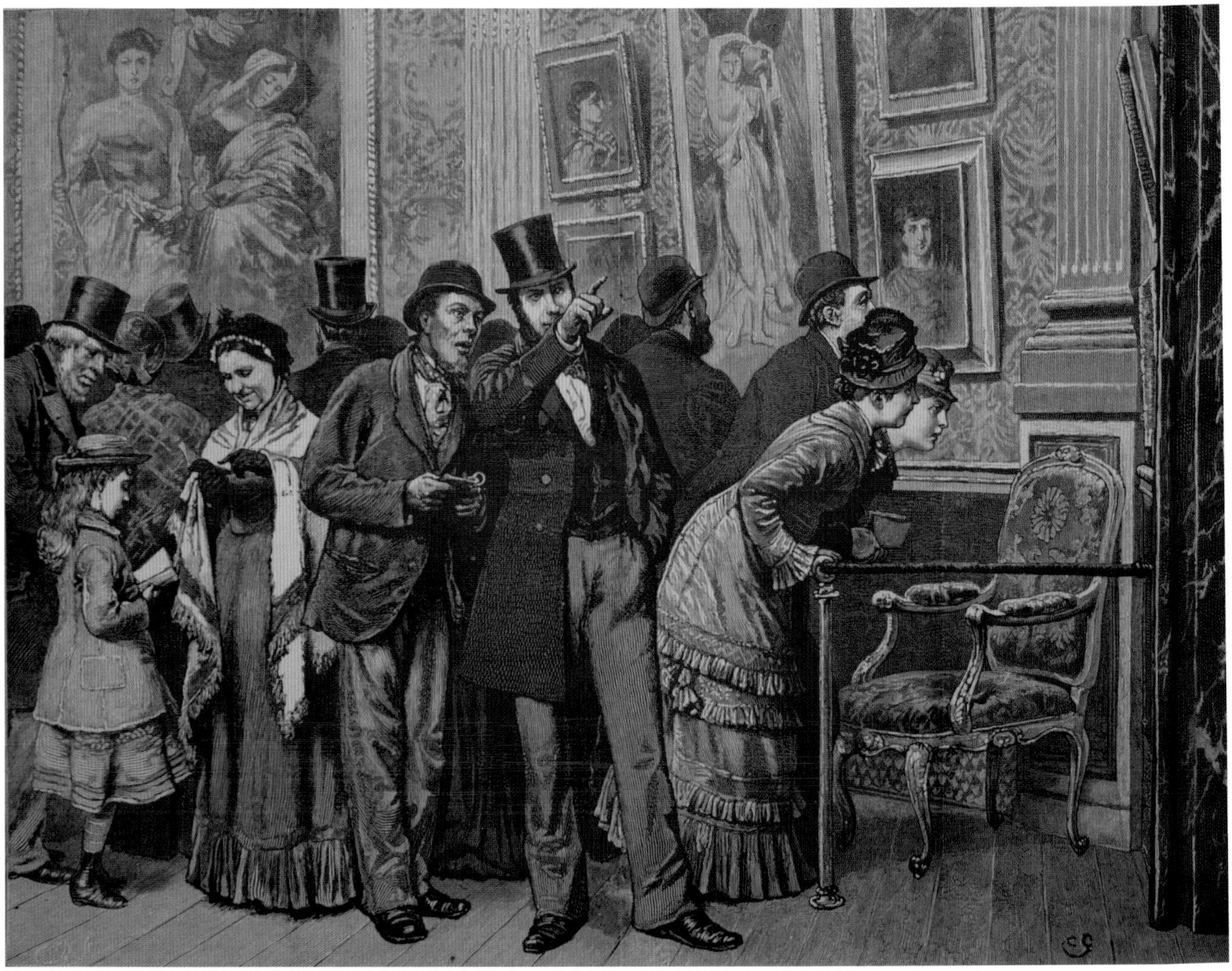

'A Sunday Afternoon in a Picture Gallery', Graphic, *8 February 1879, courtesy of the Guildford Institute. The image shows the summer exhibition of the Grosvenor Gallery in 1878, with G.F. Watts's* Time, Death and Judgement *in the background. The exhibition was opened to working-class groups on Sunday afternoons*

it began to hold annual exhibitions, initially modest. The first was held in the Brownlows' London home, 3 Carlton House Terrace.[3] The second, in 1886, was held in St Andrew's Parish Room in Bethnal Green.[4]

The association offered classes in handicrafts – woodcarving, cut and hammered brass work, pottery, leatherwork, textile work or other subjects depending on local traditions and the skills and interests of the class organizer. Classes were free to pupils, and instructors were also usually voluntary. The classes combined practical instruction with recreation, aiming to cultivate 'artistic feeling' and 'a genuine love of the work for its own sake'. Through this, 'art and its influences' were 'introduced into the humblest homes and in remote rural districts'. The association intended to 'develop dormant faculties, to encourage the perceptive powers and to establish habits of application in the pupils', noting that the training was 'a sound preparation for the serious pursuit of a trade'.[5] If a class developed a high level of skill, it could be turned into a 'developed industry' giving paid employment to its workers.

The aims of the Home Arts and Industries Association typify the late Victorian development now often termed 'cultural philanthropy'. Later Victorians questioned the effectiveness of traditional philanthropy, where poverty and social

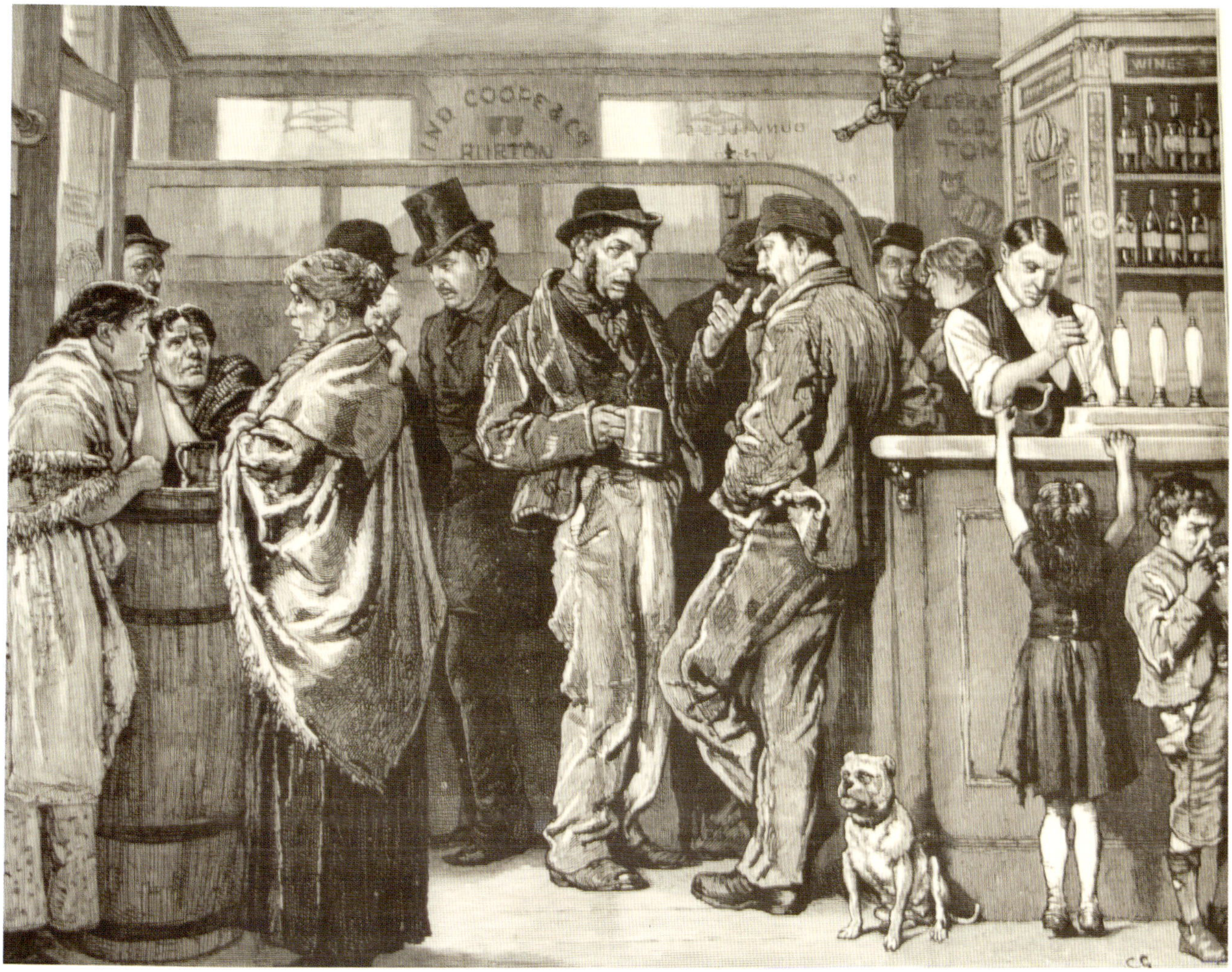

'A Sunday Afternoon in a Gin Palace', Graphic, *8 February 1879, courtesy of the Guildford Institute*

problems were addressed through donations of money, food and material help. It seemed to make no difference to levels of poverty and led to what was called 'pauperization', where the poor became dependent on handouts, sapping their will to work.[6] Cultural philanthropy, on the other hand, aimed to improve and refine the characters and minds of the lower classes, without risk of pauperization, widen their horizons through exposure to high culture and introduce them to respectable leisure pursuits, as opposed to the alternatives of idleness and drink. Its municipal aspects included the growing public provision of free libraries, museums and art galleries, often prompted by private lobbying and endowment. It also had private philanthropic aspects: Miranda Hill's Kyrle Society, for instance, was founded in 1877 to better and beautify the lives of working people by laying out parks and encouraging house decoration, window gardening and flower growing; and loan art exhibitions were organized in Whitechapel by the Reverend Samuel Barnett (1844–1913) and his wife Henrietta (1851–1936), leading to the foundation of the Whitechapel Art Gallery in 1901.[7] George Frederic and Mary Watts were closely involved in these developments. Watts's friend and neighbour, Mrs Russell Barrington, was active in the Kyrle Society and Watts was a keen supporter of the Barnetts' projects. They were friends of T.C. Horsfall, promoter of the Manchester

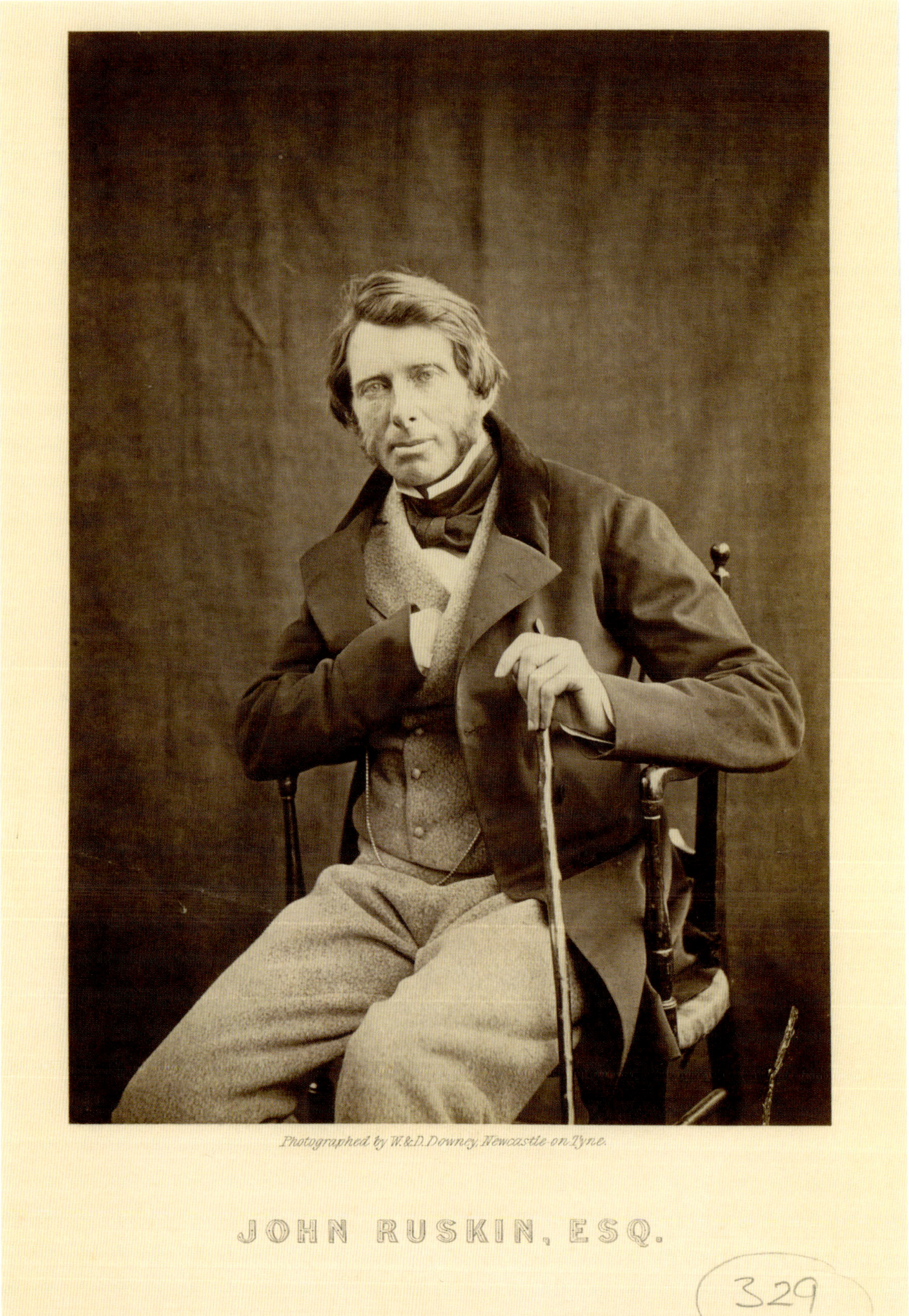
Photographed by W.&D. Downey, Newcastle on Tyne.
JOHN RUSKIN, ESQ.
329
Published by A.Marion, Son & C° 23, Soho Sq. W.

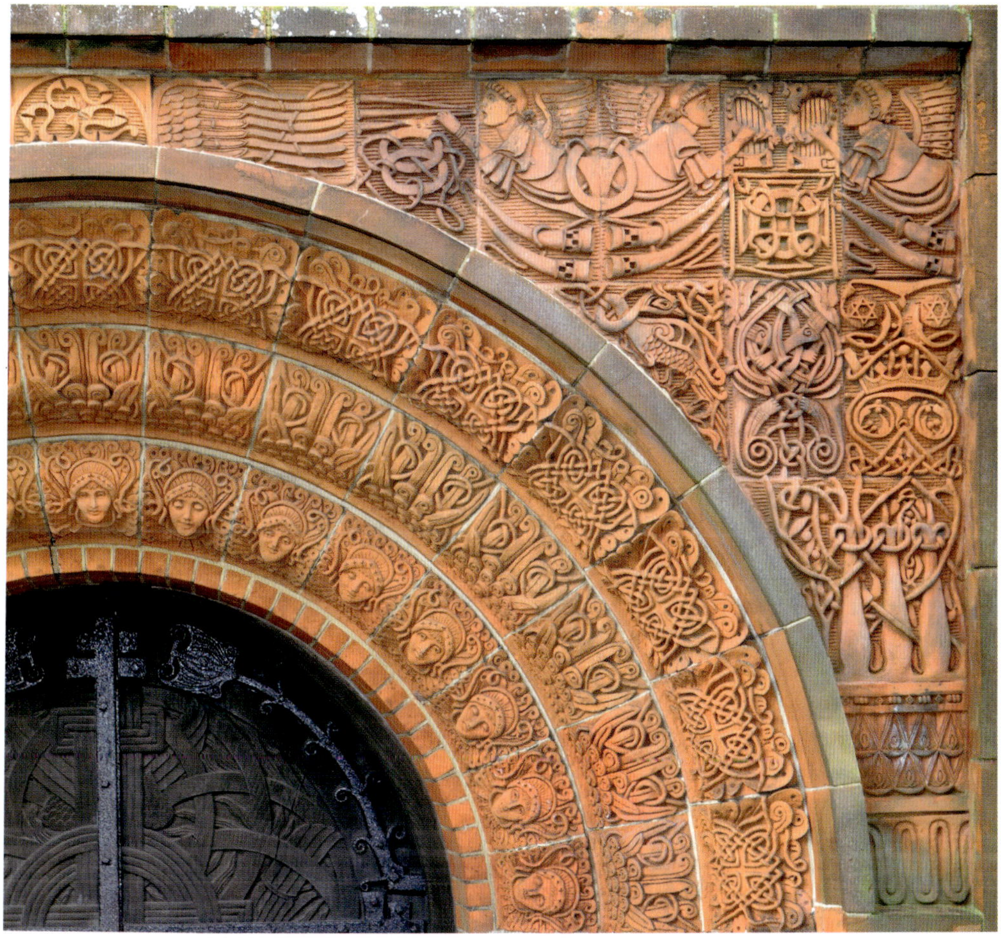

Opposite: 'John Ruskin Esq.', c.1860, carte de visite, 10.2 x 6.4 cm, W. & D. Downey, Newcastle-upon-Tyne, from The Rob Dickins Collection, Watts Gallery

Left: Part of the chapel doorway showing the innermost row of heads with eyes looking 'downwards in sympathy and upwards in hope'

City Art Gallery, and were council members from the mid-1880s of what was to become in 1891 the South London Fine Art Gallery (now South London Gallery, Peckham).[8] These organizations focused on the ennobling effects of fine art through passive spectatorship. The Home Arts and Industries Association, although part of the same trend, differed in emphasis because it concentrated on active participation in handicraft with the additional goals of self-improvement and self-realization.

This ideal derived from the writings of John Ruskin. Both Mary Watts and her husband were great admirers of Ruskin. The 1938 probate inventory of Limnerslease lists many of his books,[9] and when a servant purloined one in 1890, Watts asserted: 'He could have taken nothing from me that I value more.'[10] Ruskin's architectural writings in *The Seven Lamps of Architecture* (1849) and *The Stones of Venice* (3 vols, 1851–53) exerted a particularly strong influence. Most important was the chapter 'On the Nature of Gothic' from the *Stones of Venice.* Here Ruskin asserted the human importance of creative handiwork:

> If you will make a man of the working creature, you cannot make him a tool. Let him but begin to imagine, to think, to try to do anything worth doing; and the engine turned precision is lost at once. Out come all his roughness … all his incapacity … but out comes the whole majesty of him also,

including the capacity for 'transfiguration'.[11] Its influence can be seen in the 1895 pamphlet *Notice of the Work and Objects of the Home Arts and Industries Association*: handicraft alone allows the individual 'to put forth in some permanent form some expression of that divine and spiritual side which is his alone amidst creation' and through this to become 'a man, a living soul'.[12]

William Morris (1834–96) reprinted *The Nature of Gothic* on the Kelmscott Press in 1892. Its theory of creative work underpinned his socialist commitment and his theories of art and design. Ruskin and Morris together influenced the widely held Arts and Crafts movement principles of the value of craftsmanship and of the designer as maker, even though the movement's practices did not always live up to its ideal. These principles were valued within the Home Arts movement. The secretary of the Irish section, Miss Bourke, reported in 1895 that 'more effort is now made to encourage pupils to bring out their own ideas of beauty, instead of ... copying what is before them in a mechanical way'.[13] Mary Watts recorded a conversation with Leighton in her diary: '"Very good," Sir Frederick said of some H. A. Ind. Work, "but no use because they do not design the things themselves." Oh but they will come to that I said – "Oh! You are young and hopeful."'[14] Her espousal of this philosophy can perhaps be seen in the variations permitted in the faces that look 'downwards in sympathy and upwards in hope' over the doorway of the chapel.

Commentaries on Home Arts classes constantly emphasized their effects on the lifestyle and appearance of their pupils. When a class in Scotland 'beg[a]n to like to carve they beg[a]n to mend their clothes too'. Elsewhere 'a class-holder in Ireland, who had invited a number of the boys about her to be taught in her own beautiful home, and made a point of not asking them to come cleaner or less ragged, found that both rags and dirt disappeared before the force of that silent influence.'[15] Watts praised Mary's work in Compton on the chapel, believing it 'may have some influence for good, already I see a change in some of the people about'.[16]

From a twenty-first-century viewpoint the Home Arts and Industries agenda was not simply about the empowerment of its pupils by 'awakening the sense of self-respect, through the sense of spiritual power'.[17] We are more clearly aware of the social distance between organizers and pupils and the deference the organizers expected and hoped to perpetuate. Even in the 1930s Mary Watts expected the Compton children to curtsy to her.[18] The Home Arts movement, like other forms of cultural philanthropy, was essentially conservative in its social outlook. Home Arts class organizers sought evidence that pupils had absorbed middle-class artistic values and the virtues of respectability and self-discipline. In the mid-1880s the majority of students were boys aged thirteen to sixteen, entering the workplace after elementary education. This group had a high perceived risk of perpetuating anti-social behaviour or gravitating into 'idle' adult drinking cultures. The *Magazine of Art* noted that 'without the aid and incentive supplied by these classes, the profit and pleasure of the leisure hours of these boys would be wholly lost'.[19] There were perhaps deeper social control agendas. The association promoted a 'refined and happy home-life for the people' through the appreciation of handicraft and beauty.[20] The encouragement of private and

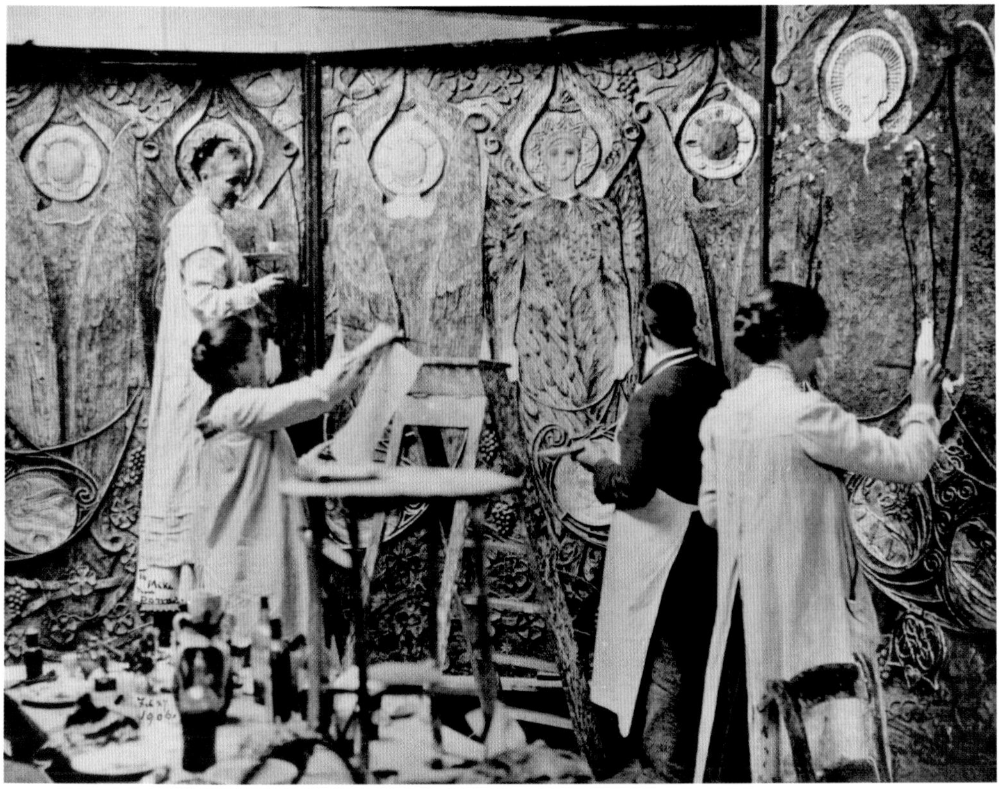

Mary Watts and students of her Home Arts and Industries Association class decorating interior panels for the chapel in her studio at Limnerslease, c.1902

domestic culture discouraged public and collective working-class behaviours ranging from drinking to political action. As early as 1853, in *The Nature of Gothic*, Ruskin had explicitly linked the promotion of handicraft with the defusing of working-class unrest. He asserted that the 'universal outcry against wealth and against nobility' was not solely caused by famine or the humiliation of the poor but because 'they have no pleasure in the work by which they make their bread'.[21] In many ways cultural philanthropy allayed middle-class fears of social breakdown and concern about the future of western society in the last decades of the nineteenth century, which were marked by unemployment and social unrest.

Cultural philanthropy, the Home Arts and Industries Association and the Arts and Crafts movement all developed in the 1880s when the social problems of the industrial city had become acute, systematic state intervention was only just beginning to have some effect, and existing remedies – charity, belief in progress and traditional religion – appeared inadequate. The decline of religion was particularly important. The intelligentsia were affected by scientific developments and Darwinism, while the urban masses largely eschewed church going. Ruskin and Matthew Arnold had given the arts and culture a quasi-religious status that promised effectiveness in a secularizing age. The Rev. Samuel Barnett used art to reach the urban poor precisely because Christianity was proving ineffectual,[22] and the rhetoric employed by the Homes Arts Association, as seen above, often had a religious tinge.

Mary Watts's first-known involvement with the Association took place in 1884. Through the winters of 1884 and 1885, when still unmarried, she organized an evening clay-modelling class at a boys' club at St Jude's school,

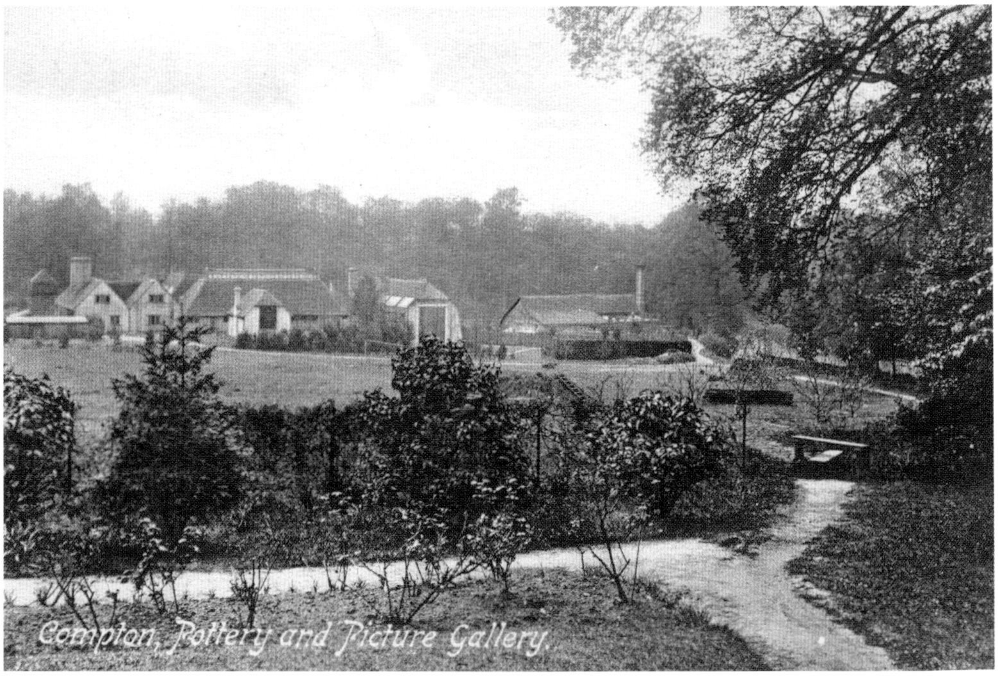

The Watts Gallery (left) and Compton Pottery (right, with tall chimney) seen from the north, after 1906, from an old postcard, private collection

Whitechapel, through a friend and fellow member of the association who ran a mosaic class there. Her pupils were 'chiefly shoe-blacks'.[23] In June 1886, shortly before her marriage to Watts, she was elected to the Council of the Home Arts.[24] G.F. Watts was already sympathetic to the organization, through Lord and Lady Brownlow, the latter being one 'of his truest friends to the end of his life'.[25]

The Home Arts and Industries Association developed and expanded in the late 1880s and in the 1890s. From 1888 the annual exhibitions were held in the Royal Albert Hall. By 1889 around 450 classes were in progress and by 1895 around 500.[26] In the mid-1890s Mary Watts was heavily involved in plans to develop and endow the association, to enable it to fund a secretary at its Albert Hall offices, to purchase examples of craftwork for circulation and to finance classes and projects where needed.[27] She solicited subscriptions and details of potential subscribers for the association in 1893.[28] She also valued Watts's support for the fund-raising, depicting him as an 'Epsom beggar'.[29] To deter her from writing begging letters, Watts painted special portrait commissions, donating £1,000 to the fund in 1895, a contribution of over one third of its total.[30] At the same time Mary developed her plans for the chapel and pottery, setting up her Home Arts clay-modelling class in her studio in Limnerslease in the autumn of 1895. Watts sold smaller paintings to fund the projects. Their philanthropic purpose made the expenditure acceptable to him, even when worryingly large. He wrote to his Liverpool patron, James Smith, 'my wife likes to give & aid largely, (I don't discourage her!)'[31] Later, while the chapel was in progress, he wrote that 'a little money could be useful. My wife has undertaken some things here in the hope of improving the conditions & improving the taste of the village which will cost I expect a great deal more than she anticipates,'[32] and, when the hostel for the pottery was under construction, 'my wife's very active philanthropy sometimes outruns strict prudence'.[33]

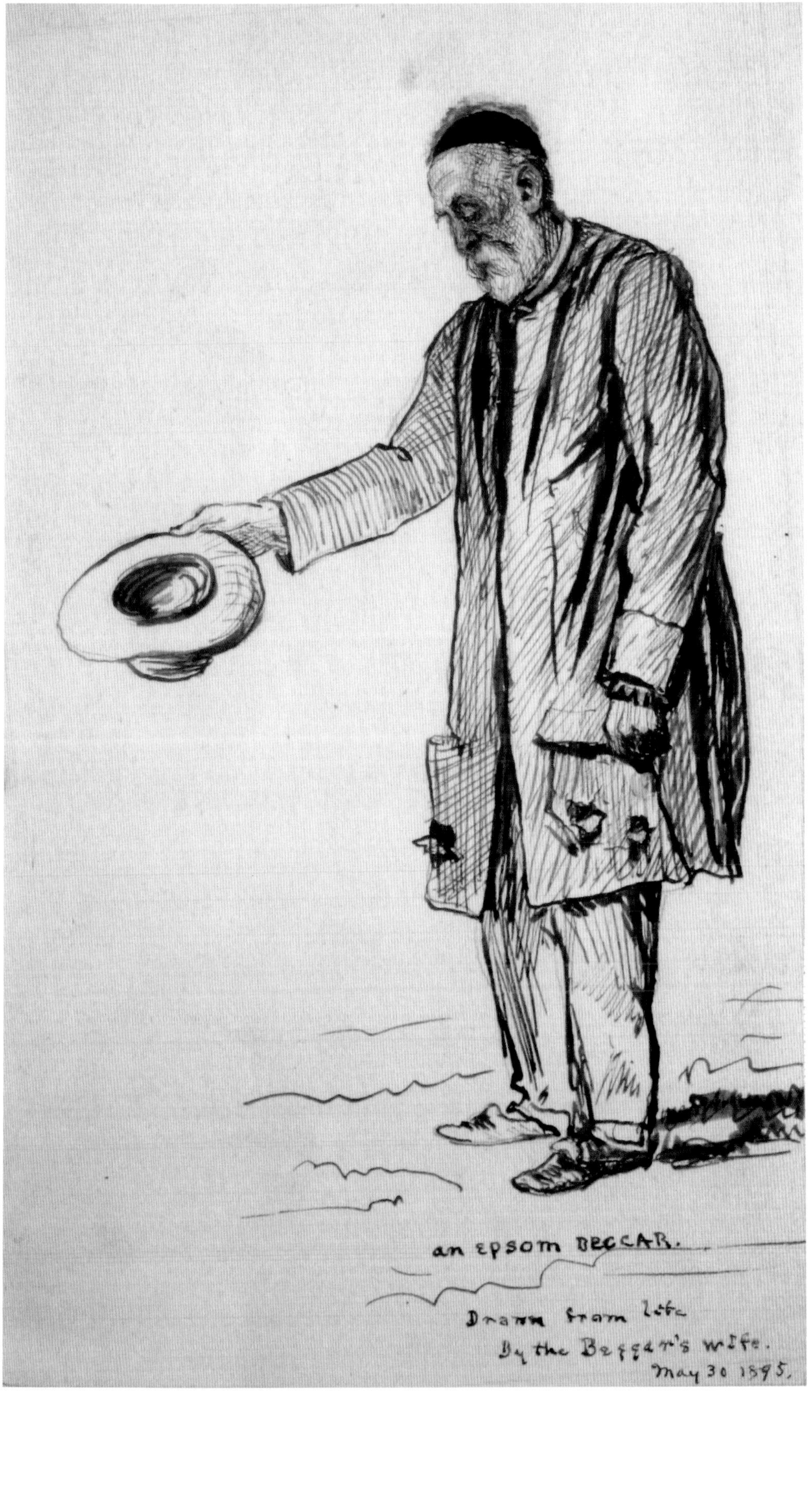

Mary Watts, An Epsom Beggar, *30 May 1895, pen and ink, 20 x 12.1 cm, Watts Gallery. G.F. Watts is shown soliciting funds for the Home Arts and Industries Association*

Most cultural philanthropy was aimed at the urban and industrial working classes.[34] Some of the classes and developed industries of the Home Arts movement were based in the cities, such as the Hon. Mabel de Grey's inlay and marquetry classes in Pimlico and the Della Robbia Pottery in Liverpool. However, the origins of the movement in the Cottage Arts Association were rural, and many of its classes remained in small towns, villages and rural areas. To that extent, Mary Watts's Compton enterprises were typical of the movement. This ruralism had a dual aspect: it reflected both the idealization of the countryside and the real problems of rural areas in the context of a developed urban, industrial society.

The idealization of the countryside has a long history, which grew with the expansion of industrial cities and their environmental and social problems.[35] In late nineteenth-century Britain the simplicity of rural life was highly valued as part of a 'back to the land' movement among the intelligentsia.[36] William Morris created a rural idyll in his socialist utopia, *News from Nowhere* (1890), and Charles Robert Ashbee (1863–1942) shifted his Guild of Handicraft (founded 1888) from the East End of London to Chipping Camden in the Cotswolds in 1902. When setting up her pottery with teenage apprentices in the new hostel, Mary Watts brought at least one boy, Lincoln Holland, from an industrial town (Macclesfield) to a rural environment.[37]

On the other hand, British rural society faced real problems from the 1870s on. Agricultural depression caused by cheap food imports from America and Australasia, combined with the erosion of local crafts and industries through the national distribution of cheap, industrially made goods contributed to lack of employment, lowered wages and rural depopulation. At its height, the pottery gave employment to at least seventeen men, mostly local,[38] a significant contribution to the economy of a village with a population of under eight hundred.[39]

An article of 1911 on the pottery and its roots in the chapel noted that 'the whole story of the work is deeply interesting, for it was decided that the decorative part should all be made of terra-cotta from local clay'.[40] Localized deposits of brick earth are found among the sandy soils that lie north and south of the North Downs, leading to a long history of small-scale pottery manufacture and brick making in these areas. South of the Hog's Back, in a narrow ridge of downland between Guildford and Farnham, the iron-rich nature of the soil produces distinctive strong orange-reds in fired clay. A seam of this gault clay was available in the grounds of Limnerslease and was used for the chapel and the pottery.

Ruskin has little to say about local materials – around 1850 he praises the appropriate use of rich and exotic building stones – but it became a common Arts and Crafts movement tenet. Appreciation of local and vernacular traditions of architecture grew in the 1860s when George Devey (1820–86) and Norman Shaw (1831–1912) developed the 'Old English' style. Shaw's office became the training ground of many Arts and Crafts movement architects. Surviving vernacular buildings were increasingly valued, as in William Morris's loving tenure of Kelmscott Manor from 1871 and the preservation work of the Society for the Protection of Ancient Buildings from 1877. As pattern-books, the mass manufacture of architectural fittings and the railway transport of bricks and

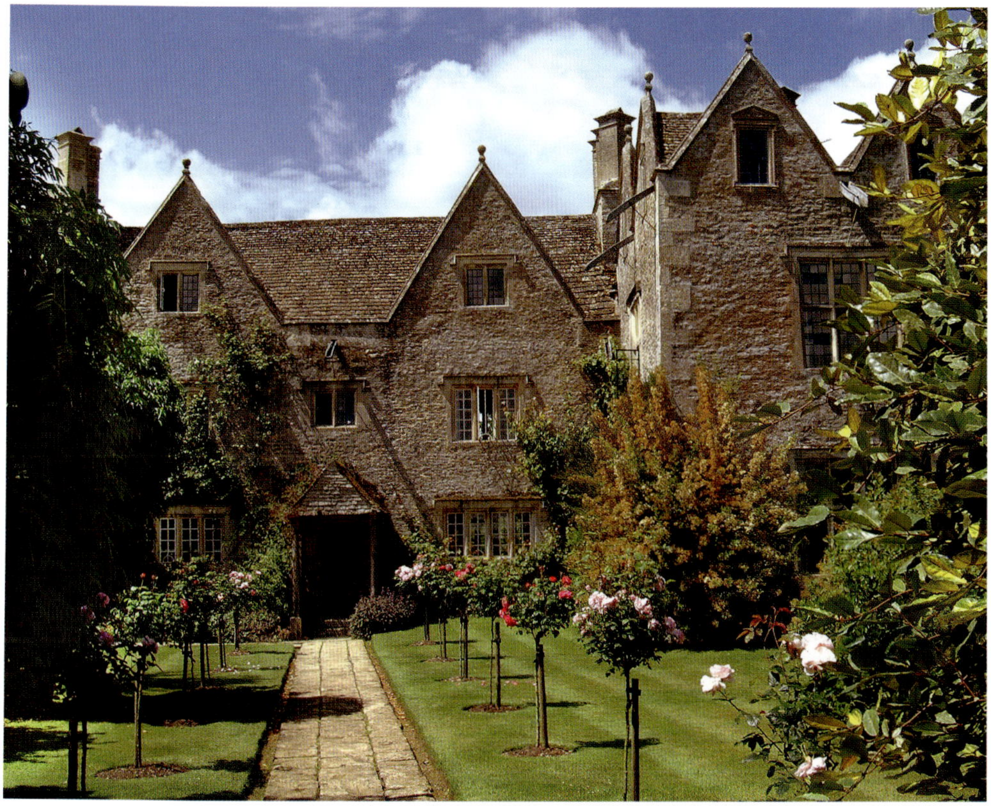

Kelmscott Manor, Gloucestershire, the country home of William Morris, photograph by permission of the Society of Antiquaries of London

Welsh slate gave rise to semi-standardized, suburbanized buildings in the later nineteenth century, many Arts and Crafts movement architects, favouring handicrafts and rural traditions, insisted on taking their materials from as close to their site as possible. Examples could be multiplied, but, for example, Philip Webb, Edwin Lutyens, Detmar Blow, E.S. Prior and Sidney Barnsley all favoured this.[41] Locally, Lutyens's Munstead Wood house for Gertrude Jekyll incorporated timber from oaks that had given her pleasure while growing.[42] This insistence on local materials helped to create a building in intrinsic harmony with its landscape.

In 1904 the pottery was named the Potters' Arts Guild, one of a series of recent 'Guild' organizations associated with Ruskinism and the Arts and Crafts movement. These included John Ruskin's own Guild of St George (1871), A.H. Mackmurdo's Century Guild (1882), the Art Workers' Guild (1884), C.R. Ashbee's Guild of Handicraft (1888), the Northern Art Workers' Guild in Manchester (1896) and the Guild of Women Binders (1898). The medieval ideal of the Arts and Crafts movement stemmed from its roots in the Gothic revival and was similarly used to criticize modern industrialized society. The 'guild' recalled an era of handicraft production and suggested a harmonious and egalitarian association of craftsmen. In fact, the Potters' Arts Guild, like other manufacturing Arts and Crafts guilds, ran on hierarchical business lines, despite its profit-sharing arrangement. Even after Mary Watts had vested her capital in the business with trustees in 1920[43] and become the director in a management committee of four that included two workers, she retained a right of veto over all pottery designs[44] and clearly exerted control for most of her life.

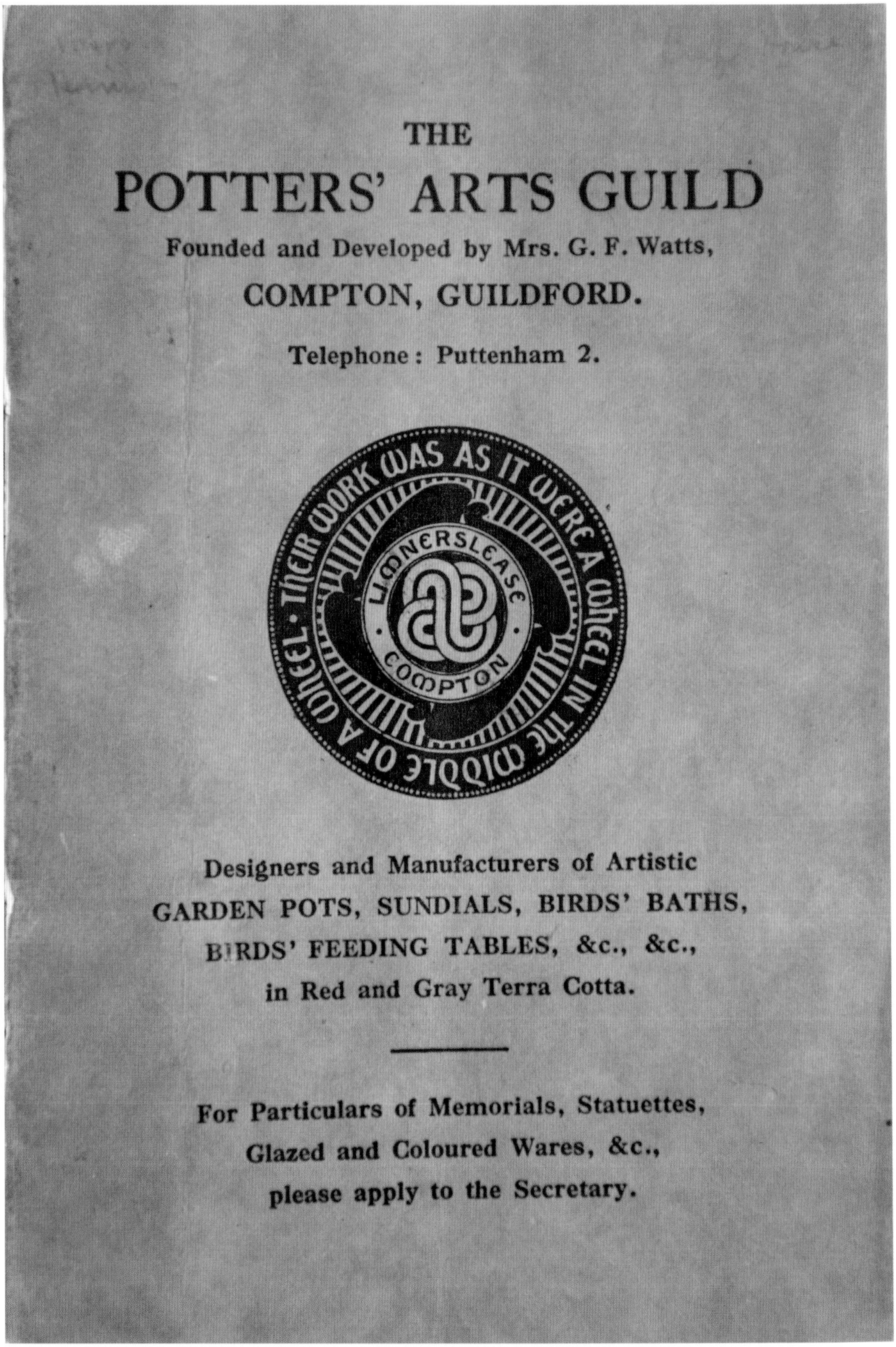

THE

POTTERS' ARTS GUILD

Founded and Developed by Mrs. G. F. Watts,

COMPTON, GUILDFORD.

Telephone: Puttenham 2.

Designers and Manufacturers of Artistic
GARDEN POTS, SUNDIALS, BIRDS' BATHS,
BIRDS' FEEDING TABLES, &c., &c.,
in Red and Gray Terra Cotta.

For Particulars of Memorials, Statuettes,
Glazed and Coloured Wares, &c.,
please apply to the Secretary.

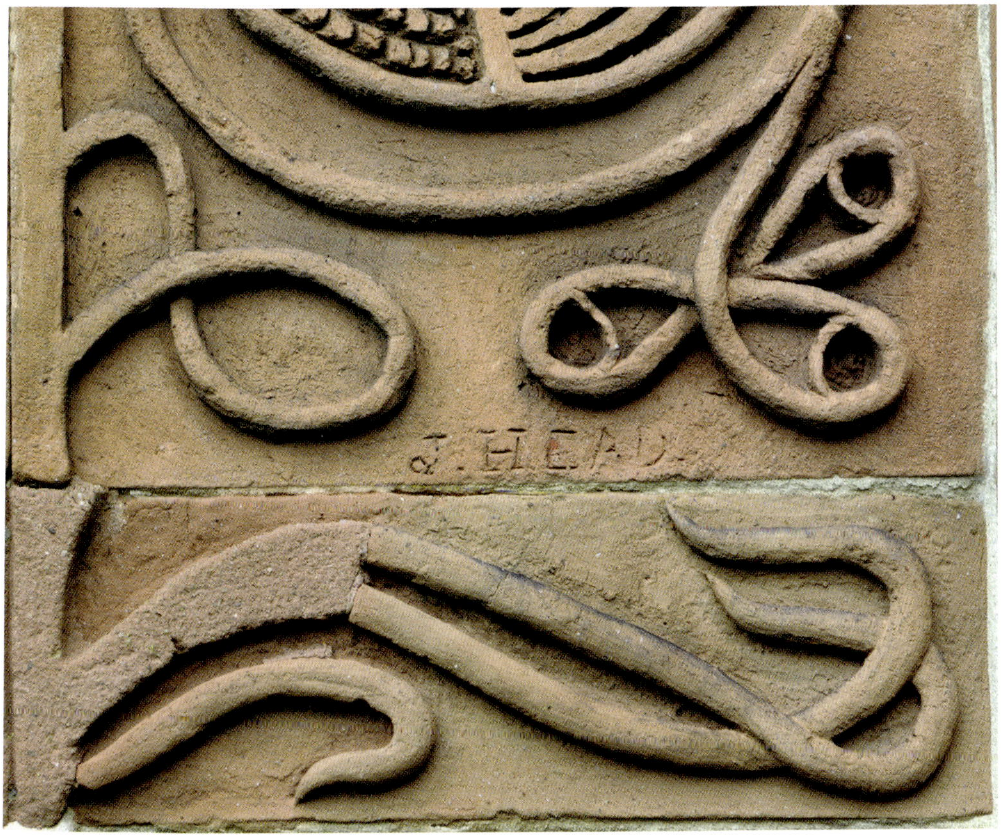

Opposite: The cover of a catalogue of Potters' Arts Guild products, undated, Watts Gallery Archive

Left: Detail from the Tree of Life frieze on the north-west corner of Watts Chapel, c.1895–98, showing the signature of J. Head

Guilds also suggested a pre-individualistic age where the creative worker was happy to remain anonymous. Mary Watts only permitted individual contributors to the chapel to sign their work on the reverse,[45] although a tile signed 'J. Head' on one of the northern exterior pillars escaped her notice. She included a list of the makers' names in the first edition of her book about the chapel, *The Word in the Pattern*, but saw this as 'only of interest to the workers'.[46] It was omitted from later editions. Of the chapel's workers, she did not like to 'mention one more than another', singling out only Louis Deuchars (1870–1927) and George Redmayne (1840/41–1912), but this was in the context of downplaying her own contribution: 'I should rather prefer if the personal element was rather less – I mean about "Mrs Watts"!'[47] In the pottery, as was common in this period, individual designers were not credited, although magazines sometimes mention the modelling skills of Thomas Wren.[48] However, because of her social status, Mary was widely credited as organizer of the pottery and as a designer, even by Liberty's, whose practice was not to acknowledge the source of its designs.[49]

Detailed accounts of the building of the Watts Chapel and the history of the Compton potteries follow in later chapters of this book but the continuing relationship of the enterprises to the Home Arts and Industries Association is shown by Compton's appearances in the association's annual exhibitions at the Royal Albert Hall. The exhibitions were without catalogues, so their contents can only be reconstructed from press coverage. Sections of the chapel were exhibited by 'Compton Terra Cotta Home Arts' between at least 1896 and 1902, including exterior capitals in 1896, the altar in 1899 and unfinished panels from the interior

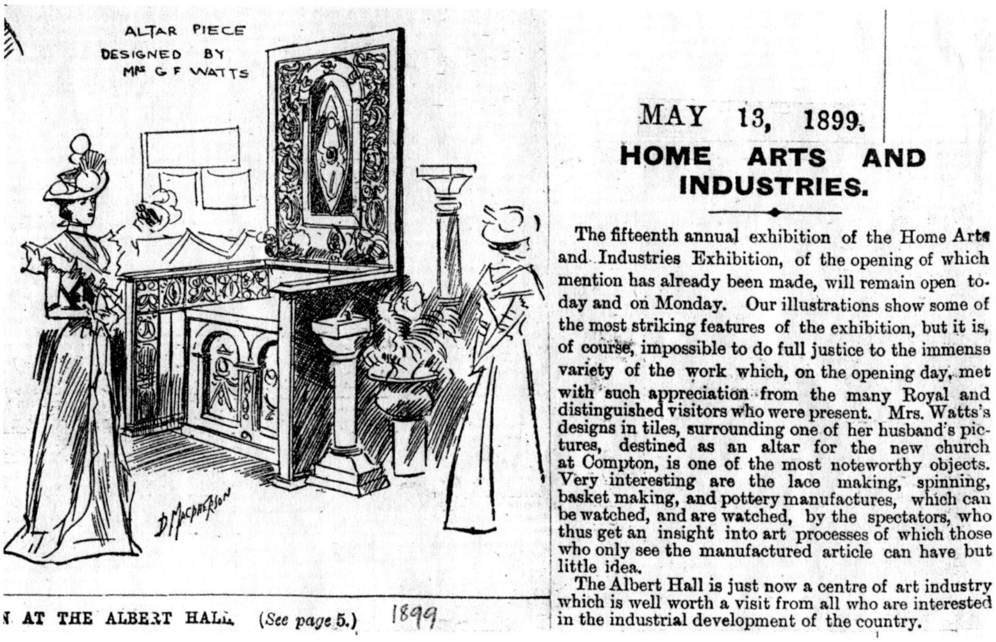

MAY 13, 1899.

HOME ARTS AND INDUSTRIES.

The fifteenth annual exhibition of the Home Arts and Industries Exhibition, of the opening of which mention has already been made, will remain open to-day and on Monday. Our illustrations show some of the most striking features of the exhibition, but it is, of course, impossible to do full justice to the immense variety of the work which, on the opening day, met with such appreciation from the many Royal and distinguished visitors who were present. Mrs. Watts's designs in tiles, surrounding one of her husband's pictures, destined as an altar for the new church at Compton, is one of the most noteworthy objects. Very interesting are the lace making, spinning, basket making, and pottery manufactures, which can be watched, and are watched, by the spectators, who thus get an insight into art processes of which those who only see the manufactured article can have but little idea.

The Albert Hall is just now a centre of art industry which is well worth a visit from all who are interested in the industrial development of the country.

The Home Arts and Industries Association exhibition of 1899, including the Potters' Arts Guild stand with the altarpiece of Watts Chapel, from an unidentified press cutting, Watts Gallery Archive

in 1902.[50] Other notable exhibits comprised the Watts sundial in 1900 and the 'Celtic Sleep Blessing' bedhead in 1901.[51] After this period detailed coverage in the art press diminishes and it is harder to identify individual exhibits.

The Home Arts and Industries Association was most active before the First World War, but existed in some form until at least the early 1930s. The Potters' Arts Guild showed in an association exhibition at Drapers' Hall in London in 1931.[52] Philanthropic handicraft industries continued to develop in the post-war period, but largely as employment projects for wounded soldiers.[53] It is probable that the association was already in decline before the war. Its exhibitions were not so prominent, its organizers were ageing, and the excitement about handicraft and vernacular traditions, which had marked the height of the Arts and Crafts movement for about twenty years after 1885, was lessening.

The Home Arts and Industries Association occupies an ambivalent place in the wider history of the Arts and Crafts movement.[54] The association and the movement share common sources of inspiration in Ruskin's ideal of handiwork and in the rural ideal, as shown above. Indeed, the Arts and Crafts movement pioneer, A.H. Mackmurdo (1851–1942), believed that, 'had it not been for the work done by the Home Arts and Industries Association, it may be questioned whether the Art Workers' Guild or the Council craft schools would have yet been established' and saw the association as the 'first fruits of the Arts and Crafts movement'.[55] However, there were significant differences between the movements. This is apparent in the organization of their respective exhibitions. The Arts and Crafts Exhibition Society, founded in 1887, mounted annual exhibitions from 1888 to 1890 and triennial shows subsequently. Until 1903 they were held in the prestigious art venue of the New Gallery in Regent Street. They lasted for several weeks and had a printed catalogue. The Home Arts exhibitions were held annually from 1885, and after 1888 in the Albert Hall, a venue associated with popular entertainment rather than high culture. They were of only a few

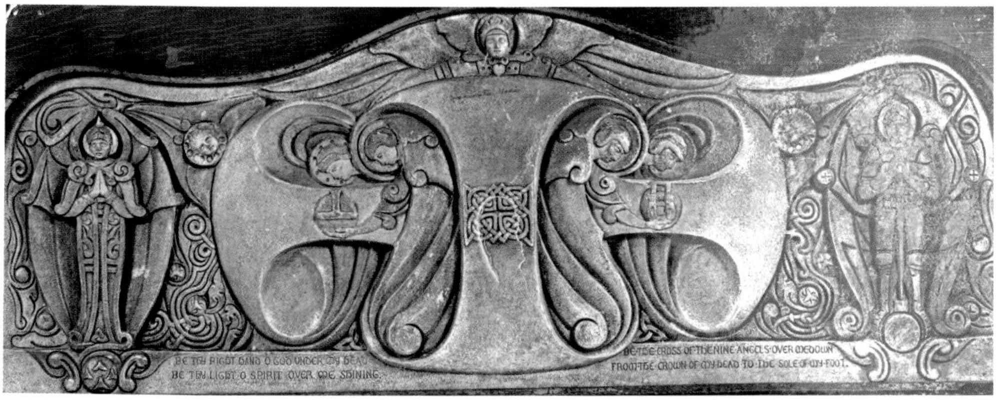

'Celtic Sleep Blessing' bedhead, 1901, painted ceramic

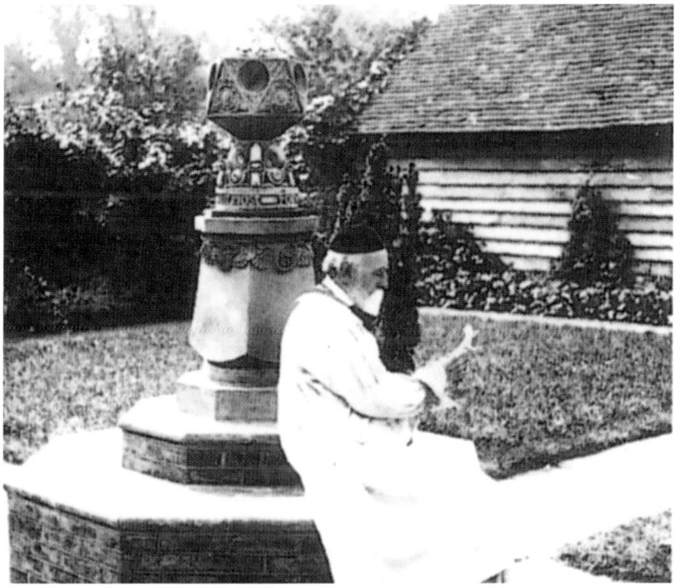

George Frederic Watts seated by the sundial in the garden of Limnerslease, c.*1899–1900*

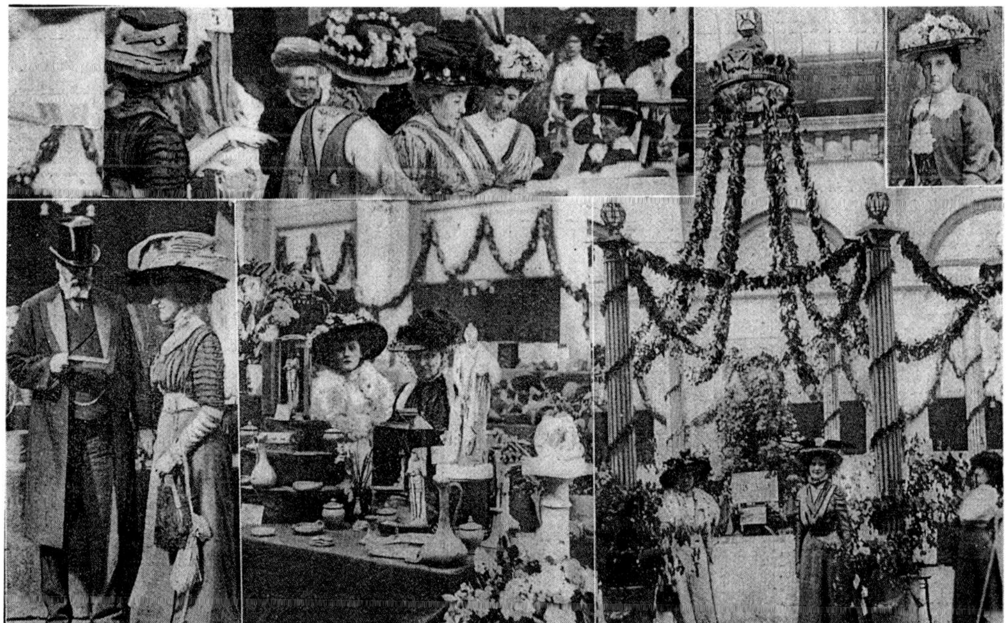

Scenes at the Home Arts and Industries exhibition at the Horticultural Hall, London, 1909, from an unidentified press cutting, Watts Gallery Archive

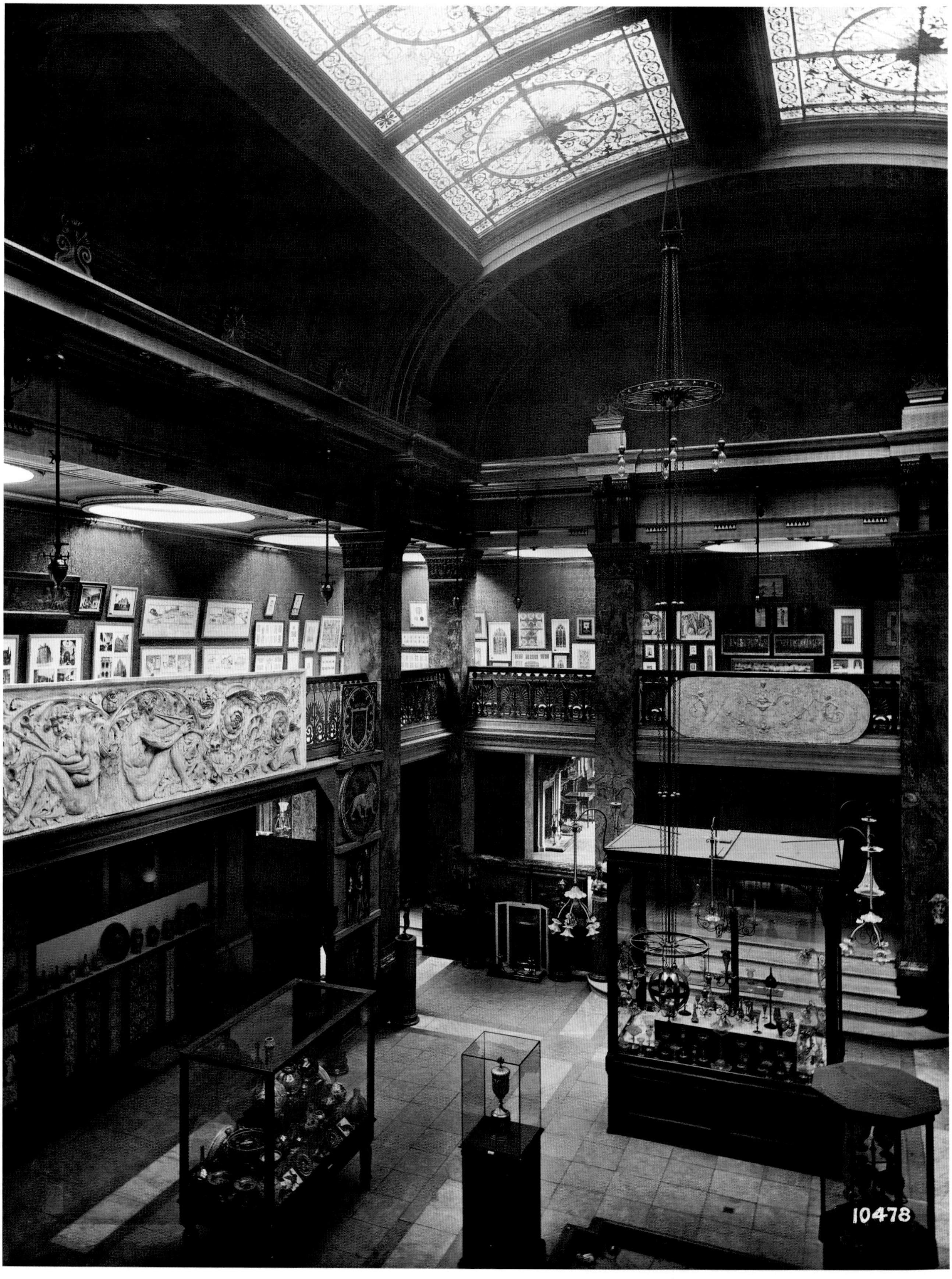
10478

days' duration[56] and produced no catalogues.[57] Classes put on their own displays at tables or stands, often staffed by the class organizers. A press cutting relating to the 1909 exhibition at the Horticultural Hall in London suggests that the association exploited its royal, aristocratic and society connections to gain publicity and raise funds. Captions include 'Princess Christian purchasing' and 'Lady Talbot finds a customer in Lord Brownlow'. The review in the *Studio* in 1895 was forced to dismiss associations with 'a sort of annual charity bazaar' in order to assert that the organization had a serious purpose.[58] The association was little reviewed in the art press after 1902. In the context of the general professionalization of society and the art world in the late nineteenth century,[59] the philanthropic background of the association and the amateur status of many of its workers and classes relegated it to a culturally marginal position compared with the wider Arts and Crafts movement, which was dominated by professional architects, designers, fine artists and commercial manufacturers.

Opposite: The Arts and Crafts Exhibition Society exhibition of 1890 at the New Gallery, Regent Street, London, photograph by A.B. Bedford Lemare and Company, reproduced by permission of English Heritage/NMR

NOTES

1 Mrs Ellis, *Education of the Heart: Woman's Best Work*, London 1869, p.14, quoted in F.K. Prochaska, *Women and Philanthropy in Nineteenth-Century England*, Oxford 1980, p.6.

2 Her fourth child, also Eglantyne Jebb (1876 –1928), was a notable philanthropist, too, and founder of Save the Children Fund in 1919. Brian Harrison, 'Eglantyne Jebb (1876–1928)', *Oxford Dictionary of National Biography*, ed. H.C.G. Matthew and Lawrence Goldman, Oxford 2004 (http://www.oxforddnb.com accessed 15/05/2009).

3 'The Chronicle of Art: Art in June', *Magazine of Art*, vol.VIII, 1885, p.xxxiii; see also 'The Chronicle of Art: Art in August', p.xlii.

4 Franklin Gould 2004, pp.196–97.

5 'The Chronicle of Art: Art in August', *Magazine of Art*, vol.VIII, 1885, p.xlii.

6 Compare present-day anxiety about 'welfare dependency'.

7 Borzello 1987. See also Wilson 2004, pp.169–83, especially pp.175–76.

8 Franklin Gould 2004, p.214. Giles Waterfield, ed., *Art for the People: Culture in the Slums of Late Victorian Britain*, exh. cat., Dulwich Picture Gallery, London 1994. This catalogue is the most detailed study of the South London Gallery.

9 Inventory of Limnerslease, 1938, Watts Gallery Archive. This is a selective rather than a complete listing of the books at Limnerslease.

10 'From Diaries 1886–1895', MSW Diary Notes, 21 September 1890.

11 Ruskin 1903–12, vol.10 (*The Stones of Venice*, vol.II, 1851), pp.192–93.

12 *Home Arts and Industries Association c.*1895.

13 *Home Arts and Industries Association c.*1895, p.7.

14 'From Diaries 1886–1895', MSW Diary Notes, 16 June 1892.

15 Both examples from *Home Arts and Industries Association c.*1895.

16 George Frederic Watts to James Smith, 27 November 1898, Watts Gallery Archive.

17 *Home Arts and Industries Association c.*1895.

18 Blunt 1975, p.237. Blunt records, 'One such child, on being reprimanded, replied, "Mother told us not

to as we're just as good as you"', a clear sign of changing times.

19 'The Chronicle of Art: Art in August', *The Magazine of Art*, vol.VIII, 1885, p.xliii.

20 *Home Arts and Industries Association c.*1895.

21 Ruskin 1903–12, vol.10 (*The Stones of Venice*, vol.II, 1851), p.194.

22 Borzello 1987, p.33.

23 Watts 1912, vol.II, pp.57–58.

24 Wilson 2004, p.183 n.27.

25 Watts 1912, vol.II, p.123. Watts had painted Lady Brownlow as Lady Adelaide Talbot in 1865–66 before her marriage, also including her in the group portrait, *Lady Constance Lothian and her Sisters* (1862; Earl of Ancram). He painted Lord Brownlow in 1868–69 (Watts 1912, vol.II, pp.21, 154).

26 http://www.artsandcraftsmetalwork.co.uk/page4.htm, accessed 22/05/2009; referencing Janice Helland, *British and Irish Home Arts and Industries 1880–1914*, Dublin 2007. For number of classes, see G.F. Watts, 'The National Position of Art', *Transactions of the National Association for the Advancement of Art and its Application to Industry*, Edinburgh meeting 1889, reprinted in Watts 1912, vol.III, p.269, and *Home Arts and Industries Association c.*1895.

27 Account of fundraising aims in *Home Arts and Industries Association c.*1895.

28 For instance, M.S. Watts to James Smith, 8 September 1893, Watts Gallery Archive. See also the circular letter that accompanied it, M.S. Watts to 'Sir', undated, and her acknowledgment of his cheque on 'September 11th' and list of potential subscribers on 'September 24th'.

29 Not only was the Derby race day at Epsom races notorious for its gypsies and beggars, Mary's stepmother had made her home there.

30 See financial accounts in *Home Arts and Industries Association c.*1895. For Watts's opposition to Mary's letter-writing campaign, see G.F. Watts to James Smith, 1 October 1894, Watts Gallery Archive. For his fundraising commission, see the *Bookman*, April 1913, p.19, in a volume of press cuttings of reviews of Watts 1912 and G.F. Watts to James Smith, 1 October 1894, both Watts Gallery Archive.

31 G.F. Watts to James Smith, 2 September 1892, Watts Gallery Archive.

32 G.F. Watts to James Smith, 12 January 1896, Watts Gallery Archive.

33 G.F. Watts to James Smith, 26 October 1903, Watts Gallery Archive.

34 Borzello 1987, p.33.

35 Raymond Williams, *The City and the Country*, London 1973.

36 Marsh 1982.

37 Calvert 2006, p.19.

38 I am indebted to Gail Naughton for her research into the birthplaces of the pottery workers.

39 Boston 1987, p.211. The population of Compton was 684 in 1911, 777 in 1921 and 771 in 1931.

40 Webb 1911, pp.101–2.

41 Elizabeth Cummings and Wendy Kaplan, *The Arts and Crafts Movement* (World of Art series) London 1991, esp. pp.44–46. Peter Davey, *Arts and Crafts Architecture*, London 1995, *passim*.

42 Gertrude Jekyll, *Home and Garden: Notes and Thoughts, Practical and Critical, of a Worker in Both*, London 1900, pp.4–5.

43 Indenture dated 15 March 1920, Watts Gallery Archive.

44 'The Scheme of Constitution during the Life-Time of Mrs Watts' (associated with the indenture of 15 March 1920), clause 6, Watts Gallery Archive.

45 Richard Jefferies, personal communication.

46 M.S. Watts to James Smith, 'Feb 13', suggesting that he should cut out the list to include the separately printed description of the interior, Watts Gallery Archive.

47 M.S. Watts to Gleeson White, editor of the *Studio*, who had sent her a proof of his article on the chapel

for correction, 'July 31', Watts Gallery Archive.

48 Webb 1911, p.102.

49 Barbara Morris, 'Liberty's Pioneer Designer', in Franklin Gould 1998, pp.12–13, discussing Liberty's March 1903 exhibition at the Grafton Gallery, *Founding a National Industry – Irish Carpets*, which included Mary Watts's Pelican rug.

50 See Franklin Gould 1998, Chronology, p.16, and Wood 1902, p.129.

51 Franklin Gould 1998, Chronology, p.16.

52 *Home Arts and Industries Association ... Catalogue of an Exhibition and Sale of British Handicrafts. The Drapers' Hall ... 26th October to 31st October 1931*, National Art Library, Victoria & Albert Museum. The later work of the association is poorly documented. Catalogues for 1931 and 1933 exhibitions survive in the National Art Library. Compton was not represented in the 1933 exhibition.

53 For instance, the Ashtead Pottery in Surrey. Mary Watts favoured former soldiers as gallery employees, such as William Westbury, gallery attendant.

54 See, for instance, Karen Livingstone and Linda Parry, eds, *International Arts and Crafts*, London 2005, where the HAIA is treated briefly on pp.96 and 106 in the essay by Mary Greensted, 'Nature and the Rural Idyll'.

55 A.H. Mackmurdo, 'History of the Arts and Crafts Movement' (MS in William Morris Gallery, Walthamstow), quoted in Franklin Gould 1998, p.65.

56 Three days in 1885 (9–11 July): 'The Chronicle of Art: Art in June', *Magazine of Art*, vol.VIII, p.xxxiii. Four days at the Horticultural Hall, 1909: press cutting, Watts Gallery Archive.

57 'The Home Arts and Industries Association, at the Royal Albert Hall', *Studio*, vol.V, 1895, p.169.

58 Ibid., p.167.

59 Harold Perkin, *The Rise of Professional Society: England since 1880*, London 1989.

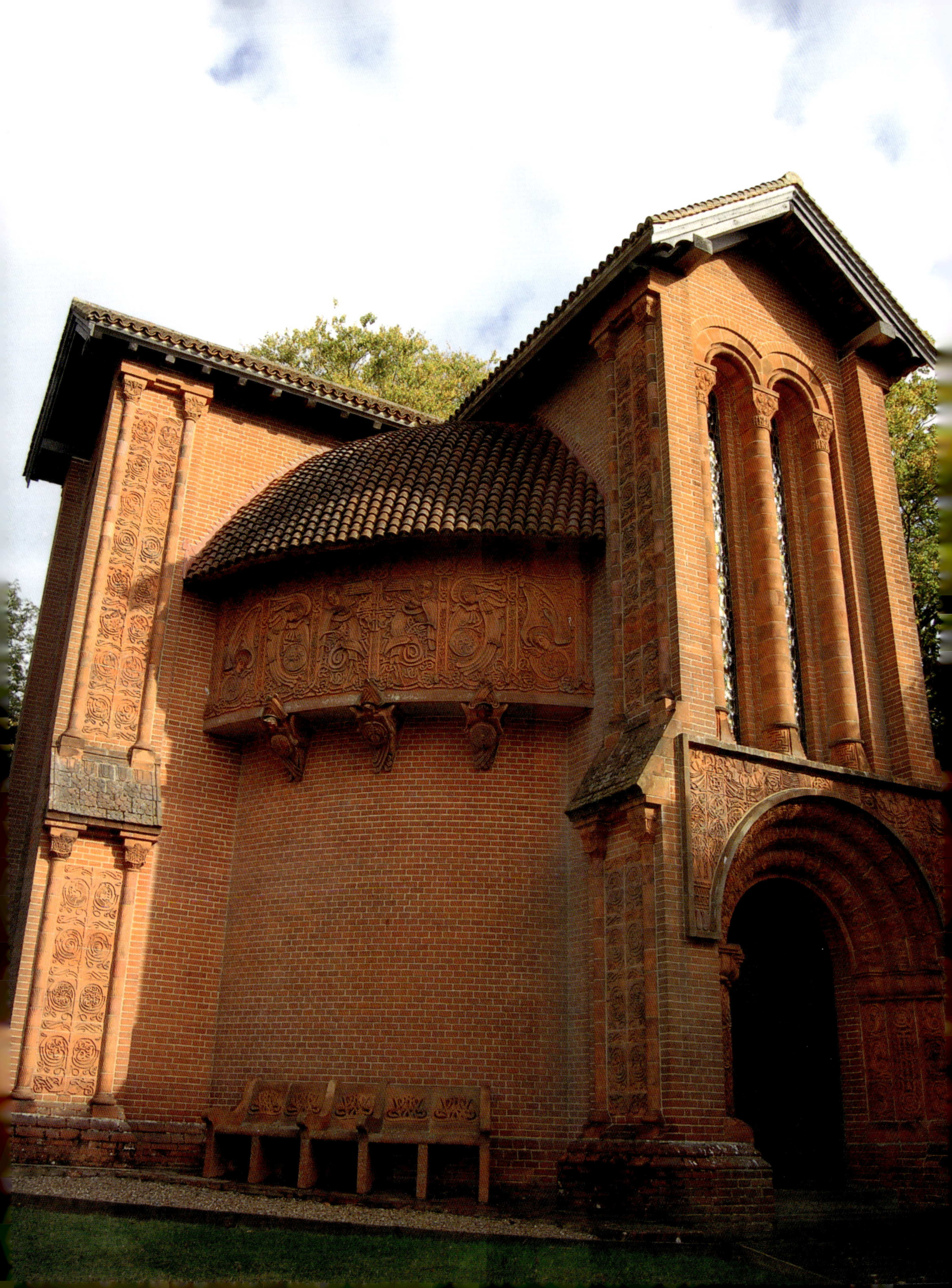

Mary Watts and the Creation of Watts Chapel

Veronica Franklin Gould

'What an opportunity wasted!' Mary Watts, depressed by the ugliness of her aunt's gravestone, sprang into action. In her mid-forties, Mary burned with creative energy. But since her marriage in 1886, her artistic life had centred largely on that of her eminent husband, the Royal Academician George Frederic Watts. Her plan that October in 1893 was to ask artist friends to design memorials to be made from local material, terracotta or stone. She would teach people to make their own gravestones.[1] Within a year she found the opportunity in her own village, Compton, which was to have a new cemetery, very close indeed to the Wattses' home, Limnerslease. Although Mary's first thought was gravestones, her enterprise was to be even more ambitious. She would herd villagers into Limnerslease and teach them to create the most extraordinary Art Nouveau building in Britain. The construction of Watts Chapel would become not only Compton's immediate functional legacy, but, as a rare fulfilment of the Home Arts and Industries Association ethos, it would lead to the foundation of a guild of potters, a new profession for Compton's working class. With idyllic working conditions in the Surrey countryside, Mary's guidance and the inspiration of the maestro (who was painting portrait commissions to pay for the chapel), this was an ideal Arts and Crafts project, there being no personal profit. As Mary wrote, 'Giving money is something – but giving ourselves is the one great & necessary gift'.[2]

Mary Fraser Tytler had studied art in Europe and London, and learned to model clay at the Slade under the Frenchman Aimé-Jules Dalou. The last two winters before her marriage to G.F. Watts, she had run clay-modelling classes for shoe-black boys in Whitechapel under the Rev. Samuel Barnett's scheme – in association with the nationwide Home Arts and Industries Association – to enrich the lives of the poor. It was this social artistic enterprise, as well as Mary's keen Symbolist imagination – Watts's preferred art form for the expression of ideas – that triggered his interest in her as a potential partner in life and art. Her church-going was less attractive to Watts, whose Sabbatarian upbringing had turned him against formalized religion. Inspired by the art critic and social reformer John Ruskin, both the Wattses yearned for the revival of handicrafts. Mary's classes, opening the minds of slum children to the joy of creativity, had given her a sense of purpose and a passion to work with the community.

Until her Whitechapel classes Mary, too aristocratic to aspire to be more than an amateur artist, had been a painter. This she had virtually given up on marriage to the academician, resolving instead to design symbolic decorative art, initially for his London home, Little Holland House in Kensington. Watts encouraged guidance from leading artists and craftsmen. Edward Burne-Jones (1833–98) arranged for Osmund Weeks to train Mary in the use of *gesso duro*.[3]

It was no small bonus for her to entertain the Burne-Joneses, the potter William Frend De Morgan (1839–1917) and his artist wife Evelyn (née Pickering,

Opposite: Watts Chapel from the north-west

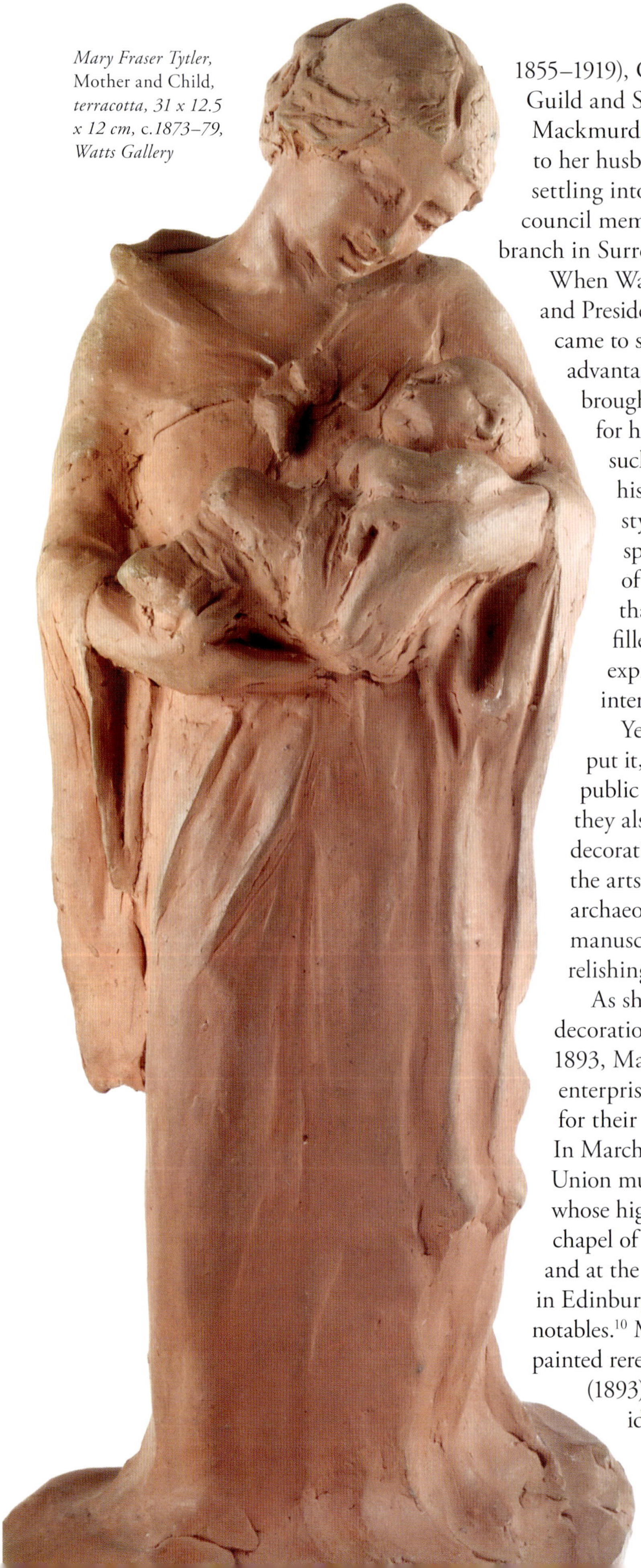

Mary Fraser Tytler, Mother and Child, *terracotta, 31 x 12.5 x 12 cm,* c.*1873–79, Watts Gallery*

1855–1919), Charles Robert Ashbee (founder of the Guild and School of Handicraft) and Arthur Heygate Mackmurdo (founder of the Century Guild), who looked to her husband to endorse their new guilds; and on settling into Limnerslease in 1891, the Wattses, active council members of the Home Arts, were keen to start a branch in Surrey.

When Walter Crane (1845–1915), the socialist craftsman and President of the Arts and Crafts Exhibition Society, came to sit to Watts that August,[4] Mary took full advantage of her duty to engage him in discussion. She brought in her own work but rejected his correct term for her application of fibrous gesso as '"stucco" – such a hideous sound to ones modern ears' – and his opinion that decorative art should ignore earlier styles. Mary wanted her symbolic patterns to spring from a style 'sympathetic for the expression of one's idea'.[5] Her husband's pivotal suggestion that she unite hitherto separate symbols – each filled with multiple meanings – led her to her expressive decorative style, the Celtic cord, or interlace, into which all her ideas could be woven.

Yearning with Watts to create, as Thomas Carlyle put it, even 'a dog-hutch',[6] to build something for the public good,[7] Mary honed her modelling skills and they also read widely together. For her pantheistic relief decoration at Limnerslease (1891–96), she researched the arts of ancient civilizations in books lent by leading archaeologists and copied details from artefacts and manuscripts at the India Office and British Museum, relishing the sensuous animation of Celtic art.[8]

As she was finishing her flamboyant painted decoration for Watts's reading niche at Limnerslease in 1893, Mary took a special interest in Conrad Dressler's enterprise with Harold Rathbone to train apprentices for their future Della Robbia Pottery in Liverpool.[9] In March 1894 she entertained the Edinburgh Social Union muralist Phoebe Anna Traquair (1852–1936), whose highly symbolic decorations in the mortuary chapel of the Royal Hospital for Sick Children (1885–86) and at the Song School of St Mary's Cathedral (1888–92) in Edinburgh featured Watts among other British notables.[10] Mary had created her first 'national work', a painted reredos for the workhouse chapel at St Albans (1893), for which Signor gave the brass cross, when her ideal opportunity cropped up closer to home.[11]

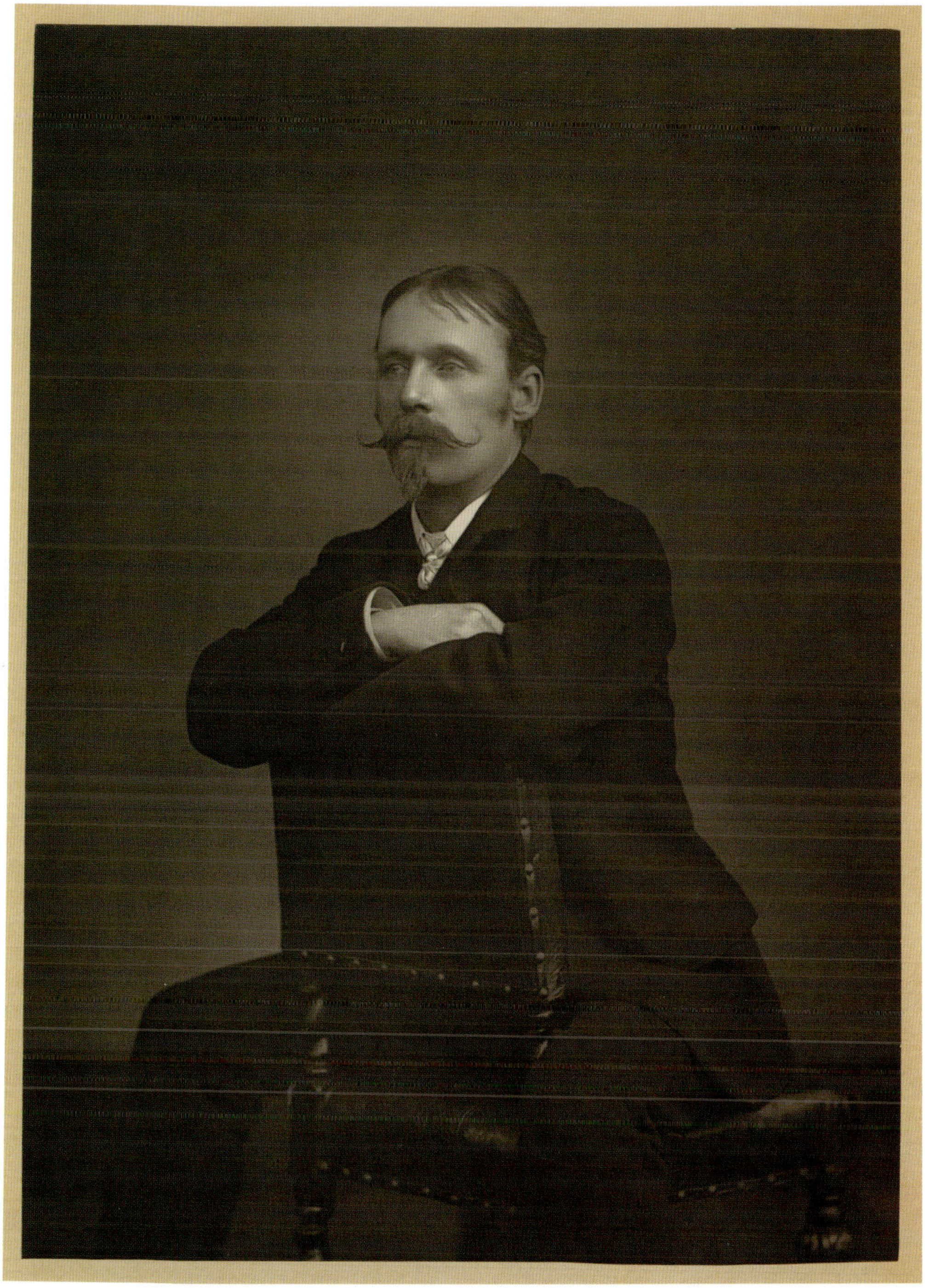

Walter Crane, c.1885, photograph by Emery Walker

On 25 May 1894 Compton Parish Council resolved to purchase 'Grass Land on Budborough Hill for the purpose of a New Cemetery'.[12] Mary's mind was now 'full of improving churchyards, memorials', as she noted in her diary on 4 September. By the 9th she had located a seam of gault clay, which resolved her medium: 'My hope is that Terra Cotta shall be my Rita', a Hindu expression meaning 'true path'. She would teach villagers to model memorials from local clay. By 21 March 1895 there had been a seismic shift. 'My fatal visit to village homes!', Mary noted in her diary. She had found her 'dog-hutch' – a terracotta

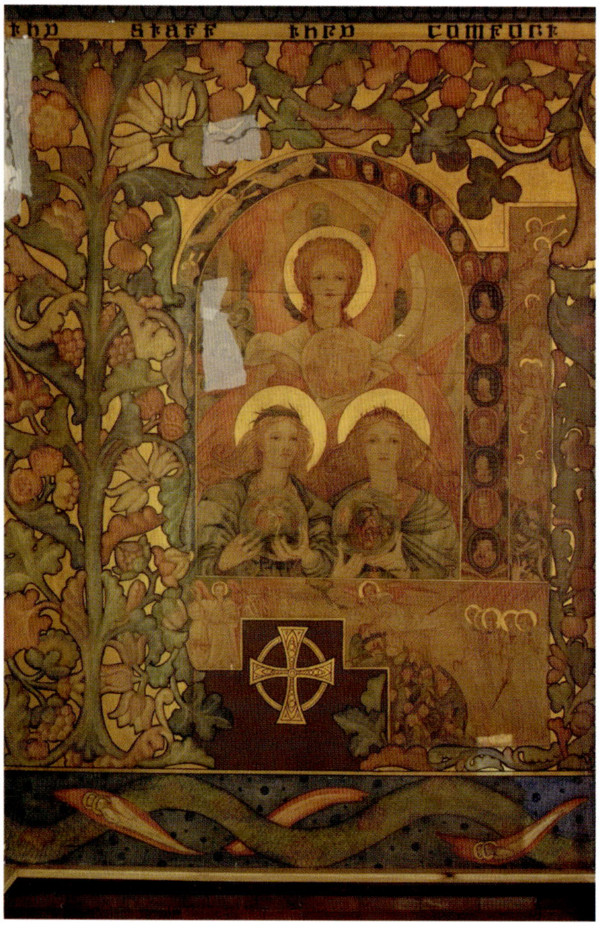

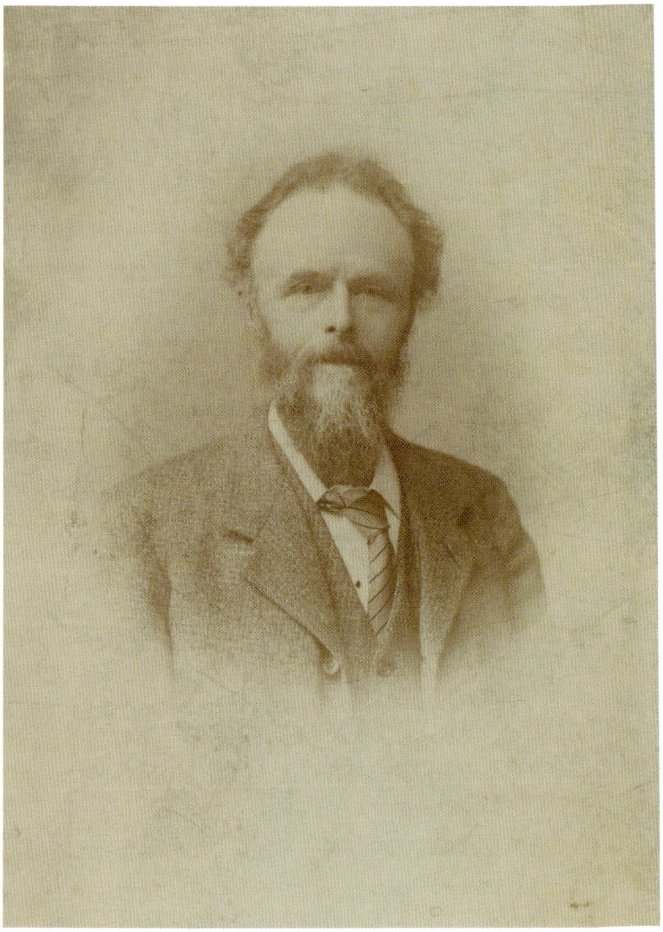

Above left: Phoebe Anna Traquair, 'Angel Powers' mural, Chapel of the Royal Hospital for Sick Children, Edinburgh, 1885–86, reproduced with permission from Medical Photography, NHS Lothian

Above right: William De Morgan, c.1900, photograph by Florence Montabone, from The Rob Dickins Collection, Watts Gallery

memorial chapel. The Archbishop of Canterbury's address to Royal Academicians in May, calling for art to give British youth a real insight into the inner spirit and beauty, was timely, for she planned to teach youngsters to model symbolic tiles for the chapel. Compton Parish Council minuted her letter offering on Watts's behalf to build a chapel in the new cemetery on 30 May. Making a cardboard model by 28 June, Mary finished the design by 9 August and discussed it with her architectural adviser George Redmayne, FRIBA. Watts, meanwhile, painted portrait commissions to make a major donation to the Home Arts, as well as pay for the construction of the chapel and the needs of Mary's Compton Terra Cotta Home Arts class.[13]

The parish council paid William More Molyneux of Loseley £74 7s for the three-quarter-acre ribbon of hillside on 2 October. Five days later, Hugh Gillett, the rector and chairman of the council, sent the Home Secretary the cemetery plan drawn up by a local architect and surveyor, John Lake; and with William De Morgan's guidance, Mary had a wood-fired bottle kiln built in the grounds of Limnerslease (on land now owned by Brixbury Cottage) across the lane from the cemetery.

Every aspect of Compton's cemetery chapel would be a symbolic celebration of spiritual and material life, from birth to death and beyond, from the distinctive ground plan of the Eternal Circle intersected by the Cross of Faith,

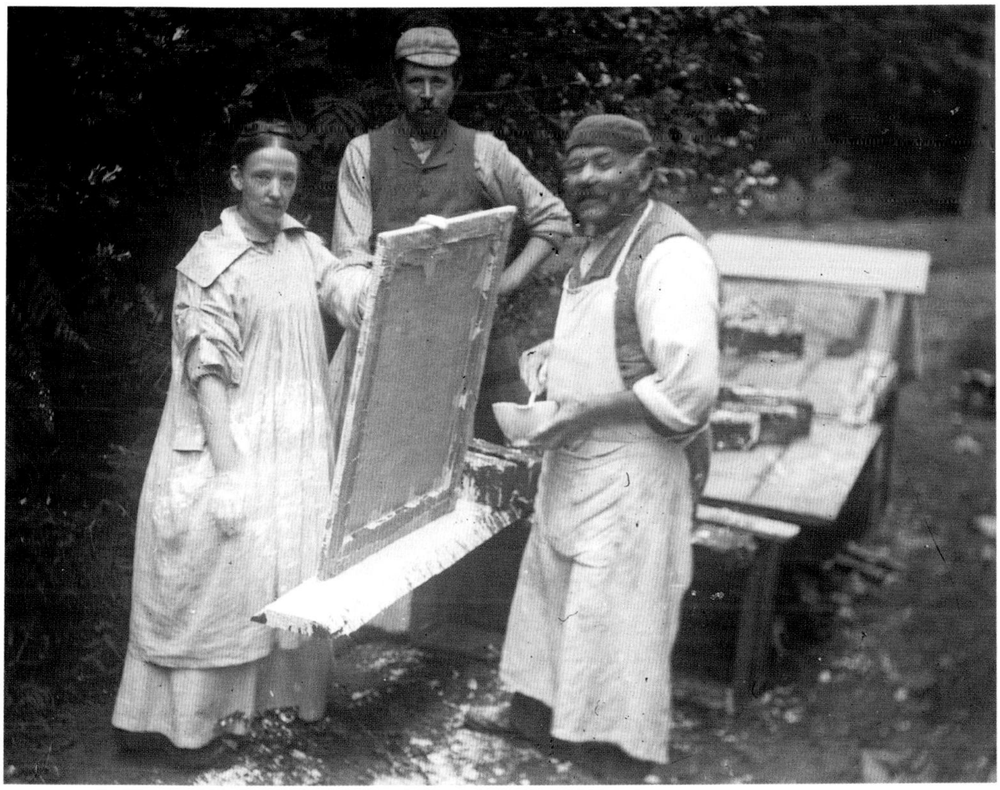

Mary Watts and helpers preparing plaster panels, Limnerslease, c.1895–96

the intricate terracotta mouldings on the building, and the wooden door and its iron hinges to the glorious painted gesso interior. Even the Roman bricks made locally by E. & A. Miles,[14] at only 1¾ inches (4.5 cm) high, give the impression of a taller, therefore more spiritual building. In harmony with Ruskinian principles, these smooth red bricks – favoured by Philip Webb for William Morris's first Arts and Crafts home, Red House at Upton, Kent – and the coarser terracotta mouldings would be worked by villagers in the tradition of 'truth to materials', the earthiness of the clay. Rising in splendour above and projecting 6 feet 2 inches (1.9 metres) beyond the circular drum – itself just 24 feet (7.3 metres) in diameter and decorated only with a frieze beneath the dome – were four tall, slender, gabled transepts with double-arched windows, forming the arms of the cross.

An elm tree was felled to make way for the chapel, which was to be built by Heal and Jackson of Compton; a small-scale model was made by their joiners George Barrow and Albert Boxall. Mary organized the transport of wagonloads of clay and, wisely catering for all abilities, prepared plaster plates for her village workers to model on. On 14 November she opened her home for the first of her Thursday-evening Terra Cotta Home Arts classes. Barrow and Boxall joined in, learning to model the terracotta tiles that were now to ornament or, as Mary put it, 'clothe' the chapel. Visitors and neighbours who were too busy or unlikely to attend – among them, the rector, the squire of Loseley and the Countess de Vesci – came privately to design a tile; a farmer's wife modelled hers under guidance from her children who were learning with Mary; and a friend departing for Canada made one so she could think about the chapel from across the Atlantic.[15] Mary was granted permission to sink a well at the cemetery's northern edge in March 1896.[16]

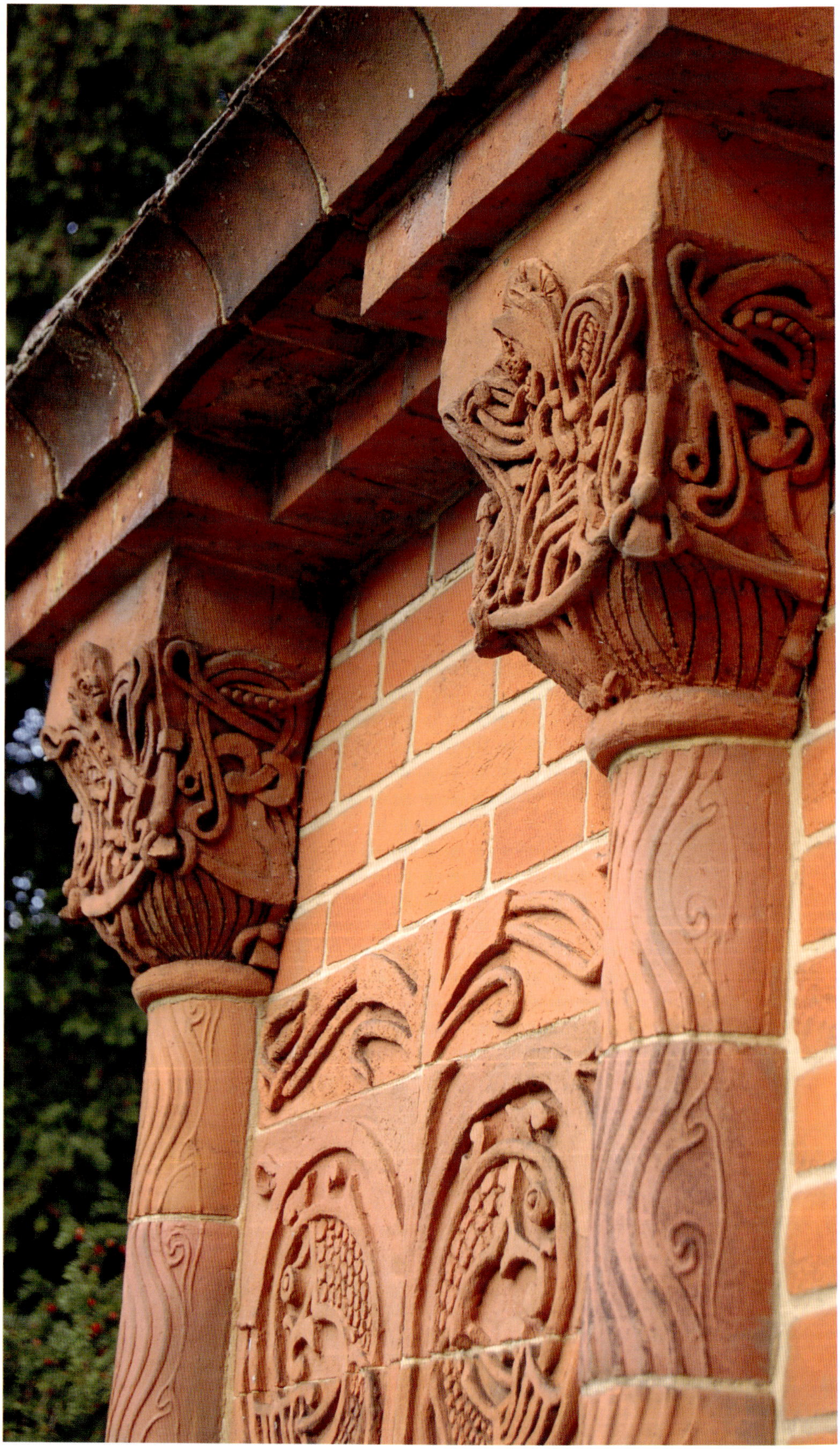

Capitals and surface fillings on the chapel exterior

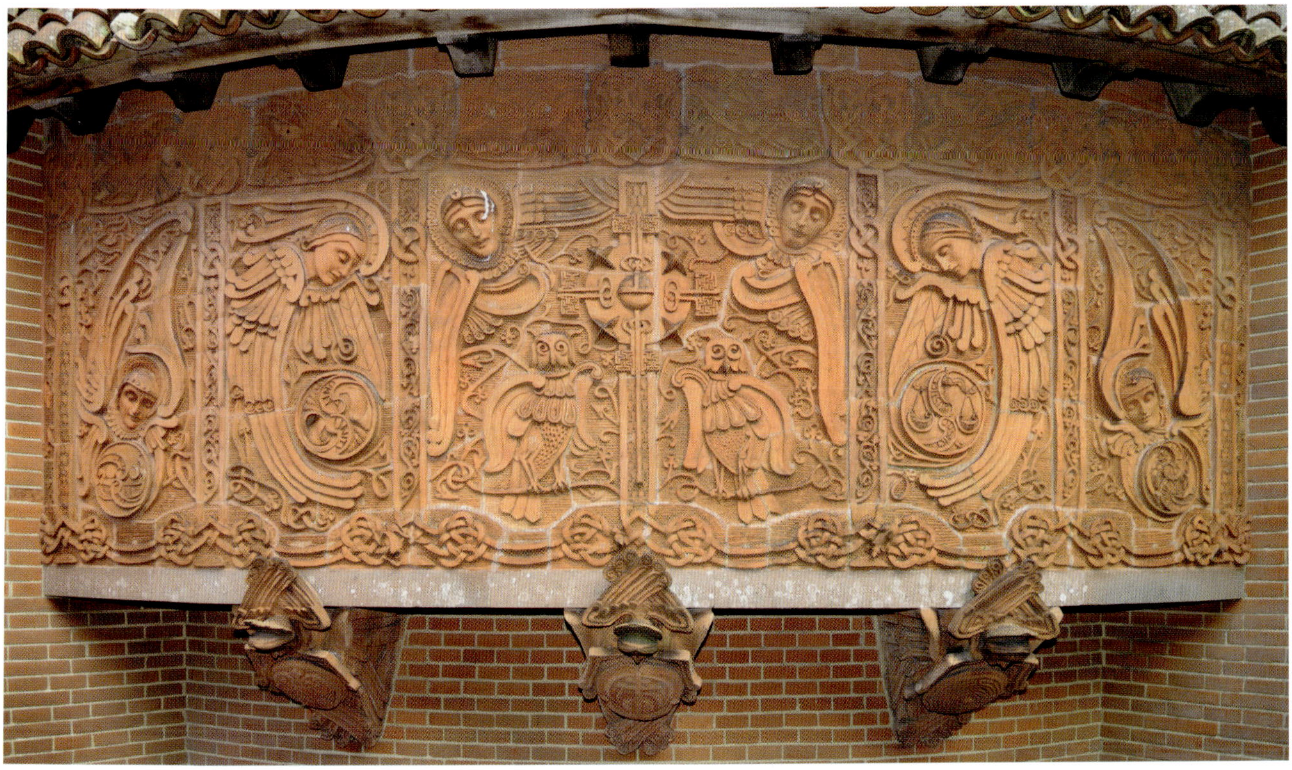

Above: Part of the Path of the Just frieze, chapel exterior

Below: The chapel bell-tower

The first capitals and surface fillings that the Compton modellers showed at the national Home Arts exhibition at the Albert Hall in May would have been the press-moulded, curved 'River of Life' decoration for the transepts, the more challenging 'Tree of Life' friezes – closer in style to Mary's Limnerslease plasterwork – that would rise up between them, and the pièces de résistance, the anthropomorphic evangelistic capitals.[17] Exhibiting before the royal family must have been an extraordinary experience for the villagers. By August, Mary was planning the 'Path of the Just' frieze to encircle the drum beneath the dome, her high-relief faces now showing the influence of Dante Gabriel Rossetti, Burne-Jones and Watts, a restful contrast from the animated, lower-relief Celtic motifs and interlace.[18] The 31-inch (79 cm) bell, to be housed in a tower above the east transept, was made by John Warner and Son of London to sound the lowest possible note, 'C', and inscribed, at Watts's suggestion, 'Be my voice neither feared nor forgotten'.[19] Plans for the cemetery lychgate were submitted in March 1897.[20]

The 'Garment of Praise' tile decoration for the spandrels above the door was designed by Mary in November and enlarged in charcoal by a Scottish assistant poached from her husband, Louis Reid Deuchars, who helped prepare designs for weaker members of her class. The spandrel decoration, exhibited at

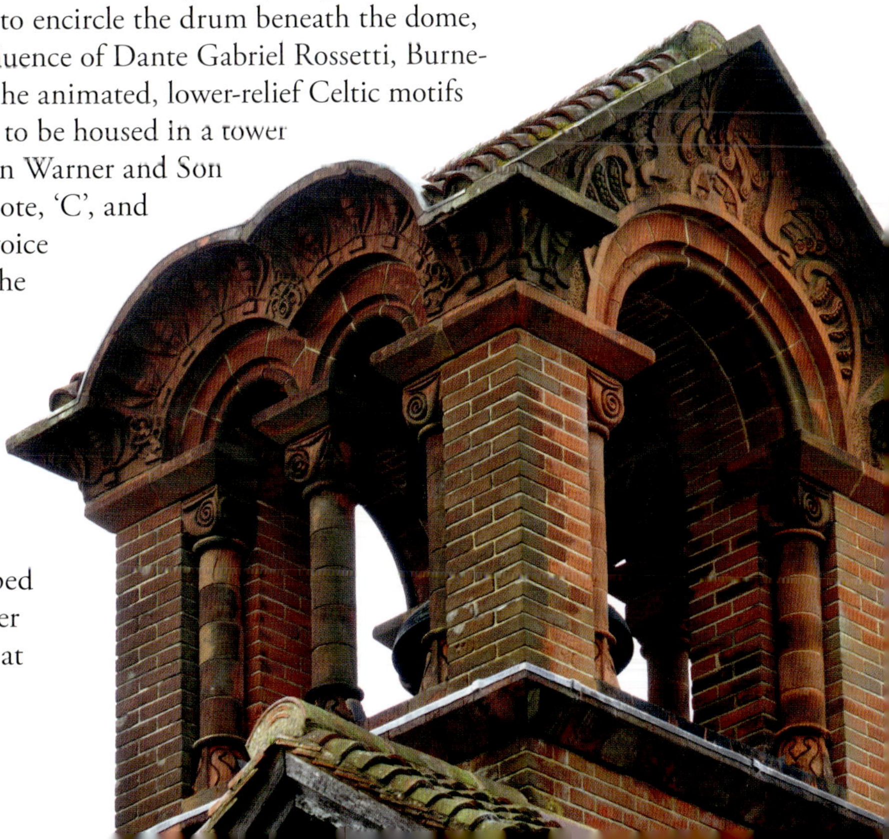

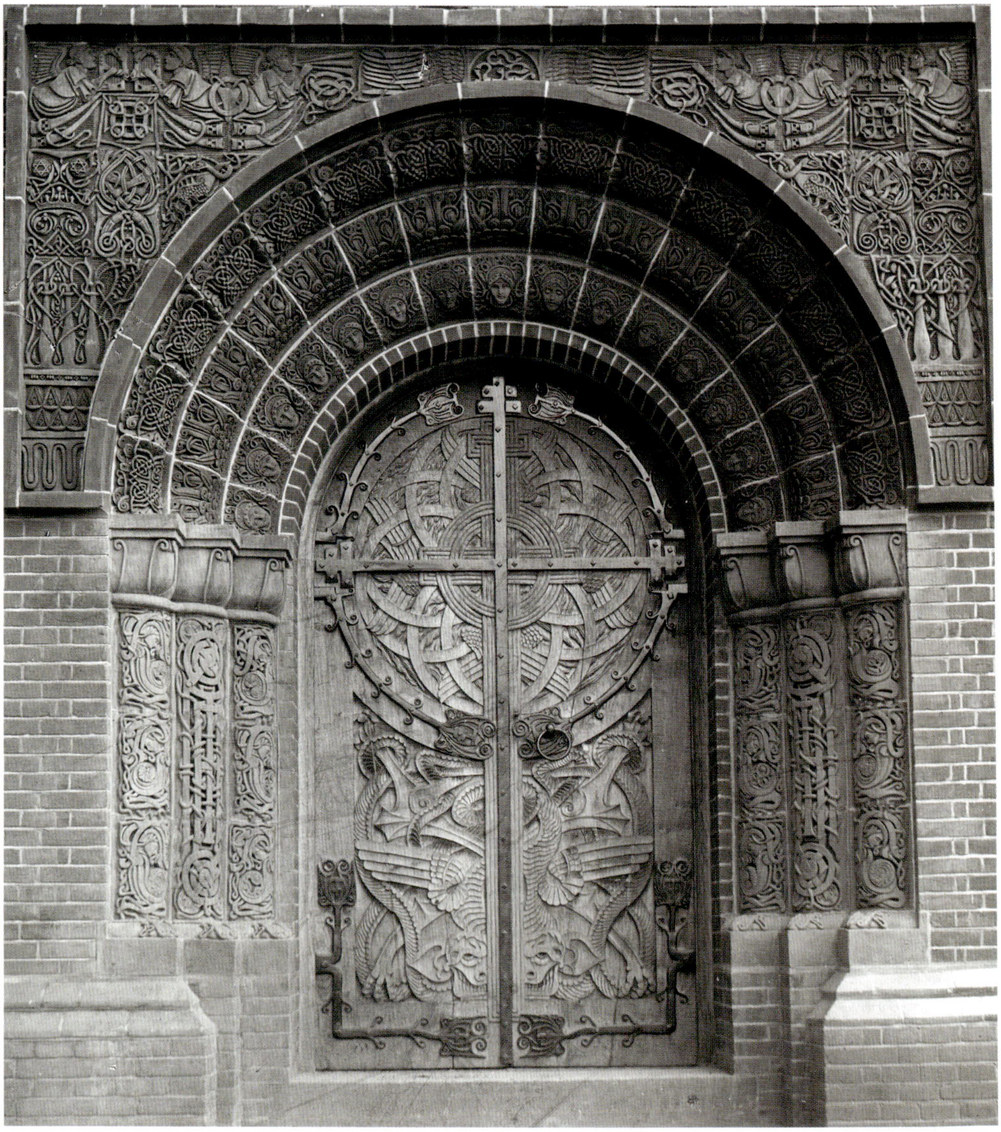

Doorway of the chapel

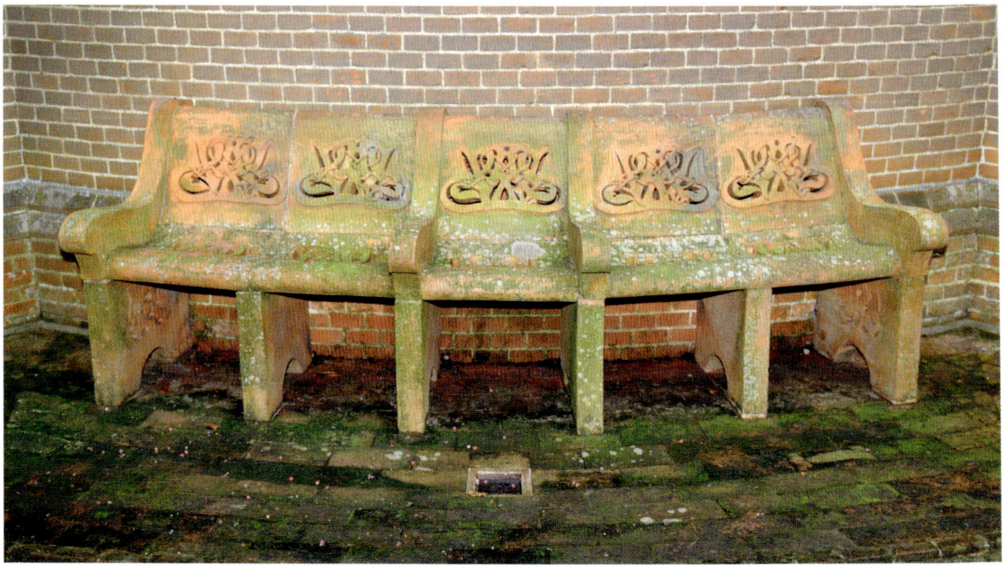

The terracotta benches outside the chapel

the Albert Hall in 1897, was highlighted in the *Studio* magazine.[21] The Wattses' coachman, Harvey Cummins, modelled the angel faces in the archivolt over the door. Such was the inventiveness of the entrance pillar decoration that this would seem to have been completed last. (For details of this fantastic symbolism, see next chapter.)[22] Barrow and Boxall prepared the oak door, to be encased in chestnut and carved with Mary's flaming interlace by the Compton wheelwright Thomas Steadman, and the delicate full-height iron hinges symbolizing the 'Breath of Life' were made by the blacksmith Clarence Sex. 'Young Mr. Sex gets his £21.5. & Compton I think good work by one of her own sons', enthused Mary on 14 March 1898.

So successful was the building that younger members of her Compton Terra Cotta Home Arts wished to become professional. The class had swelled to forty-eight; Mary would list seventy-three modellers with four or five permanent staff (including herself) in her book of the chapel, *The Word in the Pattern*, which she dedicated to the Home Arts founder, Eglantyne Jebb. To transform her terracotta enterprise into a business, Mary decided to produce three lines: tombstones, sundials and jardinières. Watts agreed to build a new potting shed, and they commissioned Ernest George, the architect of Limnerslease, to build four cottages for key workers.[23] Frank Mitchell was employed as kiln-burner and Deuchars as Mary's assistant, at a cost of £150 a year.

Mary designed at a cracking pace. On 28 March Steadman made the mould for her first tombstone;[24] two days later Deuchars made the capital for her first sundial. Setting up this village industry would delay the chapel's interior decoration, for which Mary was keen to explore asbestos for its 'light fibrous and flexible qualities'. Fortunately, no trace of this has been found inside the chapel.[25]

After classes closed on 30 April, Mary designed the terracotta chairs to stand outside the chapel and began to plan the interior. At the 1898 Home Arts exhibition, where Sex's gates were shown with the terracotta, Mary consulted the architect and designer Halsey Ralph Riccardo (1854–1928). A partner in De Morgan's pottery and specialist in coloured glazed bricks and tiles, Riccardo explained that the white clay she planned to use would be too brittle for large decorative work, nor did he think her terracotta suitable for glazing, but he approved of her free, large-scale use of terracotta.[26]

The chapel itself, stridently red in its newness, seemed nevertheless a harmonious outcrop on the hill. 'It is growing every day less red, & the green enfolds it all so beautifully now, the trees are in leaf … A sweet resting place', wrote Mary on 28 May. John Martin was elected gravedigger and caretaker of the cemetery, with space estimated to last for one hundred and fifty years, after lengthy communications between Mary, the parish council and the Home Office about the unconsecrated land reserved for non-Christian burials and, with some anguish, whether the chapel itself could be consecrated.[27] The lectern, hassocks and altar table were installed by Sunday 5 June. Days later the bier was delivered by the London funerary suppliers Dottridge and Son at a cost of £18 8s 6d.

On Friday morning, 1 July 1898, Mary placed vases of white poppies on the altar, covered for the occasion with a white cloth embroidered by May Hichens

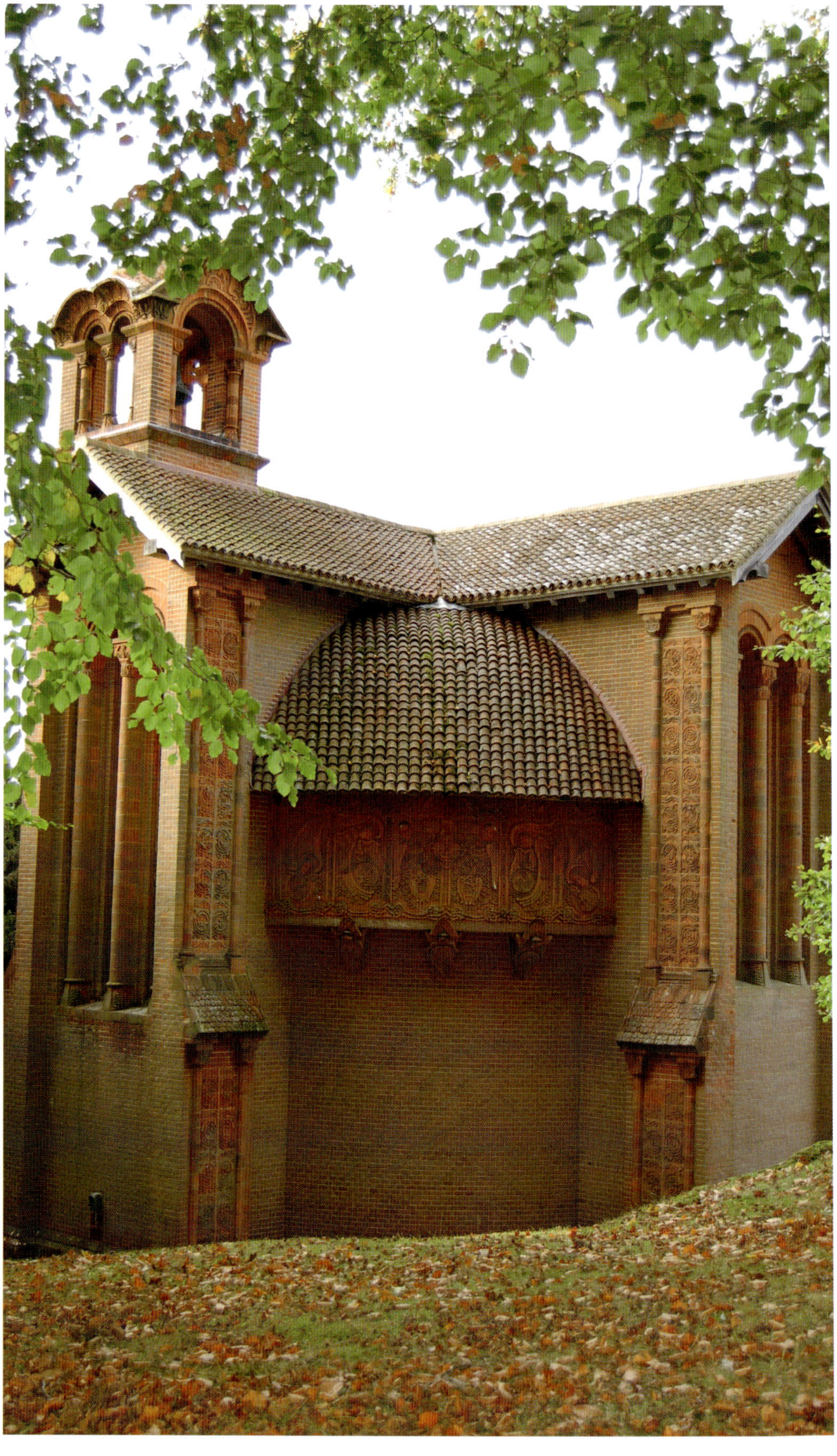

The chapel from the south-east

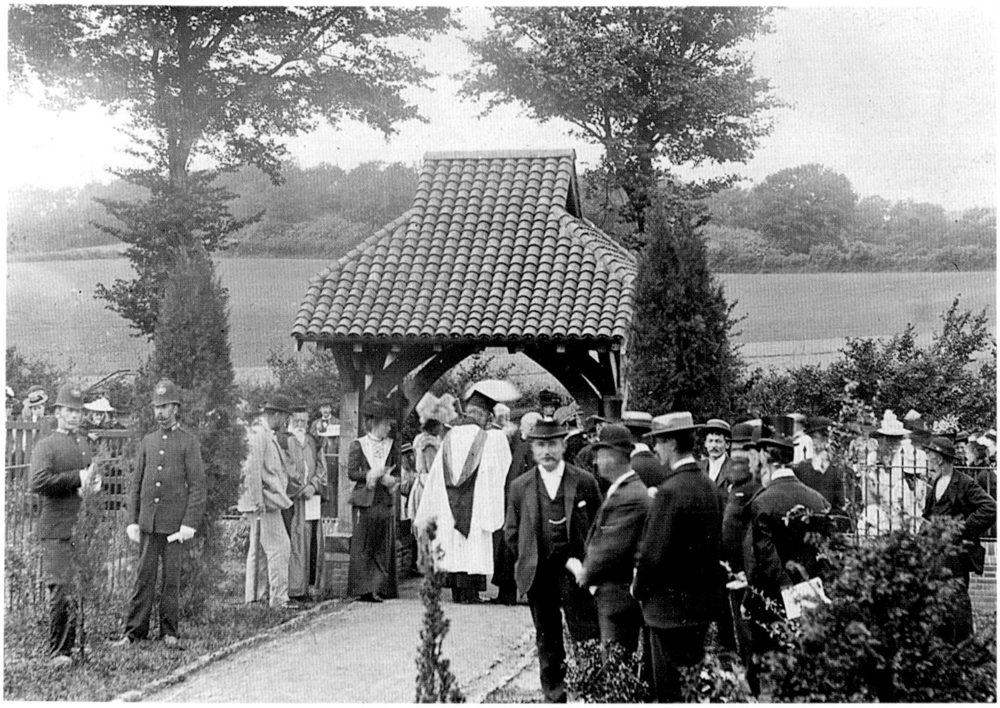

G.F. and Mary Watts and the Bishop of Winchester (by the lych-gate) before the procession to the chapel for its consecration on 1 July 1898

of Monkshatch. Gold, silver and blue curtains hanging temporarily as the reredos hinted at the glorious colour that was to clothe the brick interior. Signor, dressed in his scarlet Oxford robes, and Mary joined the Bishop of Winchester, Randall Davidson, processing up the winding path lined with young cypress trees to the assembled dignitaries and parishioners crowding around Compton's sensational cemetery chapel. With the oriental flavour of its pierced dome and Mary's riot of multi-faceted 'hieroglyphs' interweaving modern Art Nouveau with the Celtic cord as never before, it was seen as 'an architectural triumph', neither dreary nor utilitarian but 'the most original and perfect modern ecclesiastical edifice', declared the *Studio*, 'unlike any other in the British isles'. The choir of St Andrews, Wells Street, London, sang psalms in the burial ground, before the consecration inside the chapel.[28]

'Built to the loving memory of all who find rest near its walls, and for the comfort and help of those to whom the sorrow of separation yet remains', Mary began *The Word in the Pattern* a fortnight later. (Deuchars's illustrations for this, she felt, failed to express the force or flexibility of the terracotta.[29]) She completed the altar design (exhibited Home Arts 1899[30]) and resumed classes in December 1898, although after the kiln was filled on the 10th, there would be a break in the chapel decoration. On Christmas Eve Andrew and May Hichens held a party on behalf of the parish council to thank the Wattses for their generous gift of the chapel. Gillett presented them with a ceremonial book illuminated by May and spoke warmly of the potters' work now established in Compton.[31]

Mary wrote that, though Watts had not designed the chapel, 'his inspiring mind gave the impulse'. This was especially the case with the interior, through the progression of her symbolic structure and polarity of expression. 'What a grand point could be made of the development of the psyche through the

Right: A drawing of the chapel altar, Home Arts and Industries Association, 1899, unidentified press cutting, Watts Gallery Archive

Below: Cherubim holding medallions inside the chapel

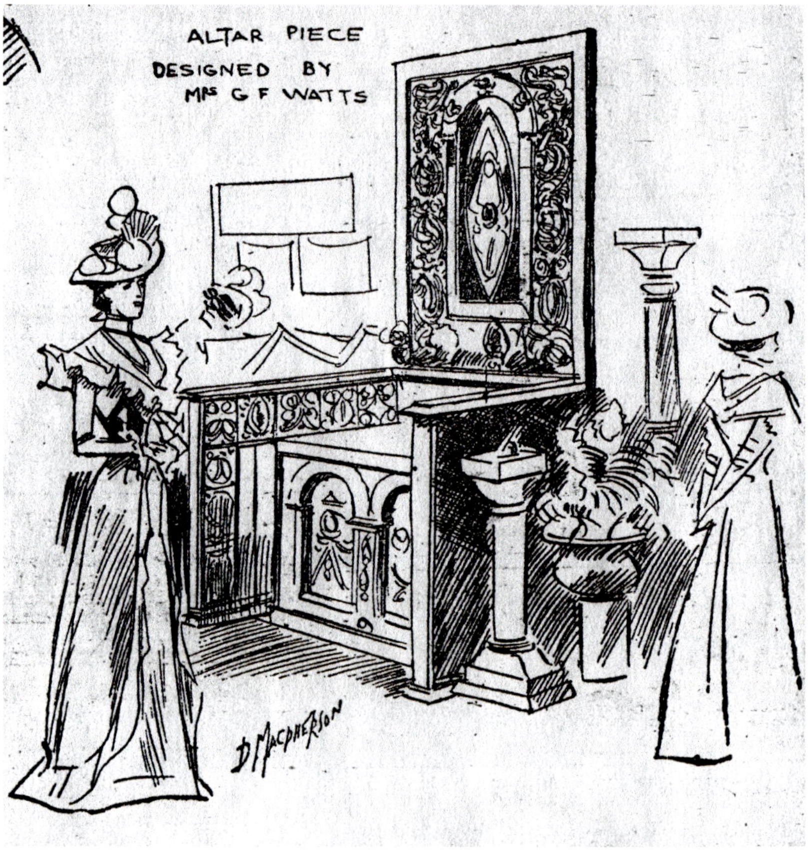

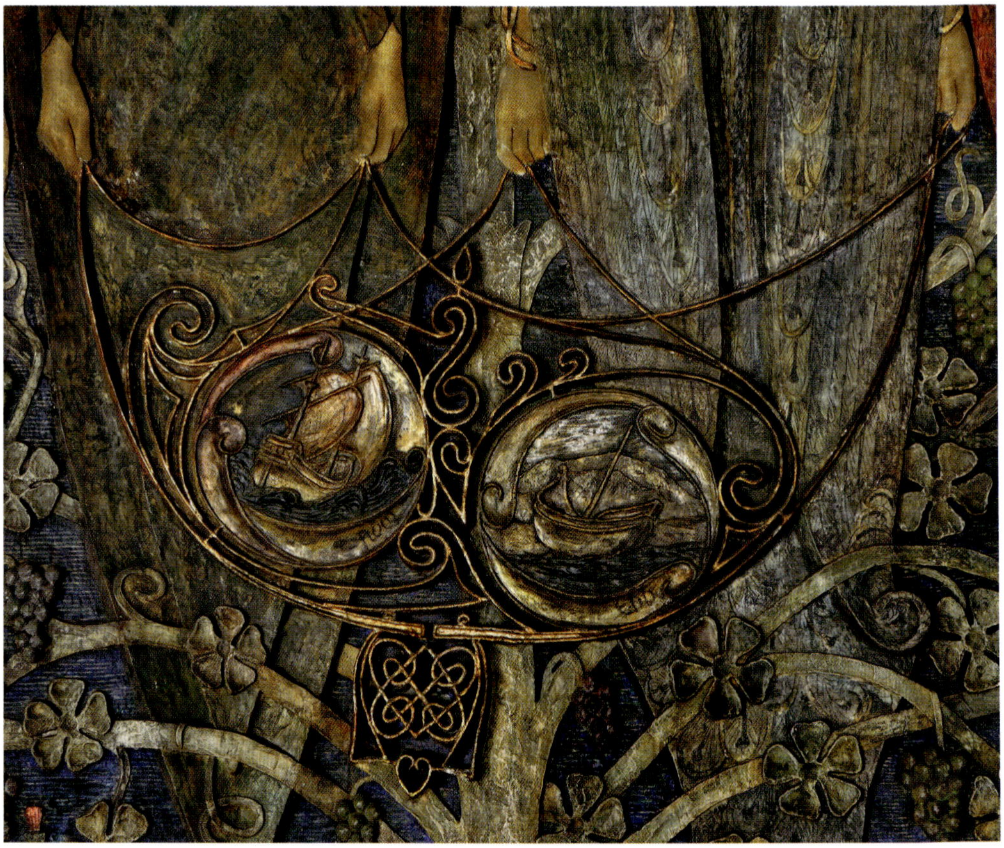

ages – The evolution of the idea of goodness in the mind of man, leading up to the knowledge that love is all', he had enthused. 'Could you not do something of this in your chapel?' Mary clearly attempted this, mindful of his observation about the dual laws of nature, 'force propelling and gravitations steadying', in her designs for the interior (see next chapter).[32]

While a Scottish manager, James Nicol, arrived in 1901 to help run her village industry, training some half-dozen boys aged fourteen to eighteen, Mary resumed chapel classes in the billiard room at Limnerslease. Having measured the interior dimensions of the drum, she had wooden frames constructed to fit tight, attached galvanized chicken wire to these and with her team wove in thick white fibrous plaster, onto which she laid low relief decoration, adding sash-cord to metal outlines. Almost every village child was invited to paint a motif in tempera; and the first panel of monumental blue cherubim bearing symbolically contrasting medallions reminiscent of the jewellery of Charles Ashbee was installed on 13 September. Though their golden fillets and rich, sober colouring, checked for permanence with Winsor and Newton, were admired at the 1902 Home Arts exhibition, the sculptor and enameller Alexander Fisher (1864–1936), seeing the panels inside the chapel on 7 December, thought the colour of the angels 'not quite monotonous enough'. Mary agreed that her angels seemed a brighter blue and red than those in the studio. She hoped to complete the decoration in 1903, when work began on a hostel for her young potters. The other half of the building would house the paintings and sculpture of G.F. Watts, a key inspiration to the apprentice potters. By now Liberty & Co. were mounting exhibitions of Mary's Celtic-style garden pottery and her first carpet, naming her, exceptionally, as 'pioneer'.[33]

On 15 April 1904 a Symbolist painting by Watts, a small version of *The All-Pervading* – the Creator holding 'the Globe of the Systems' – was hung over the altar. Signor stood inside, marvelling at his wife's work. 'He had not realised what I had aspired to in the matter of this glorified wallpaper'. Watts died on 1 July. His ashes lay on the altar steps in a casket modelled by Thomas Wren, as the bell, with the motto that Watts had composed, tolled in his memory: 'Be my voice neither feared nor forgotten'.[34] Nor would Mary's exuberant cemetery chapel be forgotten. A consummate Arts and Crafts designer, she had incorporated into the building designs in terracotta, gesso, wood, metal, glass and, consistent with her concept of the decoration as clothing, textile. The decorative motif that adorned her book *The Word in the Pattern* was even made into a brooch marketed by Liberty & Co. In the creation of the chapel – the flowering of her style from the Limnerslease niche, the chapel transept capitals, the Path of the Just frieze, the sophisticated door pillars and the altar to the coloured interior – Mary reached her apogee, the fount from which her designs, many produced by her new Compton Potters' Arts Guild, would spring.[35]

Their Celtic-style terracotta memorials began to fill the cemetery at Compton and other burial grounds around Britain. Mary kept a firm eye on memorials, concerned that they should not be inharmoniously high or spoiled by artificial materials. In 1906 the well was crowned with an ornamental wellhead, its design reminiscent of the altar, triskeles – Celtic symbol of three conjoined spirals

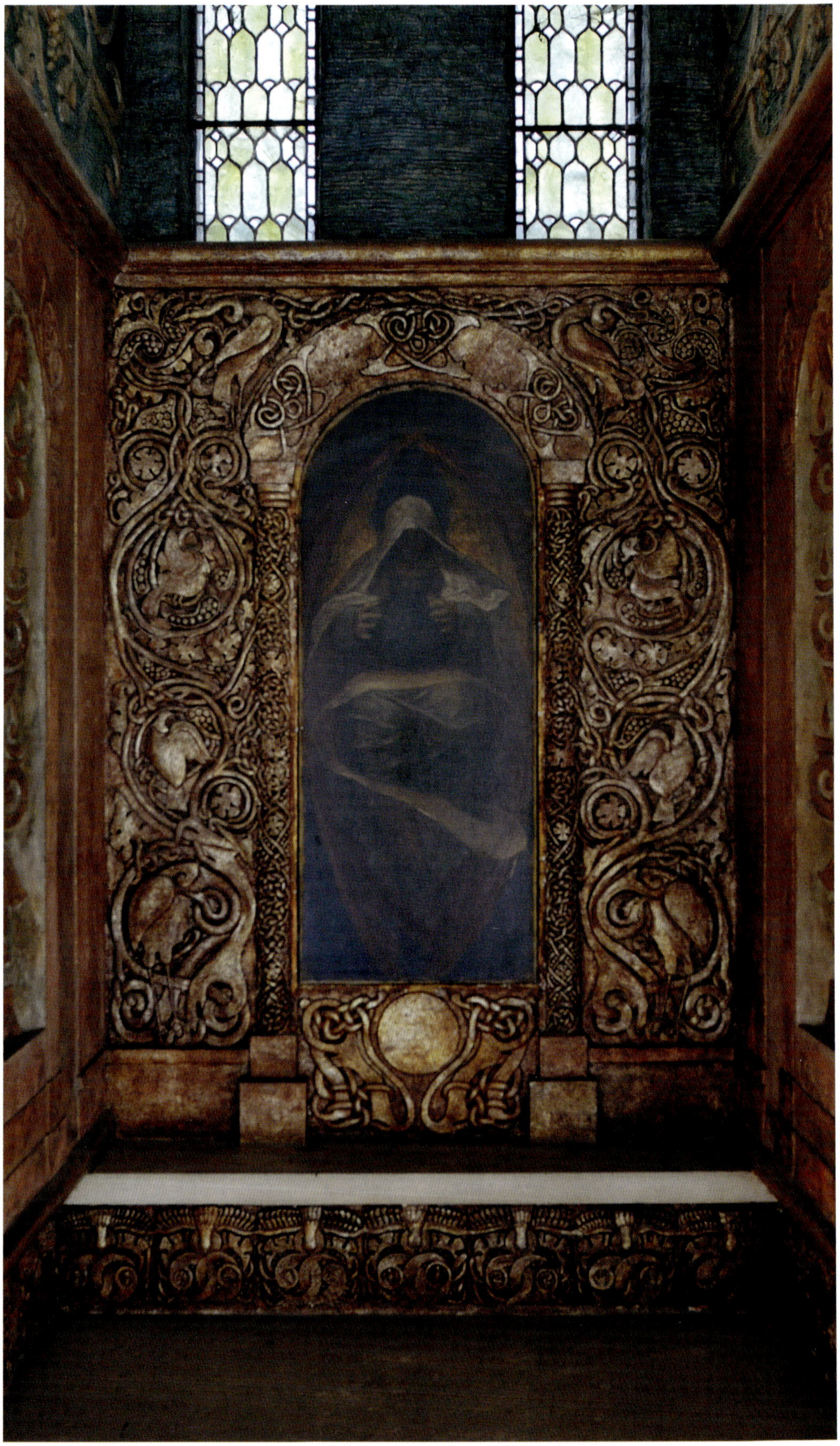

Altar in the chapel with G.F. Watts's painting The All-Pervading

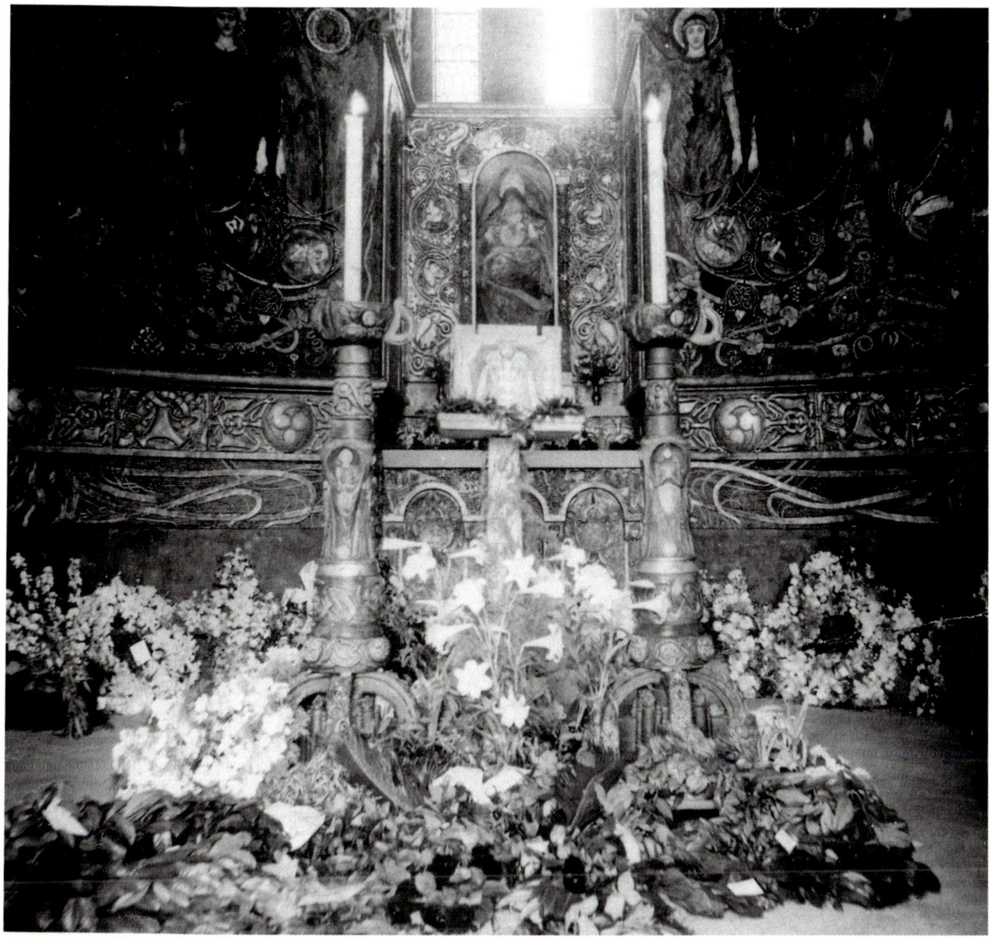

Left: The Potters' Arts Guild casket containing the ashes of G.F. Watts (on a stand behind the candlesticks) and wreathes in his memory in front of the chapel altar, July 1904

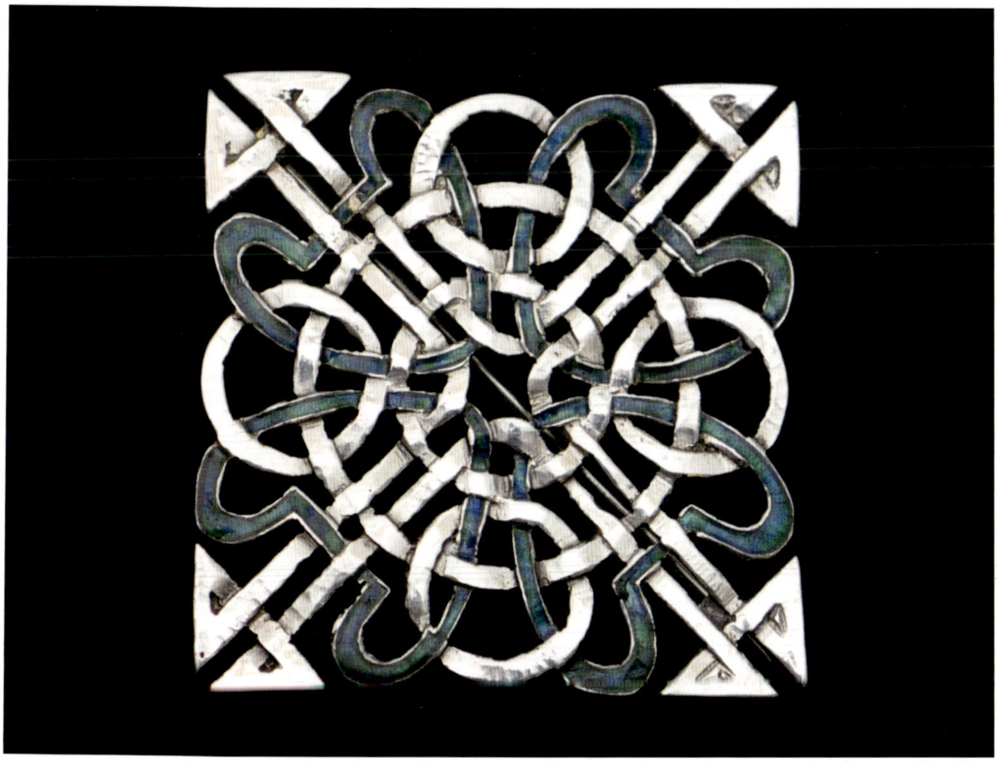

Below: Brooch with a motif from The Word in the Pattern*, marketed by Liberty & Co., 1906, private collection*

Right: The wellhead in the chapel cemetery

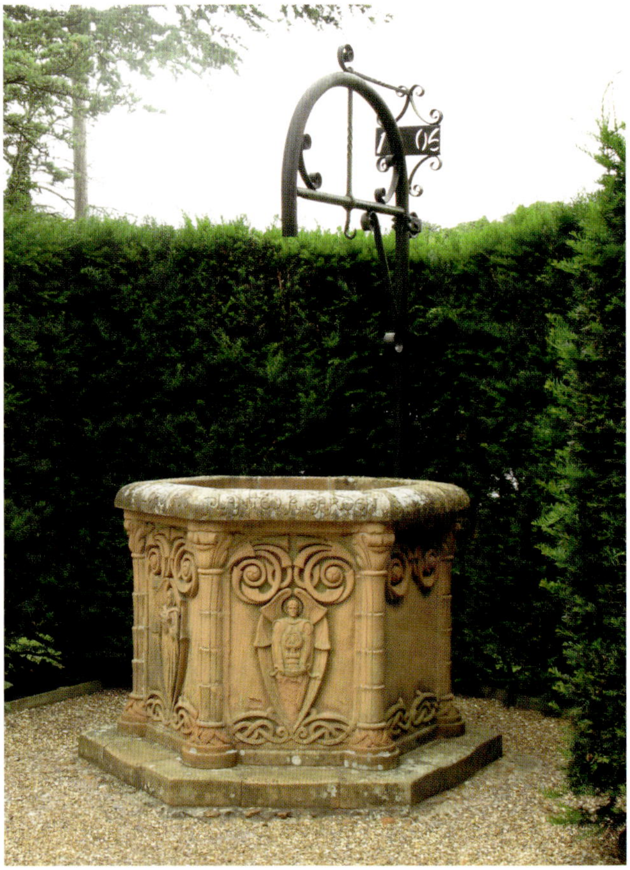

Below: Clarence Sex's gates opening onto the Watts memorial inside the cloister

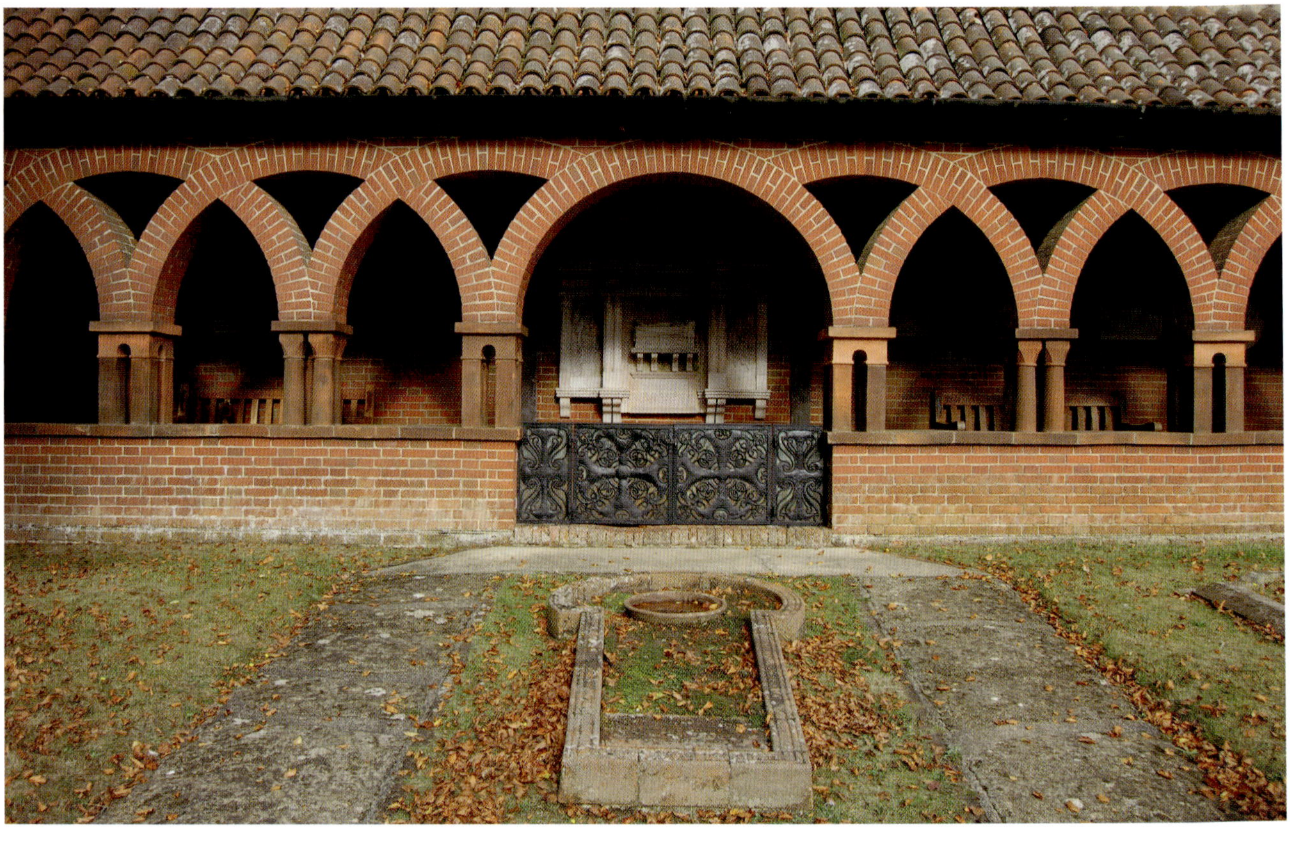

– and lettering inside the chapel. The cloister, built above the chapel to the east, was completed on Watts's birthday, 23 February 1911. His grave is marked by a low coping stone and Celtic-style birdbath. Behind this, Clarence Sex's gates open into the cloisters, which centre on a terracotta memorial to Watts. Made by the Potters' Arts Guild from a wax sketch by Mary, the recumbent figure of her husband was modelled by Tom Wren and flanked by relief panels from the artist's paintings, *Destiny* and *The Messenger*, modelled by Russell Davey and Andrew Marchant. Mary was jointly commemorated in both memorials after her death in 1938.

What a remarkable woman was Mary Watts to motivate villagers' interest in a project devoted to dying. Her husband's novel artistic representation of Death as a tender figure rather than a skeletal horror had a profound effect on the art-going public and fascinated Mary, who passed on to her young students her ideas of its restfulness, and of the joys and sorrows of life, material and spiritual: 'Between the mystery of birth and the mystery of death, material life is lifted to the glorious consciousness of its affinity with the Infinite.'[36] For Mary, immortality was the key. The rich endeavour that began with the decoration of Watts Chapel led Compton modellers to produce ornaments to her design long after her death; and today architectural enthusiasts marvel at this profound, iconic building.

NOTES

1 MSW Diaries, 1 October 1893.

2 MSW Diaries, 24–25 November 1895.

3 MSW Diary Notes, 29 July and 4 October 1887.

4 Watts was painting portraits of leading nineteenth-century figures to present to the National Portrait Gallery (see Franklin Gould 2004, pp.300–3).

5 MSW Diaries, 16, 19, 22, 24 and 30 August 1891 and 31 January 1893.

6 Letter from Thomas Carlyle to John A. Carlyle, 7 April 1822, 'The Carlyle Letters Online', vol. 2, 1822–23, http://carlyleletters.dukejournals.org/ accessed 13/9/2010.

7 MSW Diaries, 25 October 1891 and 13 January 1892.

8 MSW Diaries, 31 January 1893.

9 MSW Diaries, 3 and 13 August 1893.

10 Elizabeth Cumming, ed., *Phoebe Anna Traquair*, exh. cat., Scottish National Portrait Gallery 1993, pp.13–28.

11 MSW Diaries, 1–9 December 1893.

12 Compton Parish Council Minute Book, 1894–1911, vol.I.

13 MSW Diary Notes, 4 and 9 September 1894; MSW Diaries, 21 March and 6–7 May 1895; *The Times*, 6 May 1895, p.7; Compton Parish Council Minute Book: 30 May 1895; 'A Mortuary Chapel, designed by Mrs. G.F. Watts', *Studio*, 1898, vol.14, p.239.

14 E. and A. Miles produced the bricks at the Guildford works and the roof tiles in Cranleigh.

15 Franklin Gould 1993, p.5; letter from Hugh Gillett to the Secretary of State, Home Office, 7 October 1895 (Public Record Office: HO45/9869/B14130); MSW Diaries, 14 November 1895; 'The Cemetery Chapel', *Compton*, Guildford n.d., p.23.

16 Compton Parish Council Minute Book, 26 March 1896.
17 *Studio*, vol.8, 1896, p.91.
18 MSW Diaries, 30 August 1896.
19 MSW Diaries, 26 October and 3 November 1896.
20 Compton Parish Council Minute Book: 30 March 1897.
21 MSW Diaries, 11, 24 and 26 November 1896; *Studio*, vol.II, 1897, p.112.
22 For further detail, see Franklin Gould 1993, ch.3.
23 See Franklin Gould 2004, p.297; Watts 2000, p.36.
24 Mary and G.F. Watts had designed the Marchioness of Waterford's gravestone in 1891.
25 MSW Diaries, 22–29 March 1898.
26 MSW Diaries, 16–17 May 1898.
27 Compton Parish Council Minute Book: 18 April 1898.
28 MSW Diaries, 1 July 1898: *Studio*, 1898, vol.14, p.235; *Surrey Advertiser*, 4 July 1898; Franklin Gould 1993, p.15.
29 MSW Diaries, 15 and 17 July and 3 December 1898; Watts 2000, p.1.
30 Esther Wood, 'The Home Arts and Industries Exhibition', *Studio*, 1899, vol.17, pp.99 and 103.
31 MSW Diaries, 12, 30–31 August and 7–10, 17 and 24 December 1898; Franklin Gould 2004.
32 MSW Diary Notes, 11 November 1897; MSW Diaries, 3 December 1898.
33 Bateman 1901, p.12; MSW Diary Notes, 13 September 1901; 'The Potter's Wheel' *Country Life*, 15 March 1902, pp.328–30; Wood 1902, vol. 26, pp.129–33; MSW Diaries, 7 and 31 December 1902; MSW Diary Notes, 23 February 1903; Watts 1912, vol.II, p.305.
34 MSW Diaries, 15 April 1904; Watts 1912, vol.II, p.321.
35 MSW Diaries, 12 May 1899; *Studio*, 1899, vol.XVII, p.99.
36 Watts 2000, p.1.

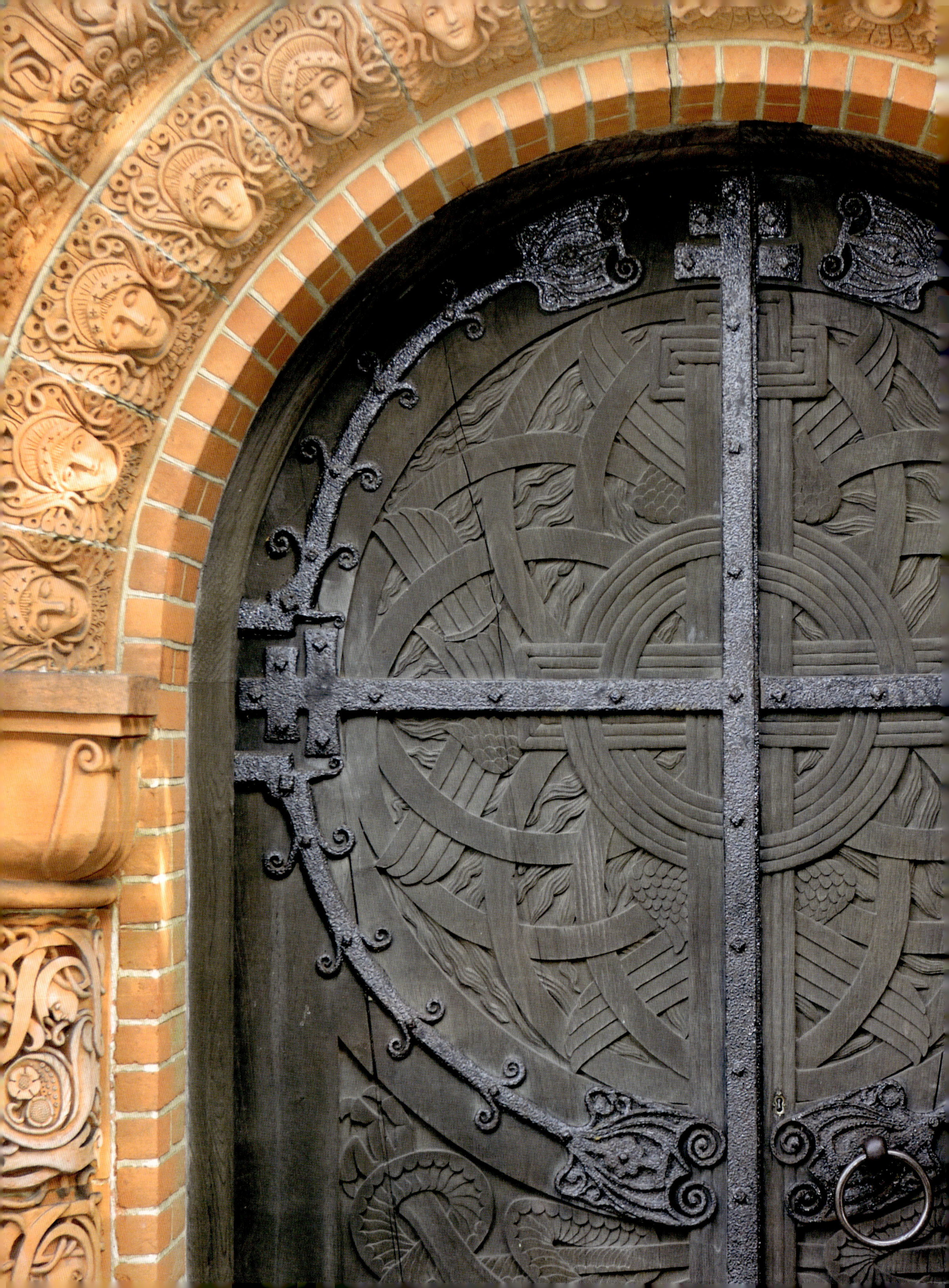

The Symbolism of Watts Chapel

Desna Greenhow

When Mary Watts wrote to the clerk of the parish council, offering to build a mortuary chapel on Budburrow Hill in Compton, she had in mind a scheme that would not only fulfil its funerary function but would give her the opportunity to decorate it in a way that reflected her own deeply religious nature. It would allow her to develop her art and explore a rich symbolism that drew on her belief in the importance of imagery in expounding and revealing spirituality.

Mary had been trained in painting and in clay modelling, but after she married George Frederic Watts, one of the greatest artists of his generation, her artistic ambitions turned to her skills in decorative modelling. She worked on this in their house in Melbury Road, Kensington, and then, when they built Limnerslease at Compton, she designed and decorated a ceiling in what they called the Red Room, and a niche where they could sit in the evenings while she read to her beloved 'Signor'.

Mary's designs had a very clear sense of purpose and direction. She and Signor discussed their broad-based views on religion and spirituality at length in the evenings at Limnerslease, as Mary's diaries show.[1] The term 'Symbolist' was beginning to be applied to his work, as he sought to examine the universal ideas of love, death and life in his canvases, and Mary, too, was interested, from her own experience and background, in the universal symbols that humanity had used from time immemorial. She saw, with Signor, the impetus towards renewal and resurrection in nature and man's spirit, and felt that she had a chance to express these truths if she could successfully build and decorate the cemetery chapel.

Mary's enthusiasm for universal truths, combined with her typical nineteenth-century Christian upbringing that instilled a strong belief in one God and His Son Jesus Christ, led her to want to make a statement opposing the materialism that both she and Watts saw everywhere in society. The title of the book, *The Word in the Pattern*, that she later wrote to explain the meaning of the symbols she adopted comes partly from St John's Gospel: 'In the beginning was the Word … And the Word was made flesh and dwelt among us.' 'The Word' is a translation of the Greek *logos*, referring to the one God as the Creator and great force of the universe. The 'Pattern' indicates the symbols that Mary used to decorate the walls and carry the message that she took from many sources, not only Christian.[2]

The plan for the building was finished in only four months and Mary showed it to the architect George Redmayne in August 1895. Its design is based in part on the Church of the Holy Sepulchre in Jerusalem, built on what Christians believe to be the site of Christ's death and resurrection – a fitting model for a cemetery chapel. The ancient and multi-layered symbolism of the ground plan is drawn from 'the Circle of Eternity with the Cross of Faith running through it', a symbol, as Mary writes in her design notebook and her diary, that was seen in

Opposite: The carved door with its iron cross and the wooden one behind it, based on an early stone cross from Iona

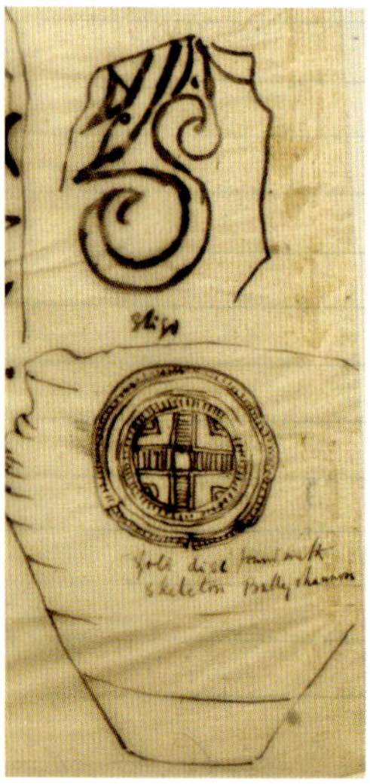

Pre-Christian Celtic 'solar cross' on an Irish funeral urn illustrated by Mary in her Chapel Notebook, Watts Gallery Archive

pre-Christian cultures as a 'solar cross', representing the sun's power over the four corners of the earth. This symbol, Mary argues, has a universal significance to be found in Christianity in the Greek cross, which to early Christians showed 'the power of redeeming Love, with arms outstretched to all the world'.[3]

Mary meticulously thought through the imagery and meaning in the chapel decoration to achieve what Wilfrid Blunt called her 'carefully calculated symbolism'.[4] Her choice of sources was influenced by the Celtic Revival aesthetic that was current in the 1890s, the images reflecting the stone crosses and doorways that she had seen in her native Scotland, probably since childhood, and had sketched in her notebooks. Mary was already working on the chapel in 1896 when she saw her first Celtic illuminated manuscript in the British Museum, the Lindisfarne Gospels, and was astonished by its intricacy and imaginative power.

She drew on symbols from both the Old and New Testaments – as messages of comfort for the mourners whom she imagined visiting the chapel in the future. She also took comforting symbols from other religions and cultures, ancient Egyptian, Buddhist and Judaic. Very much an artist of her period, she was influenced visually by Art Nouveau images, which were all around her, and also by the artists, writers and poets whom she and Signor discussed daily. Meanwhile, in forming her ideas of universal spirituality, she learnt much from him.

Mary's aristocratic and literary Scottish background attracted her to early Celtic Christianity, which was imbued with its own particular symbolism. She makes it clear that she was not trying to discover the meanings of symbols that might have been intended by the Celts. Her knots, interlace, triskeles, ribbons and spirals, which she uses in all parts of the chapel decoration to join one theme to another, show 'the unity of a divine life and law'.[5] Visually, they are allied to the earlier, gentler phase of Celtic art, found in the flowing lines of the decoration in the Lindisfarne Gospels, which had led Mary to write:

> It takes one's breath away to think of all that devouring love of beautifying and enriching the book as the holy man poured [*sic*] over it and wrought these marvellous lines & coloured in that delicate tender way his beautiful devices – under the magnifying glass only can one realize what the finish & perfection was.[6]

She perhaps softened the lines to fit the Art Nouveau influences of the time, but after her first visit to the British Museum she spent many hours studying this and other manuscripts, and her decoration is very close to the Lindisfarne Gospels and to the Book of Durrow, both dating from the seventh century.[7]

Mary intended her doorway to welcome and comfort mourners. Celtic cords on the side pillars draw the eye into the intricate, elongated words in Celtic lettering, 'I Am', held in place, as in Scottish and Irish stone crosses, by hands representing the 'hand of God', or Dextera Dei.[8] Abstract Celtic symbols appear throughout the chapel, including spirals, indicating the balance between inner and outer consciousness; human hearts, held stylistically in interlace squares, representing 'divine love, sacrificing, suffering, dying, to give spiritual life';[9] alternating black and white chequers, symbolizing day and night; and Celtic

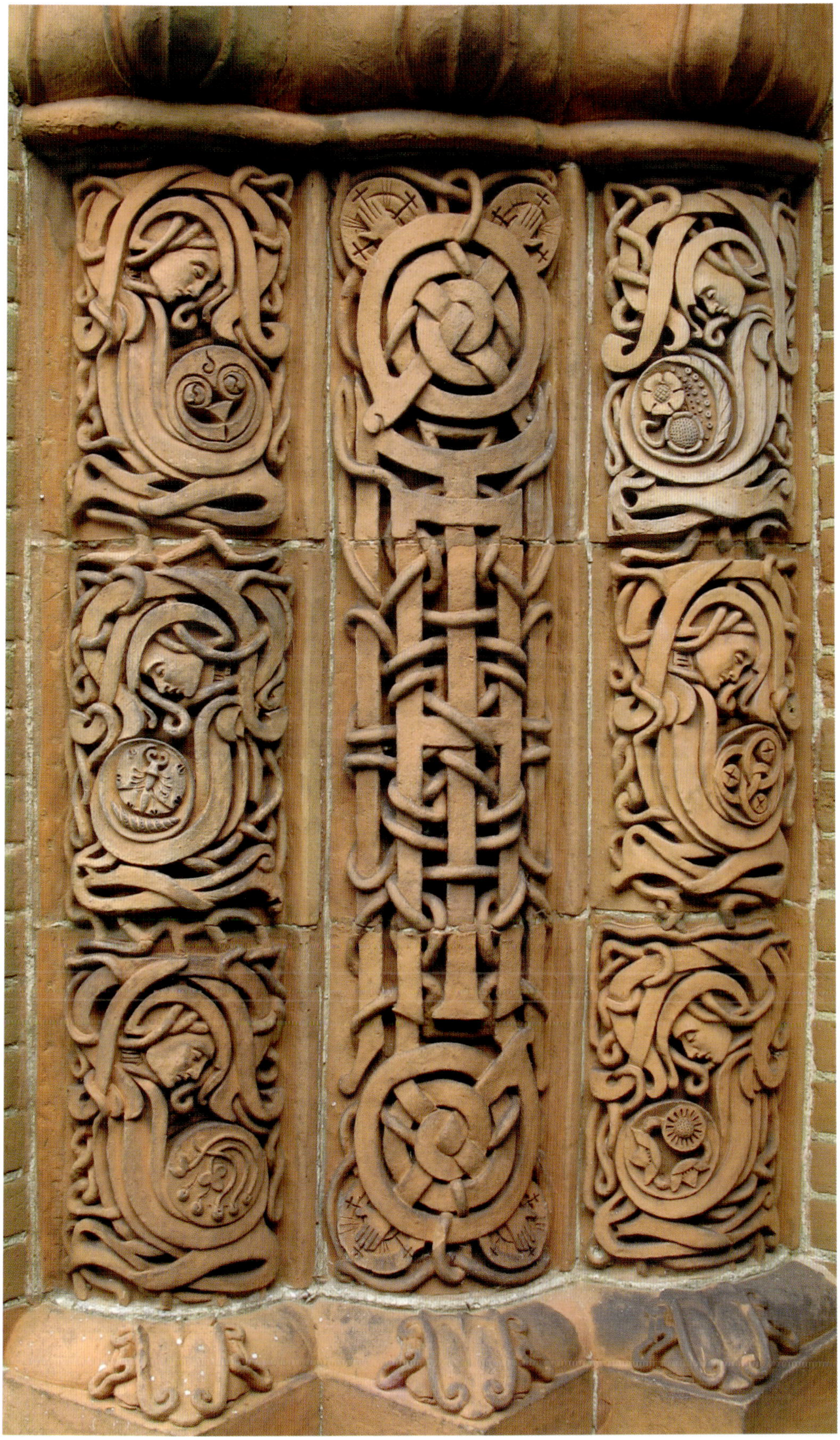

Decoration on the columns on each side of the chapel doorway showing Celtic knots and interlace that link figures studying representations of renewal in nature

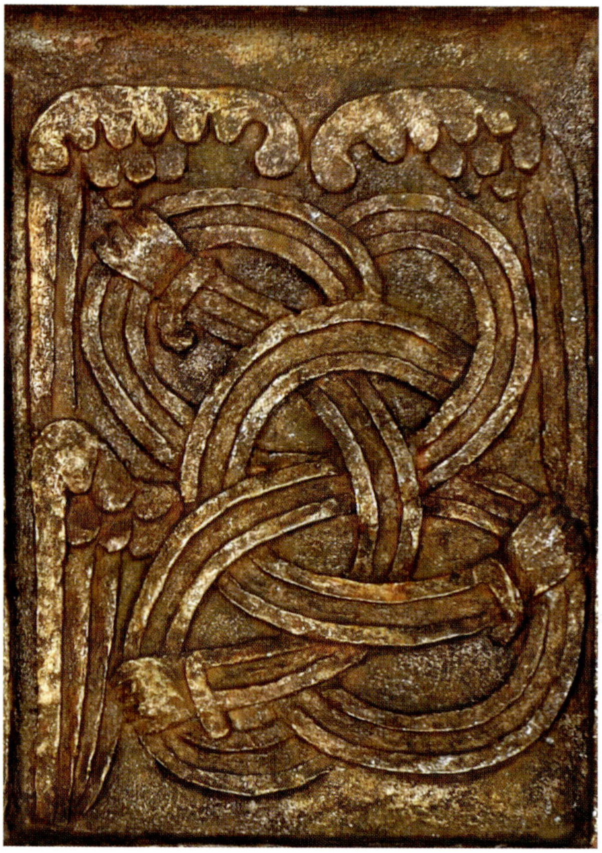

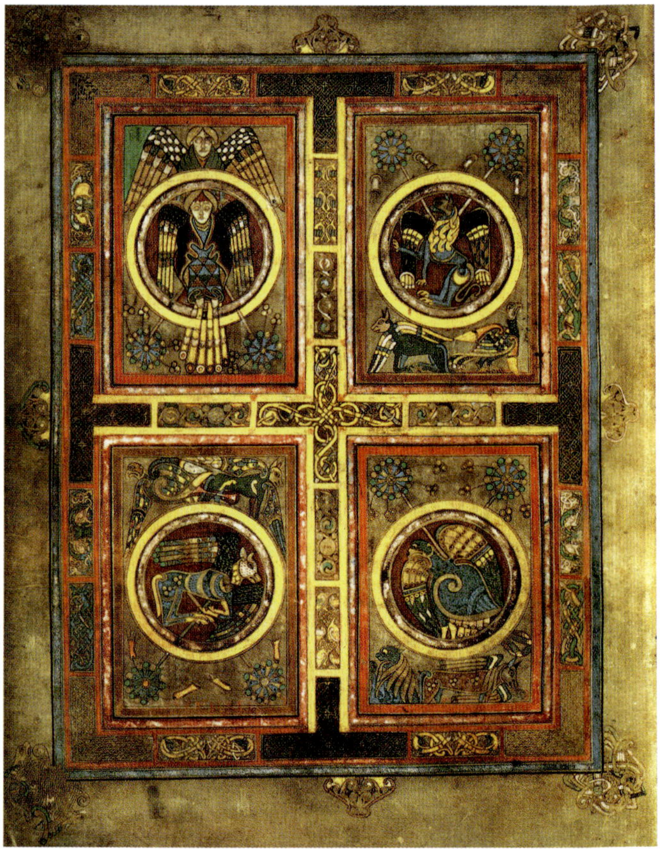

Above left: Decoration inside the chapel showing a Celtic knot with the Dextera Dei

Above right: Folio 27v of the ninth-century Book of Kells showing the symbols of the Four Evangelists, reproduced with permission from Trinity College Dublin

crosses. On the door an iron cross cuts a pagan dragon in two, and behind it is another interwoven wooden cross copied from a gravestone on Iona. She comments that its design may have been based on an earlier one of wattle, which was probably the only material that Columba and his monks found to make their crosses when they first arrived on Iona from Ireland on their mission to spread Christianity into northern Britain.[10] The dragon severed in half by the cross is a symbol used in Celtic Saints' Lives and represents the Christianizing of pagan 'fear and evil', to be replaced by Christian 'love'.[11]

Mary's Celtic designs are not solely abstract. At the heads of the pillars on the 'buttresses' that form the arms of the cross on the building are the symbols of the Four Evangelists – Matthew, a man; Mark, a lion; Luke, a calf; and John, an eagle – carved in reliefs that are very similar to the illustrations in the great ninth-century illuminated gospel manuscript, the Book of Kells.[12] The symbol of the eagle for St John on the pillars is almost identical to several in Kells and appears again as the centrepiece of the Spirit of Light frieze on the outside wall: like the eagle, the bird that can see into the far distance and look at the sun, St John is the most far-sighted of the Gospel writers and the closest to Christ.[13]

Running round the circular outer walls of the chapel is a frieze that Mary names the 'Path of the Just'. Central to each of its four quarters is a bird symbolizing an aspect of the human spirit. The peacock, a universal symbol, is shown as the Spirit of Hope. It often appears in Celtic manuscripts and also represents both 'watchfulness', as the 'eyes' in its tail look upwards when it trails

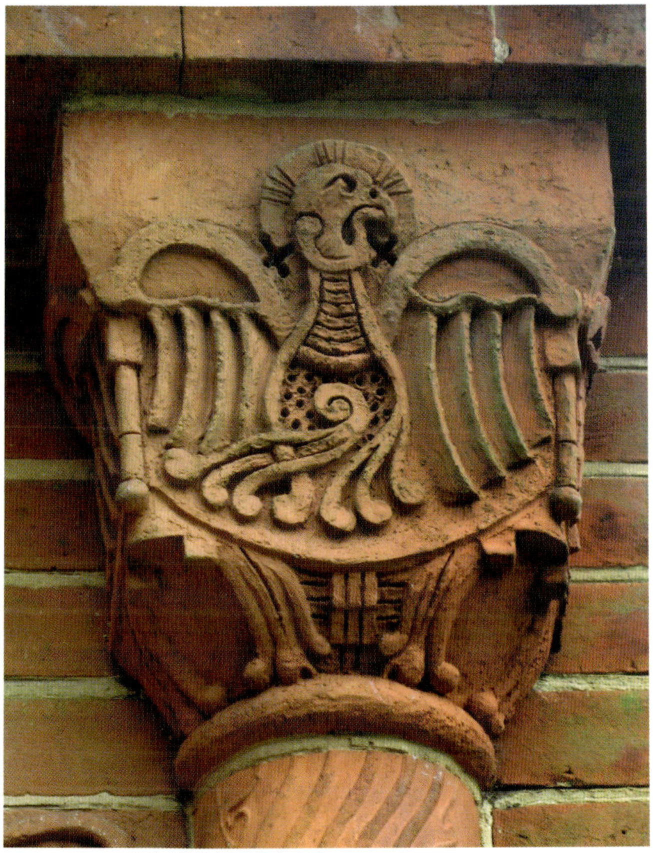

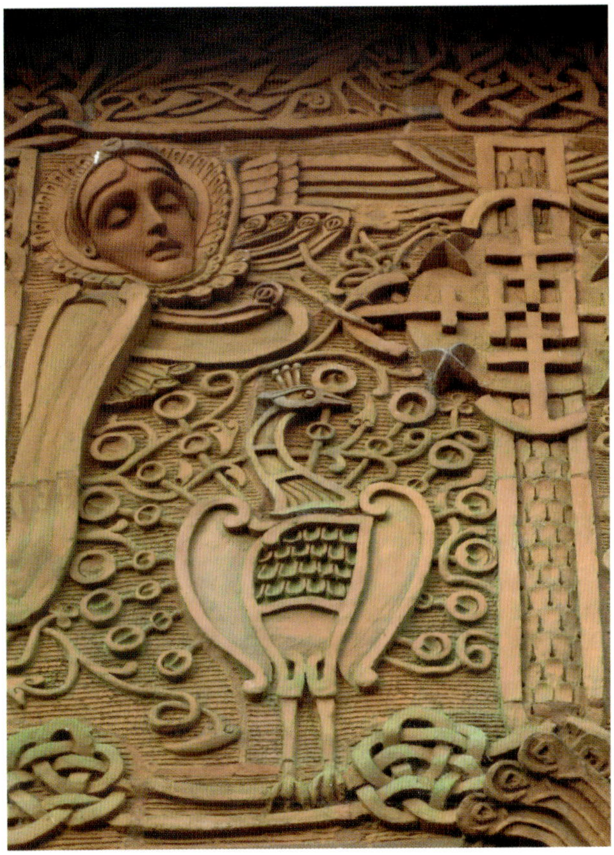

Above left: A capital with the eagle of St John based on Celtic manuscript illustrations

Above right: Part of the Spirit of Hope section of the Path of Just frieze showing a peacock (the bird of Hope) flanking a cross with the anchors of Hope

them along the ground, and 'renewal', as it loses its tail feathers in autumn and grows them again the following spring. Early Christians regarded it as a symbol of the incorruptibility of Christ, as its flesh supposedly never putrefies. Mary prefers a poetic reference to 'those wonderful blue eyes surrounded by rays shining with the colour of light'.[14] In Hinduism, as Mary notes, the peacock is sacred, and in some narratives Krishna wears a peacock feather in his turban. Another Hindu image is that of the peacock striking a rock with its beak, out of which water flows and creates a sacred lake. The owl portrayed in the Path of the Just is the Spirit of Truth, and the pelican, the Spirit of Love. To illustrate the last, Mary quotes in her book from the Buddha's 'Teaching on Unselfish Joy', which describes a good traveller: 'The whole wide world, above, below, around and everywhere, doth he continue to pervade with heart of love.'[15]

There are numerous biblical references in Mary's symbolism. From the New Testament she draws predominantly on St John's Gospel and the Book of Revelation, widely believed in the nineteenth century to have been written by St John. The opening phrases of St John's Gospel, so important for Mary's theme, appear in Celtic lettering around the dome inside the chapel, and for the Spirit of Light she refers to the words in his First Epistle: 'God is Light, and in Him is no darkness at all' (1 John 1:5). Revelation, that most obscure book of the New Testament, is also the most open to free interpretation, which fitted Mary's spirituality. In the centre of the altar frontal, gold lettering based on uncial script is almost obscured by the decoration round it, challenging

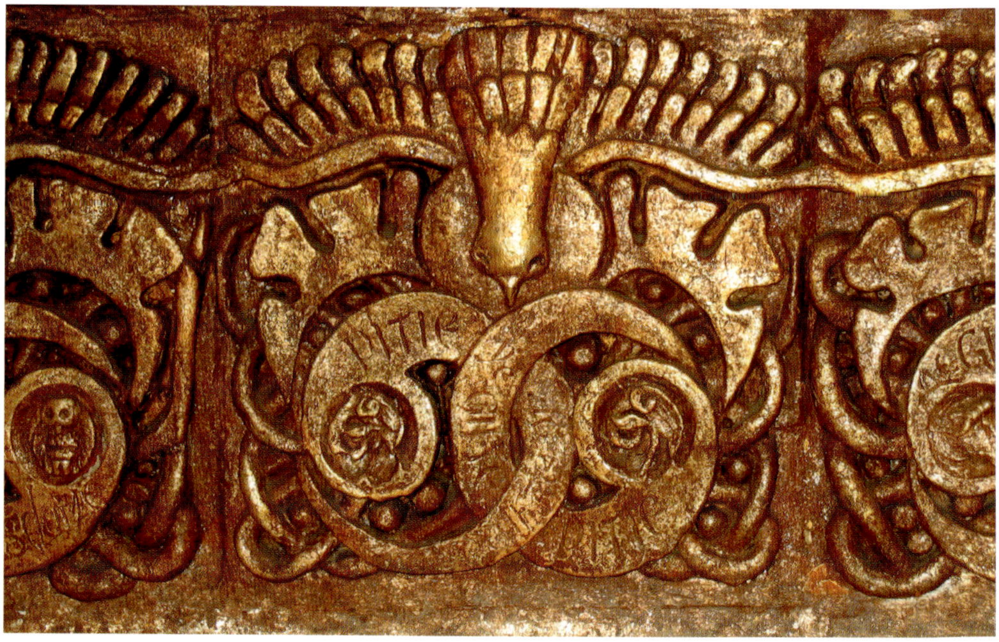

Detail of the doves below the altar illustrating the gifts of the Holy Spirit

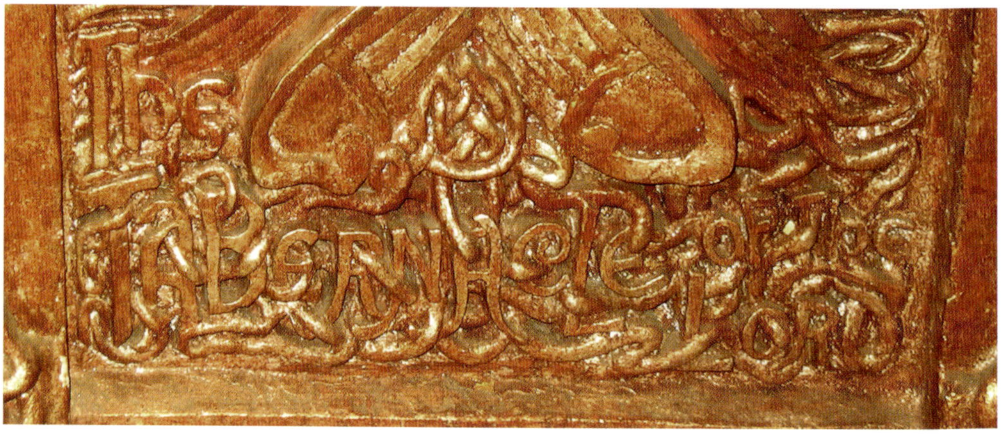

The Tabernacle of the Lord inscription below the altar with Celtic lettering influenced by contemporary design

the reader and leading us into Mary's 'holy of holies'. It is a quotation from Revelation: 'The tabernacle of God is with men, and he will dwell with them' (Rev. 21:3).[16] Other symbols from Revelation are found throughout the chapel. Images above the doorway show angels blowing trumpets and playing harps to comfort the visiting mourners, and seven golden candlesticks flank the altar to remember 'the seven lamps … before the throne' (Rev. 4:5). This image is common to both Judaism in the menorah (the seven-branched candlestick in the temple at Jerusalem) and Christianity, where it symbolizes the seven gifts of the Holy Spirit, as do the doves below the altar. Mary calls the Tree of Life, which is an often-repeated motif in her decoration, 'that mystic tree of St John's vision' (it appears in Rev. 22:2),[17] and her idea of light and darkness, God as the 'I Am', and the far-seeing eagle are also metaphors taken from John. From the Old Testament Mary quotes the prophet Isaiah's affirmation that there is one God, and that to hope in him is to fill the loneliness of the human heart (Isaiah 21:11).[18] Other notes of encouragement for mourners she takes from Proverbs, Psalms and Lamentations.[19]

One of the symbols that Mary regarded as most important comes from Judaism. This is the 'wall veil', the name that she gave to the heavily decorated section above the entrance archway, taking the phrase from John Ruskin's *Stones of Venice*.[20] At the time of the doorway's design she and Signor were reading a book on Judaic beliefs, *On the Origin and Growth of Religion as Illustrated by the Religion of the Ancient Hebrews* (1893) by Claude Montefiore.[21] A Jewish reformer and a controversial writer, Montefiore looked to form a bridge between aspects of Christianity and Judaism. The 'veil' in a Jewish temple was the important symbol hiding the 'holy of holies' (in Jerusalem the Ark of the Covenant), but it could also be lifted to allow closer access to the mysteries inside. It was made either of stone, when it was at the entrance to the temple, or of richly decorated textiles, when it was inside. It had great significance, as witness 'the veil of the temple' which was 'rent in two' when Jesus died on the cross. The wailing wall in Jerusalem still has the same importance to Jews as the 'wall veils' of the past. Mary says of her 'veil', which in the chapel entrance consists of the two heavily decorated terracotta spandrels above the doorway arch, that 'it is intended to represent an embroidered hanging, and is called the "Garment of Praise"'.[22] Her design for this and her readings of each symbol may be partially understood from her own key in *The Word in the Pattern*.

Panel at the side of the altar showing the golden seven-branched candlestick, a symbol in many cultures, including in Christian contexts where it represents the seven gifts of the Holy Spirit

Since her honeymoon Mary had been captivated by the symbolism of ancient Egypt and the hieroglyphs of Babylonia, Assyria and Egypt that were at the time being deciphered by Archibald Sayce.[23] She and Watts spoke and read about them, and he, with his interest in meaning in art – which itself might only act as a pointer to the truth behind it – wrote in his introduction to the catalogue for the New Gallery exhibition of his paintings in 1896: 'The great majority of these works should be regarded rather as hieroglyphs than anything else, certainly not as more than symbols, which all art was in the beginning.'[24]

Mary had used Egyptian symbolism in her ceiling at Limnerslease, but although there are hints of it in the chapel, particularly in the design of the panels showing the seven lamps beside the altar, she does not employ it directly. Egypt did fire her imagination, however, to embark on the project, and in August 1896 she wrote in her diary:

> Since Egypt my desire to say something in art has been a casting back, to send out a shout from the heart again, & I find myself, in this, in a sort of harmony with things generally of this time. If this is so then my little effort is alive at least.[25]

The Tree of Life, which appears in Revelation, is also cited as a powerful universal symbol that dates back to Babylonian times. Mary uses it as the quintessential vision of hope and renewal on the sides of her buttresses, with the idea of roots growing in darkness but feeding the upper trunk and branches and 'converting all it meets with, even death and decay, into a rising stream of life sent up again into the topmost bough'.[26] It is the main theme inside the chapel, where each of the four quarters of the circular design show the entire tree, with its roots spreading in free curvilinear sweeps, and the trunk and branches sheltering her

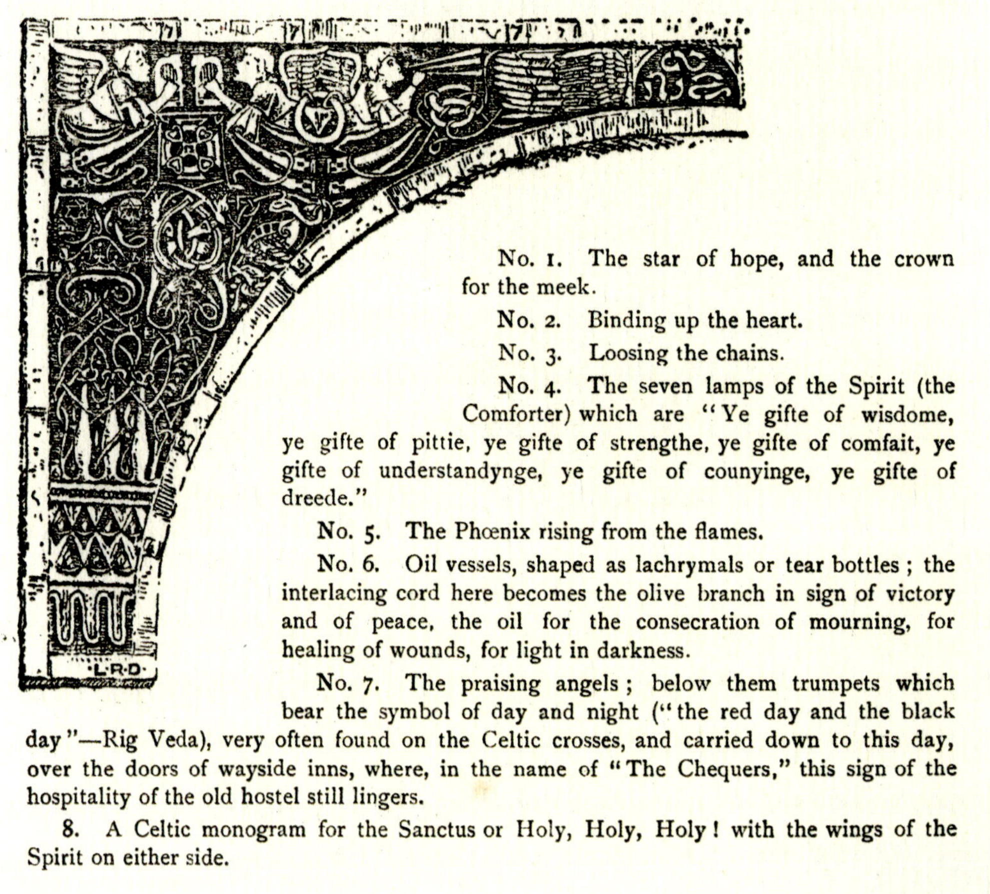

No. 1. The star of hope, and the crown for the meek.

No. 2. Binding up the heart.

No. 3. Loosing the chains.

No. 4. The seven lamps of the Spirit (the Comforter) which are "Ye gifte of wisdome, ye gifte of pittie, ye gifte of strengthe, ye gifte of comfait, ye gifte of understandynge, ye gifte of counyinge, ye gifte of dreede."

No. 5. The Phœnix rising from the flames.

No. 6. Oil vessels, shaped as lachrymals or tear bottles; the interlacing cord here becomes the olive branch in sign of victory and of peace, the oil for the consecration of mourning, for healing of wounds, for light in darkness.

No. 7. The praising angels; below them trumpets which bear the symbol of day and night ("the red day and the black day"—Rig Veda), very often found on the Celtic crosses, and carried down to this day, over the doors of wayside inns, where, in the name of "The Chequers," this sign of the hospitality of the old hostel still lingers.

8. A Celtic monogram for the Sanctus or Holy, Holy, Holy! with the wings of the Spirit on either side.

A page from Mary's book The Word in the Pattern *showing the 'Garment of Praise' or 'wall veil' with her explanations for each part of it*

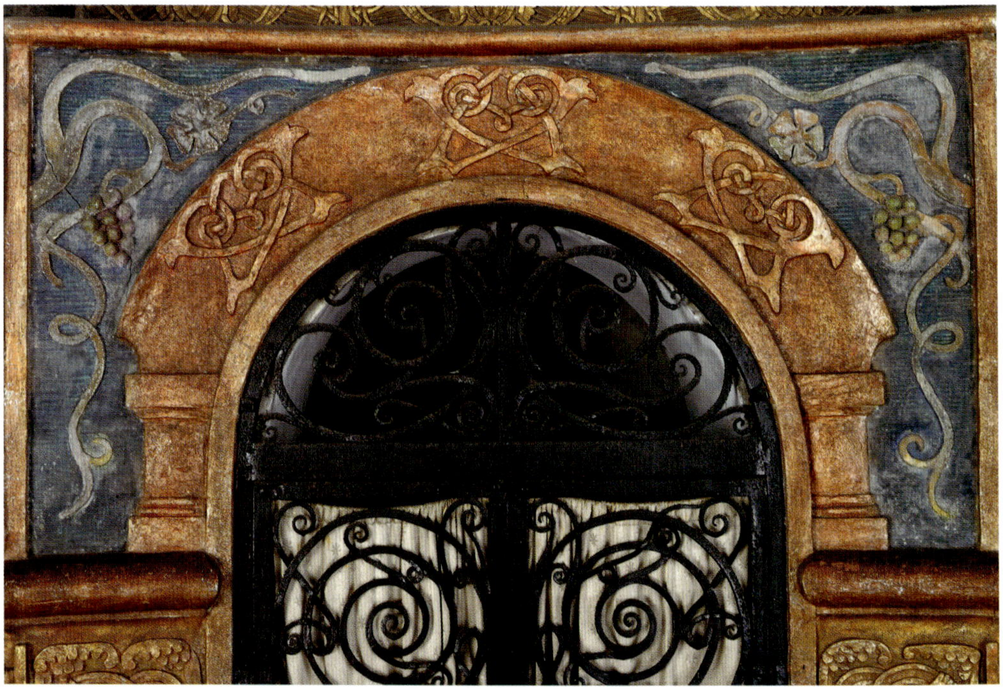

Doorway arch and surround on the north side of the chapel with decorations incorporating Mary's Celtic, Egyptian and Art Nouveau influences

winged messengers that carry roundels revealing the opposing positives and negatives in life and in nature.[27] Above the tree four seraphs give their blessing, and the domed roof is surrounded by cherubim, while in the centre, echoing W.R. Lethaby (1857–1931), is 'the circle of the Eternal – without beginning, without end; the shelter of wings from everlasting to everlasting; the infinite Love; the Sun of righteousness'.[28]

A universal symbol that Mary uses both inside and outside the chapel is that of the maze, representing the difficult path through life leading to eternity for those who follow God: 'The maze of life may bewilder, but the path of light runs through it'.[29] The decoration on the columns supporting the sides of the buttresses is based on a maze from a stone cross at Carew, Wales. It shows a swastika entwined with a 'Tau' cross, far older than Christianity. The swastika is found in all civilizations and in Mary's lifetime had none of the associations with Fascism that it has today. The word comes from the Sanskrit *svastika*, meaning 'well-being' or 'luck', and Mary traces its provenance in her notebook. It was used in Mycenae, Illium, Cyprus and Athens, and in Greece it was called the *gammadion*, a cross with hooks. It appears in Hittite images as a symbol of felicity and is the Anglo-Saxon *fylfot*, the 'many-footed'. The Tau cross is so-named from the last letter in the Hebrew alphabet, pronounced 'taw', and also from the Greek letter 'T', but is itself based on the Egyptian 'key of life'.[30]

While she was working on the chapel design, Mary read, along with many of her contemporaries, William Lethaby's *Architecture, Mysticism and Myth*, published in 1892. In it Lethaby poses a philosophical reading of architecture as a system of symbols, and creates a new perspective on the buildings and decoration of previous cultures. His book includes a chapter on the significance of labyrinths and mazes.[31] In the corbels holding up the friezes on the outer walls of Mary's chapel, three angels hold roundels illustrating the Way, the Truth and the Life. The Way is represented by another version of a maze highlighted by Lethaby and based on the Cretan labyrinth through which Theseus found his way, helped by Ariadne's thread, symbolic of our own tortuous progress through the maze of life.[32] In the Truth Mary uses her only symbol from Scandinavian mythology, which itself dates back to the Egyptian 'Boat of the Sun', believed to sail daily across the sky. Mary's is a stylized Viking boat that steers day and night by the sun and the moon, the black and white chequers on its side symbolizing light and darkness, its sails, the breath of life, and its mast, the double-armed cross guarding its journey.[33]

Mary was not alone in working on freely expressed symbols in her chapel decoration. In Edinburgh a remarkable group of painters, architects and designers was exploring the past, and mysticism generally, in what was part of the Celtic Revival of the late nineteenth century, Several of them were friends of W.B. Yeats in Ireland, and an enthusiasm for all things Celtic inspired them, as indeed it did Mary. Among them was the artist and craftswoman, Phoebe Traquair, who was well known to G.F. and Mary Watts and stayed with them in 1894. She was many-talented, worked in the Arts and Crafts tradition and produced several stunning murals in Edinburgh, well publicized in the art journals of the time. Her techniques and effects were different from Mary's,

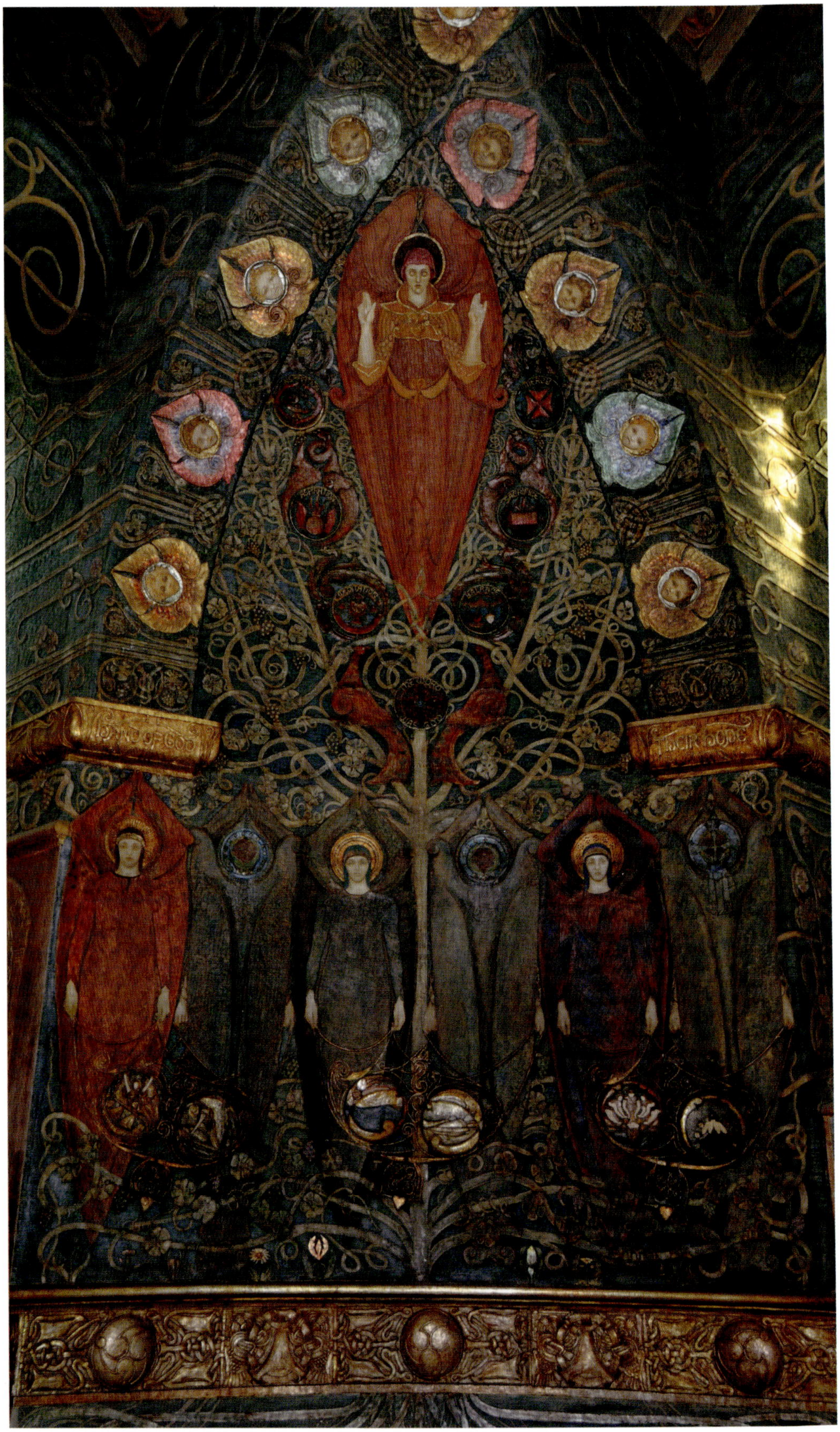

One of the Tree of Life panels inside the chapel with winged messengers and positive and negative roundels connected by Celtic symbols

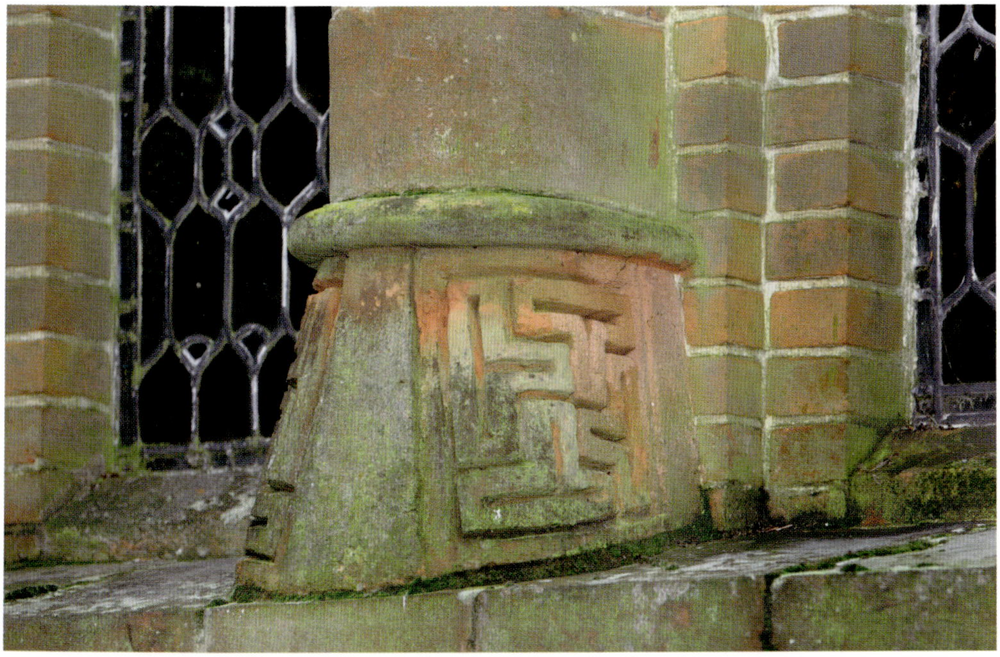

Left: The base of an external pillar decorated with a maze composed of swastikas and Tau crosses derived from a cross at Carew in Wales

Below left: The corbel below the Path of the Just frieze illustrating the Way with a labyrinthine maze, symbolic of the difficult path through life

Below right: The corbel illustrating the Truth with the symbol of a Scandinavian boat that steers day and night by the sun and the moon

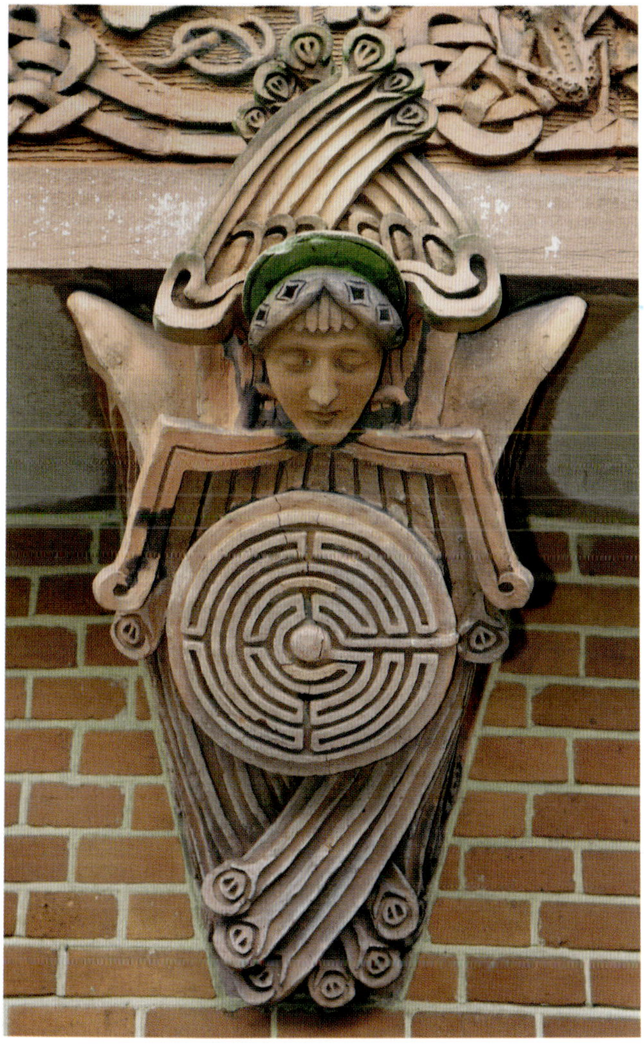

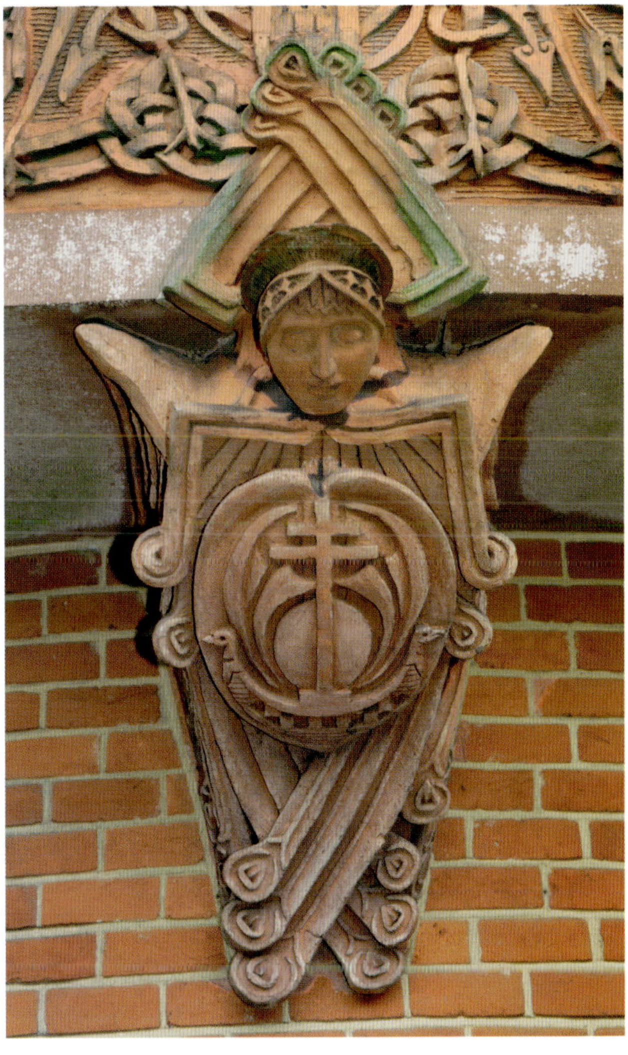

Opposite: Celtic swirls beside a window in the chapel linking with the heads of cherubim and winged messengers

but her aims were similar. She was first commissioned to paint murals in the mortuary chapel of the Royal Hospital for Sick Children, and later produced notable murals for the Catholic Apostolic Church, both in Edinburgh. Her embroidered panels illustrating 'The Progress of the Soul' come closest to Mary's intentions to illuminate the spiritual in man. Traquair's friend and colleague John Duncan painted mystical canvases showing Celtic saints and heroes with views of Iona in the background.[34] The group was close to Walter Crane, William Morris, William Lethaby and Edward Burne-Jones, all of whom were well known to the Wattses, so that ideas and discussion flowed in both directions. Walter Crane and Burne-Jones gave Mary advice and encouragement, and her winged messengers and seraphs inside the chapel are reminiscent of Burne-Jones's elongated figures, while the translucent effect of her tempera finish is also influenced by his murals. Walter Crane's designs, using abstracts to fill in the background to his narrative paintings and illustrations, and his flowing Art Nouveau figures were part of the ambience of the 1890s that Mary absorbed. The faces and the figures in her chapel decorations, however, owe nothing to Celtic or other artistic influences, but are characteristic of the late nineteenth century, as if they are showing 'modern man' reacting to the meaning of universal symbols from the past.

Mary's quotations in *The Word in the Pattern* pay homage to contemporary poets, particularly Tennyson, one of Watts's closest friends. She describes the lily in her Spirit of Love frieze as 'the white flower of a blameless life', referring to Prince Albert, who is remembered in this way in the dedication to Tennyson's *Idylls of the King*.[35] Mary's second quotation from Tennyson is very significant to her theme. She is writing of Watts's contribution to the chapel project, his painting *The All-Pervading* above the altar. She describes the sphere, symbol of the universe held by the Creator, as 'the rush of suns and roll of systems'. This is taken from Tennyson's poem 'God and the Universe', and a line from the same poem completes Mary's message: 'Fear not thou the hidden purpose of that Power which alone is great'.[36]

The complexity of Mary's rich tapestry of symbols with their traditional and arcane references makes it difficult for a visitor to understand their significance without a guide. Clearly, this was something that Mary was aware of and inspired her to write *The Word in the Pattern: A Key to the Symbols on the Walls of the Chapel at Compton*. Couched in flowery language and only partially explaining her sources, it nevertheless gives a valuable insight into the depth of Mary's desire to create a spiritual whole. Mark Bills, Curator of Watts Gallery, has also recently written a new comprehensive guide, *Watts Chapel: A Guide to the Symbols of Mary Watts's Arts and Crafts Masterpiece* (2010), a unique and much needed reference work.

The impact of the chapel on almost everyone who visits it is great. It is impossible not to react to such a concentration of images, which, even if one does not understand them all, have clearly been put together with purpose, meaning and love. The contrast between the terracotta exterior, whose motifs have to be examined and appreciated intellectually, and the revelatory, flowing, translucent designs inside, which produce gasps from many who see them for the first time, creates a lasting impression. Some people may not warm to late nineteenth-century decoration, but Mary's intention shining through the ambiguity of her symbols and the dedication that brought it all together cannot but be acknowledged and admired.

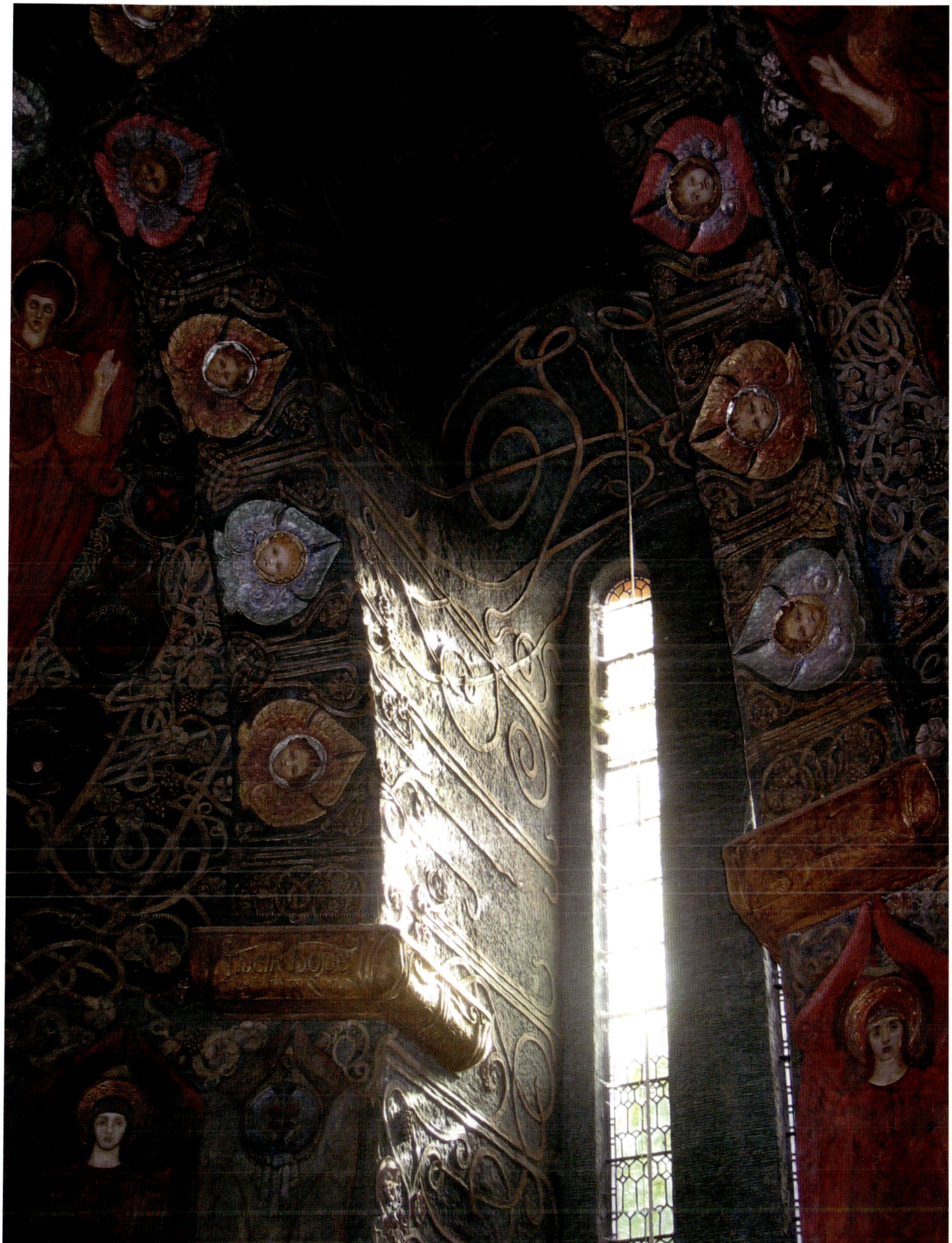

NOTES

1 Discussions during the honeymoon, on the Nile and in Constantinople: MSW Diaries, 21, 22, 23 and 27 January, 4 and 6 February, and 31 March 1887. Evening reading at Little Holland House and Limnerslease: MSW Diaries, 4 and 9 January, 6, 9 and 15 February, 27 March, 5 and 11 April, 22, 24 and 31 May, 28 June, 26 July, and 6 August 1891.

2 M.S. Watts, *The Word in the Pattern: A Key to the Symbols on the Walls of the Chapel at Compton by Mrs George Frederic Watts*, London 1905, reprinted Compton 2000.

3 Watts 1905, p.4.

4 *Apollo*, April 1966.

5 Watts 1905, p.11.

6 MSW Diaries, 9 September 1896.

7 A.T. Lucas, *Treasures of Ireland: Irish Pagan and Early Christian Art*, Dublin 1973, pp.58, 68–73.

8 Francis Joseph Bigger, *The Dextera Dei Sculptured on the High Crosses of Ireland*, Dublin 1900, pp.79–84.

9 Watts 1905, p.13.

10 *Bede's Ecclesiastical History of the English People*, ed. B. Colgrave and R.A.B. Mynors, Oxford 1969, pp.221–23; W. Brindley and W.S. Weatherley, *Ancient Sepulchral Monuments*, London 1887, pl.102.

11 Adomnan of Iona, *Life of Columba*, trans. Richard Sharpe, Harmondsworth 1995, p.330.

12 The Book of Kells, f.27v (symbols of the Four Evangelists).

13 Bernard Meehan, *The Book of Kells: An Illustrated Introduction to the Manuscript in Trinity College*, Dublin 1994, p.57.

14 Watts 1905, p.18.

15 Watts 1905, p.21.

16 Watts 2000, p.35.

17 Watts 1905, p.4.

18 Watts 1905, p.13.

19 Watts 2000, pp.17, 18 (Proverbs 4:18), 18 (Psalms 31:24, 42:1 and 5; Lamentations 3:6).

20 Ruskin 1903–12, vol.9 (*The Stones of Venice*, vol.1, 1851), ch.5, 'The Wall Veil'.

21 See also Lethaby 2004, p.35.

22 Watts 1905, p.14.

23 A.H. Sayce, *Fresh Light from the Ancient Monuments*, London 1884, pp.15–17.

24 Franklin Gould 2004, p.308.

25 MSW Diaries, 30 August 1896.

26 Watts 1905, p.5; Lethaby 2004, pp.10–11.

27 Watts 2000, pp.32–35. Panel I (left of the door): Day and Night, Flow and Ebb, Growth and Decay; Panel II: Life and Death, Good and Evil, Labour and Rest; Panel III: Joy and Sorrow, Spirit and Flesh, Real and Ideal; Panel IV: Freedom and Limit, Union and Conflict, Stability and Change.

28 Watts 2000, p.32.

29 Watts 1905, p.15.

30 MSW Chapel Notebook.

31 Watts 1905, p.17; Lethaby 2004, ch.7 'The Labyrinth', pp.149–54.

32 Lethaby 2004, p.153.

33 Watts 1905, p.17.

34 Murdo Macdonald, *Scottish Art*, London 2000, ch.7 'Modernity and Revivals: Arts, Crafts and Celtic Revival in Edinburgh', pp.151–57; *Builder*, 2 April 1892, p.259.

35 Alfred, Lord Tennyson, *The Idylls of the King* (1859), Oxford 1912, p.531.
36 Alfred, Lord Tennyson, *The Death of Oenone, Akbar's Dream, and other Poems*, London 1892.

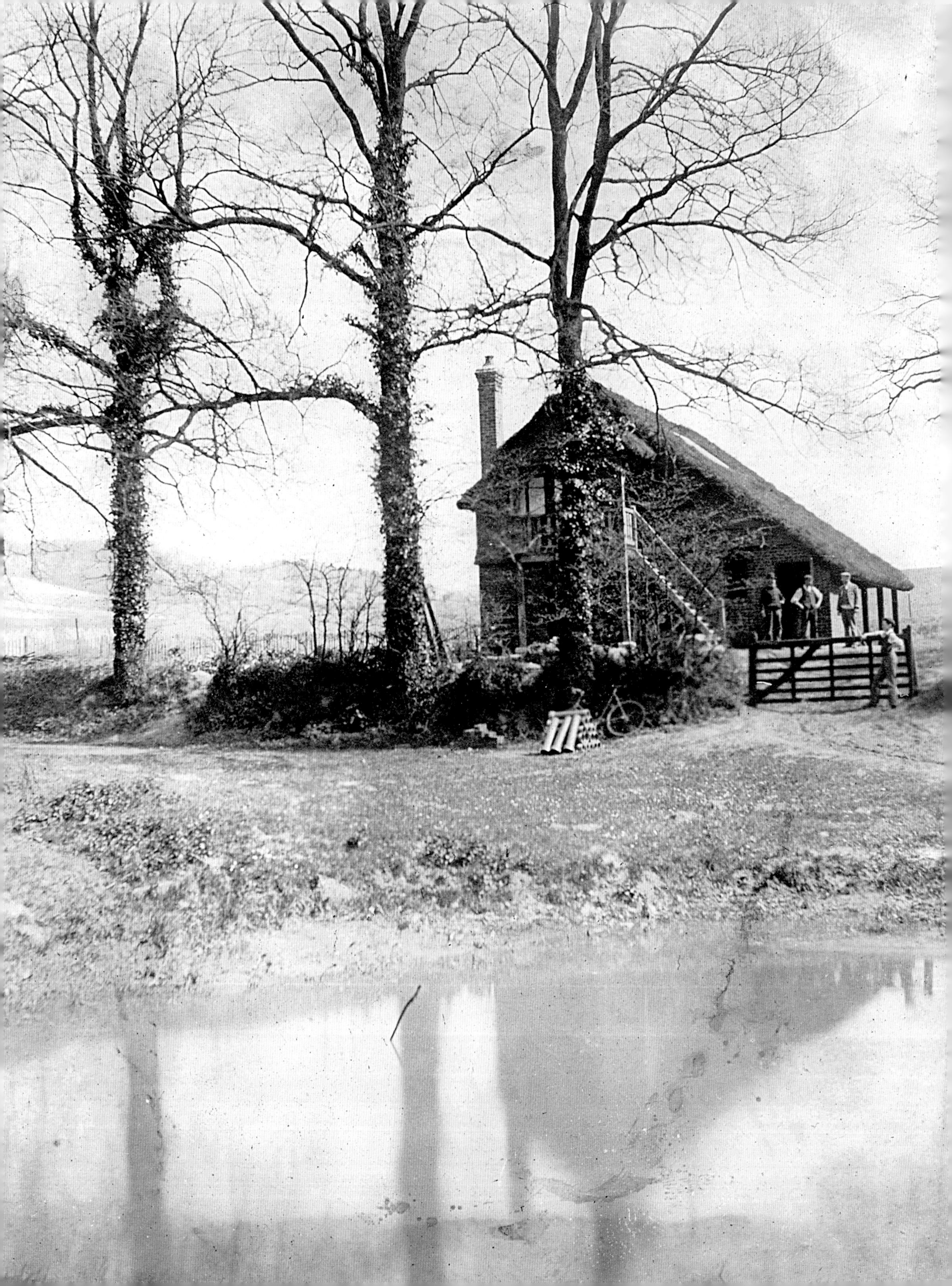

Compton Pottery

Hilary Underwood

Mary Watts's background gave her ideal skills to develop a pottery at Compton. She had trained in the specialist techniques of terracotta sculpture under Aimé-Jules Dalou. Her involvement in the Home Arts and Industries Association provided her with the intellectual and social framework in which to work and an initial outlet to display and sell her products. Her 1885–86 Home Arts clay-modelling class gave her experience of teaching youths and volunteers. In addition, her raw material, clay, was fortuitously to hand in the grounds of Limnerslease. She founded the pottery only after her more personal work decorating Limnerslease was complete and after Watts deterred her from more fundraising for the Home Arts and Industries Association, but she had been developing the idea since the early 1890s. She considered Watts's praise of work in December 1891, when he declared 'Education begins in work', the 'germ of my potter's work'.[1] She was also inspired by Conrad Dressler (1856–1940) and his project to found a pottery on guild lines in 1893, with its ideals of creative handicraft and the active involvement of the workers in the organization.[2] Dressler's idea materialized as the Della Robbia Pottery in Birkenhead (1893–1906). Mary had designed the recumbent cross for the grave of Lady Waterford at Ford in Northumberland in 1891[3] and was considering starting a Home Arts class in memorial design by the autumn of 1893.[4] The final impetus for her work came from the project to design and build a chapel for the new cemetery in Compton, which has already been discussed. On 14 November 1895 she started a Home Arts clay-modelling class in her studio in Limnerslease to realize the project.[5]

The infrastructure needed for the chapel also helped to establish the pottery. With support and advice from William De Morgan,[6] a wood-fired bottle kiln made of brick and with twin stoke-holes was constructed in the garden of Limnerslease and is still extant. Wood, rather than the more modern and hotter-burning coal, was used as a fuel, 'to obtain a delicate and broken colour'.[7] The kiln was still in use as late as 1911,[8] although it was later superseded by a larger one within the main pottery complex. The specialist kiln-burner left when the exterior of the chapel was finished, but the successful clay-modelling class continued. During the chapel project it had met twice a week with thirty to forty pupils aged from ten to sixty.[9] Mary Watts re-employed the kiln-burner to fire their work, and provided him with a wheel to make additional pots to offset his wages.[10] Orders grew and 'several of the younger members of the class were so attracted by the artistic nature of the work that they expressed a desire to devote their whole time to it'.[11]

Around 1900 Mary Watts decided to turn the successful class into a Home Arts 'developed industry', which would provide paid employment for its workers. She overcame the anxieties of her husband, who was to provide the capital, and planned new premises and a manager. Conrad Dressler recommended James

Opposite: The pottery building, pre-1903

Right: Compton Potters' Arts Guild ornamental ware, Watts Gallery

Below right: The restored kiln on Down Lane, Compton, recent photograph, private collection

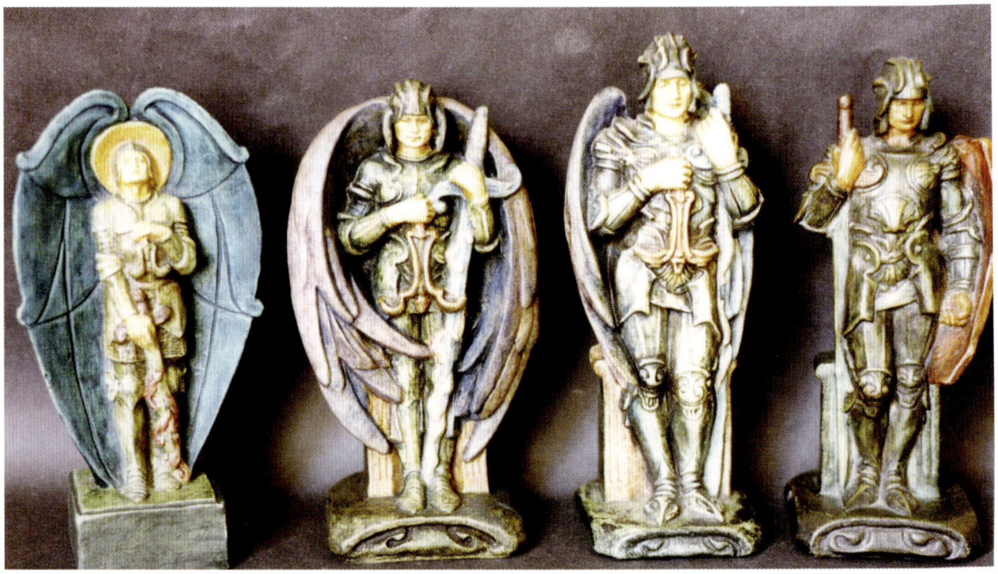

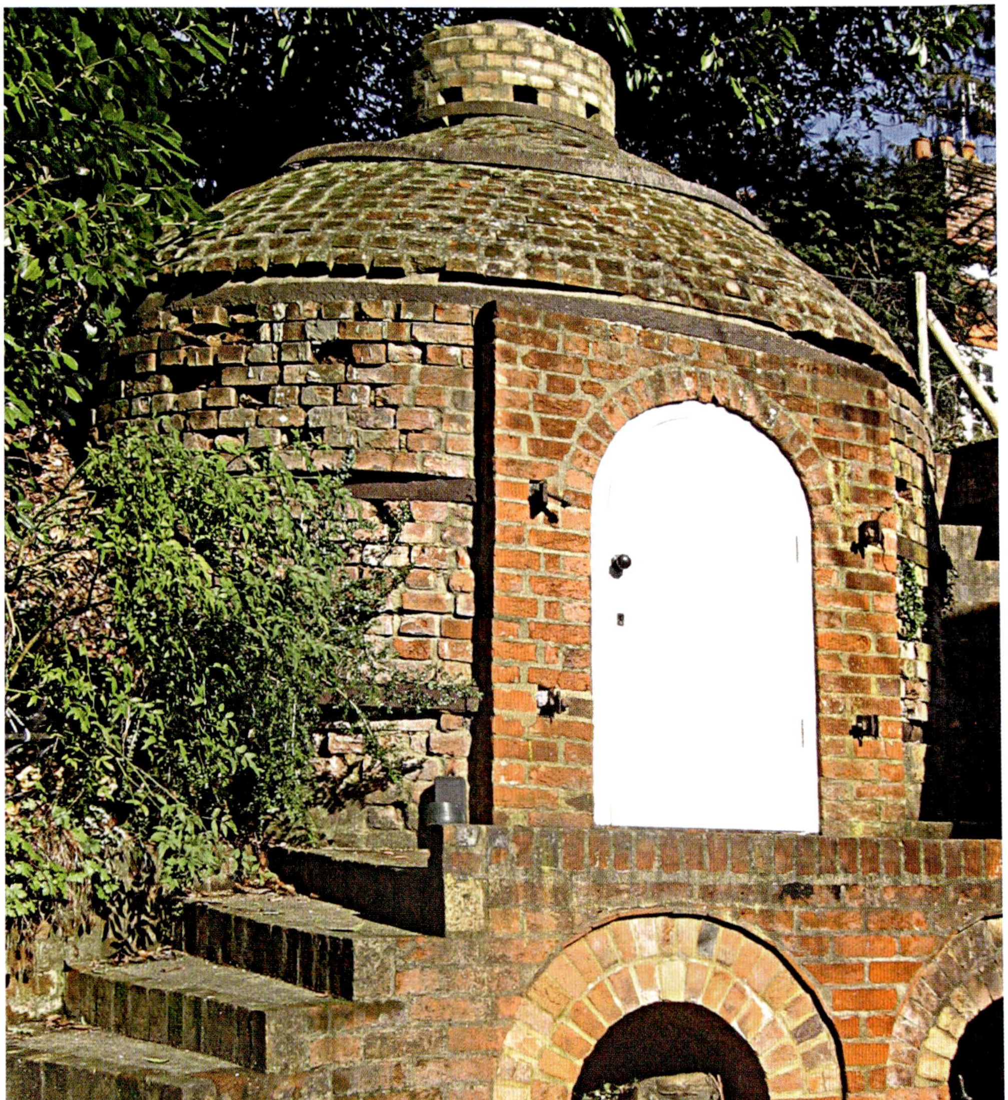

Nicol, who had been working at the Cumnock Pottery in Ayrshire for more than twenty years. Two letters in December 1900, offering him 'a *delightful* village industry – beautiful things beautifully made, by people in beautiful country' and then more practically a 'big salary', persuaded him to Compton in February 1901.[12] Land was bought from the Loseley estate on the east side of Down Lane adjacent to the Limnerslease estate on the west side. A house, Helmstead, was built for the pottery manager to the north of the site and by 15 January 1901 the pottery buildings had been planned. First to be constructed was a small two-storey workshop and drying area in creosoted lapboard with heather thatch and a brick chimney.[13] At the same time Mary Watts initiated the Aldourie Pottery at Dores in Inverness-shire near her childhood home of Aldourie Castle. Louis Deuchars was sent from Compton as manager in 1900. He was a painter and sculptor who had trained at Glasgow School of Art. He had assisted George Frederic Watts with his sculpture and become one of the full-time workers on the chapel. The Aldourie Pottery produced similar terracotta garden ware to Compton, but it was a smaller operation with a more limited product range and relied on expensively imported Compton clay, which was unreliable in the Scottish climate. This short-lived project probably closed after five or six years.[14]

Meanwhile, the Compton Pottery developed and expanded. By 1904 the thatched workshop was much enlarged. It housed a drying area and a workshop for large mould-made pots on the brick-built ground floor. The potters' wheels, hand-cranked by junior workers, were also located there. An external wooden staircase led to a skylit upper studio for modelling, making smaller pots and painting the ornamental ware. The 1901 plan included a large adjacent brick-built kiln that would also heat the drying room in winter by a removable pipe. The kiln was added at right angles to the main workshop at a later date, its bottle shape partly concealed by a surrounding brick building with a tiled roof.[15] The Watts Gallery building, designed and constructed between 1903 and 1904, incorporated accommodation for up to twelve teenage apprentices and their housekeeper in its flanking wings, including dormitories in the roof, and a shared dining room and a recreation room. Early postcards title it 'The Hostel'. Mary Watts continued to provide accommodation for her workers in their adulthood, commissioning four cottages by Ernest George and later two further cottages by Clough Williams-Ellis. Known collectively as Oak Cottages, they stand near the Withies Inn in Compton. She offered Bowler's Cottage in the gallery grounds to potters Martha 'Cis' Wonham and Thomas Brunt-Nye on their marriage, and Cis Nye lived there until her death in 1992.[16]

The pottery was constituted as the Potters' Arts Guild in 1904 and distinctive logos were designed for the terracotta and the ornamental ware. As recorded in a constitution of 1920, the guild organization divided the annual profits between the manager and workers of more than five years standing.[17] Half the profits were retained by the guild as capital but credited to the individual workers' accounts, paying interest and available to them on departure.[18] From 1920 the pottery was headed by a committee of four: Mary Watts as director, the manager (at that time still James Nicol) and two workmen – but, as director, Mary Watts retained the right of veto over new designs.[19]

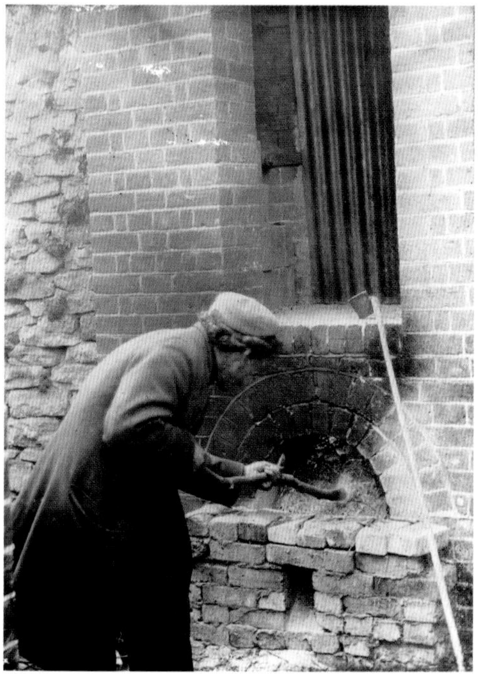

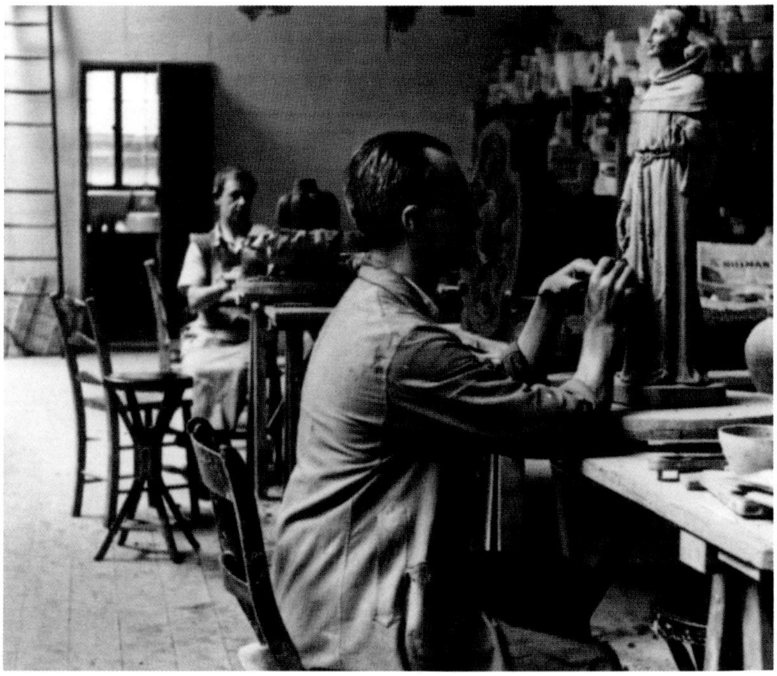

Above: Loading the kiln, from the Country Home, *November 1911, Watts Gallery Archive*

Above right: The modelling room of the pottery with Tom Wren working on a figurine, from the Country Home, *November 1911, Watts Gallery Archive*

Mary Watts's creative energies were not solely devoted to her decorative work for Limnerslease, the Compton chapel and the pottery. She designed book bindings. One, for a catalogue of a G.F. Watts exhibition, was executed by the Guild of Women Binders (1897; Watts Gallery). Another, for her book on the chapel, *The Word in the Pattern*, was executed by E. Gertrude Farran and exhibited in the prestigious Arts and Crafts Exhibition Society exhibition in 1906 (1906; Watts Gallery).[20] She also designed a small number of significant Arts and Crafts textiles. The wool-pile carpet, 'The Pelican', was designed in 1899 for Alexander Morton & Co., hand-woven at Killibegs in Donegal and marketed through Liberty & Co. Examples were exhibited at Liberty's Grafton Gallery exhibitions in London, *Founding a National Industry – Irish Carpets* in March 1903 and *Modern Celtic Art* in March 1904. As in the chapel, Mary Watts used Celtic design elements and a similar image of a pelican feeding its young with its blood, a traditional symbol of self-sacrifice. Characteristically, she wrote a long letter explaining the spiritual significance of the design for the weavers.[21] She was also commissioned to design two painted, appliquéd and embroidered silk banners by the Governor General of Canada, Earl Grey. *Our Lady of the Snows* (1906; McGill University) was presented to McGill University, Montreal, by Queen Alexandra, and *The Spirit of the Flowers of the Nation* (1907; Victoria & Albert Museum) was originally hung in Government House, Ottawa. These works are stylistically close to the chapel interior and have a similar rich iconography.[22]

Mary Watts undertook the gesso decoration of a second chapel at the Cambridge Military Hospital in Aldershot in 1916 in the middle of the First World War. To create a fitting chapel for wounded soldiers and for the coffins and funeral services of those who had died, she represented Shadrach, Meshach and Abednego unharmed in the burning fiery furnace on the west wall. The subject from the Book of Daniel is a metaphorical image of divine protection

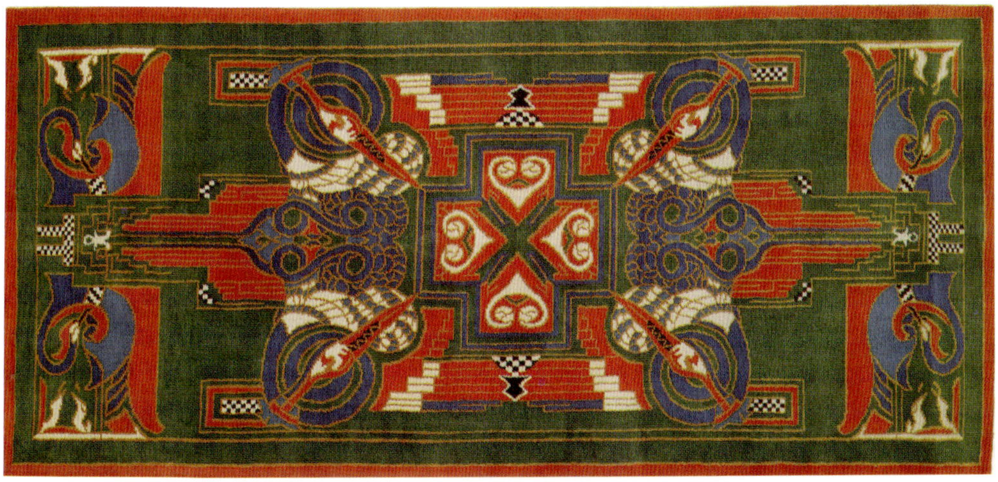

1899 Pelican carpet, Watts Gallery

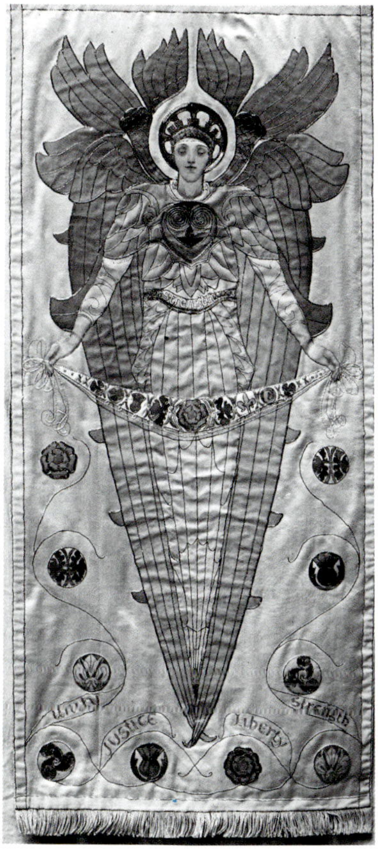

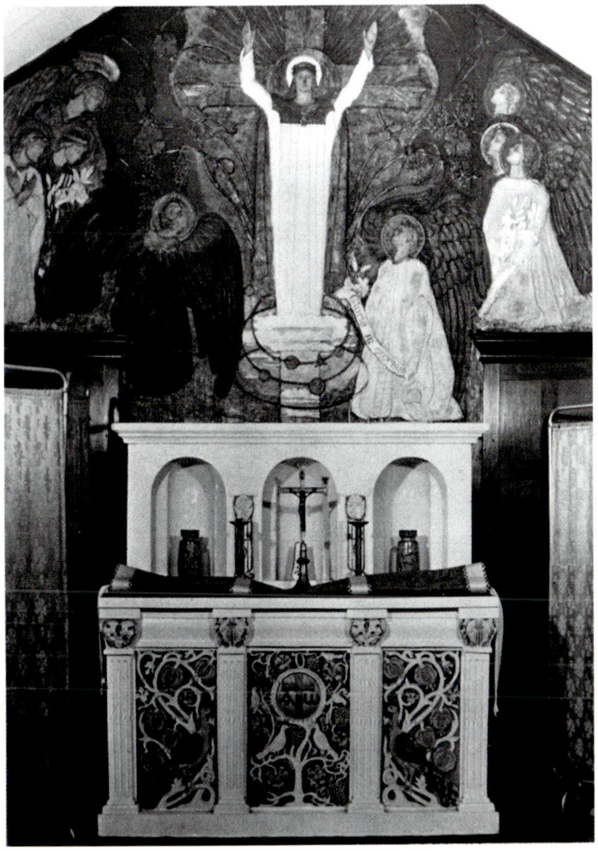

Left: Mary Watts, The Spirit of the Flowers of the Nations, *1907, embroidered and appliquéd hanging, Victoria & Albert Museum, London, from a glass plate negative, Watts Gallery*

Right: Mary Watts and Potters' Arts Guild, altar wall relief, c.*1916–21, painted plaster, Watts Gallery (formerly Mortuary Chapel, Cambridge Military Hospital, Aldershot)*

from the horrors of war. The east, altar wall was dominated by a triumphant Christ, standing before a cross and tree of life and surrounded by angels. Friezes on the side walls represent musical angels with lettered scrolls. The style is more conventional than that of the Compton chapel. A few friends had raised a subscription to beautify the mortuary chapel. Mary Watts was approached and 'readily agreed' to design the work.[23] The Aldershot chapel was to be executed by her Potters' Arts Guild, and Thomas Wren modelled the head and arms of Christ. However he, like the other potters, was called up for military service. Mary Watts completed the work herself as late as 1921.[24] When the site of the hospital was

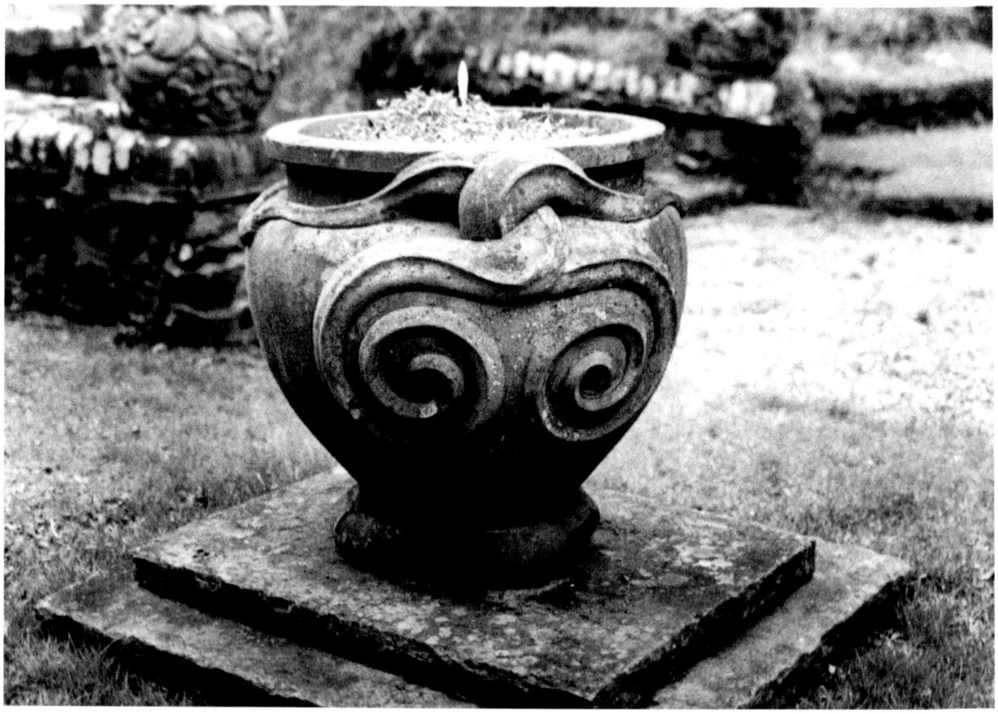

Potters' Arts Guild, Scroll Pot, in production by 1903, terracotta, Watts Gallery

redeveloped and the chapel was demolished in 1996, the army kindly permitted Watts Gallery to remove and preserve the decorative work.[25]

The most important and popular work of the pottery was large-scale terracotta garden ware, riding on what Mary Watts called 'the present fashion for gardening and garden decoration'.[26] Most pots were available in a variety of sizes, the largest sometimes standing up to 2 ft 6 in (76 cm) high. Most, like the popular Celtic and Duchess pots, were press-moulded in plaster moulds. Others, like the Snake (or Cobra) pot, were wheel-made with applied decoration. In the 1920s the pottery's first post-war apprentice, Roy Saywell, developed the skills to throw particularly large pots. Most of the early designs were provided by Mary Watts, but the Jekyll Bowl was designed by the famous gardener Gertrude Jekyll and used in her own garden schemes as well as sold by the pottery. To match the pots to stone buildings the pottery bought in grey clay, although the grey range was more expensive and more vulnerable to frost. Miniature Compton pots were used in the garden that Gertrude Jekyll created for Queen Mary's Dolls' House designed by Sir Edwin Lutyens in 1921.

Liberty's sold the pottery's garden wares. Liberty's policy was to market designs anonymously under their own brand, even those of well-known Arts and Crafts designers such as C.F.A. Voysey (1857–1941). They made an exception in crediting the Potters' Arts Guild and Mary Watts, partly because she was the 'talented wife of our greatest living artist'.[27] However, they did rename her pottery, often giving her Celtic designs Germanic and Wagnerian titles. The Snake pot became the 'Fafnir' and the Scroll pot became the 'Wottan [*sic*]'.[28] Compton Pottery was included in the Liberty's *Book of Garden Ornaments* of 1904 and in several of its exhibitions, including the Grafton Gallery exhibitions of 1903 and 1904 mentioned above. It also featured and was a medal-winner in Liberty's displays

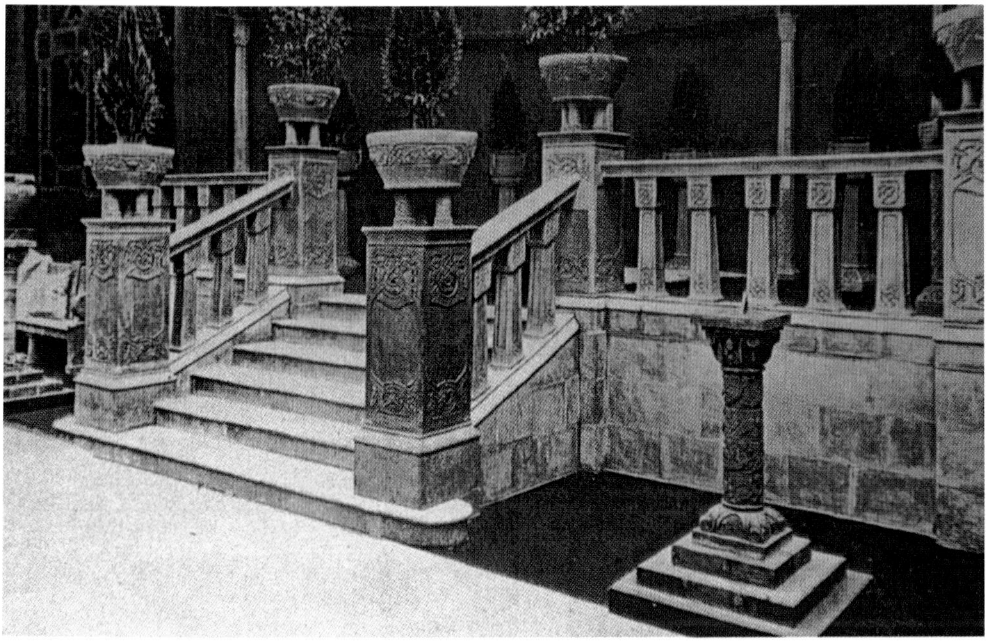

Mary Watts and Potter's Arts Guild, Winged Hours sundial (foreground) and garden pottery by Archibald Knox, marketed by Liberty and Co., from Ffoulkes 1903, courtesy of V&A Images

at the Royal Botanic Society and the Royal Horticultural Society in the 1905–12 period.[29]

The pottery marketed its own work, including displays at the Home Arts and Industries exhibitions. It produced regular catalogues from at least 1909 to 1932, mainly of twenty-four pages, which illustrated and priced garden pots, 'birds' baths' and sundials, and showed representative garden statues and occasionally tombstones, soliciting commissions.[30] In some catalogues the foreword announced that the pottery was 'glad to undertake work from designs entrusted to them by Architects or Artists'.[31] Among such architectural work was a commission from the architect Herbert Baker in 1910.[32] Goods were despatched throughout Britain by rail, and to aid their enterprise, the pottery had one of the first telephone lines in the district, with the number 'Puttenham 2'.[33]

Well-designed gravestones had been one of Mary Watts's aims for the pottery and they were produced from 1895 onwards. The most striking were individually designed, using a similar visual language to the exterior of the chapel. In Compton Cemetery the graves of Arabella Ellice (died 1910) and Gertrude Vernon (d. 1913) bear large elaborate recumbent crosses, the second with a Celtic interlace pattern. The grave of Harriet Greenfield (d. 1905) has a small standing cross where cherubs in the arms surround a Celtic roundel. That of Margaret Gillett (d. 1907) has a semi-circle of four profile angels at its head. That of Julian Russell Sturgis (d. 1904), novelist and owner of the Voysey-designed Greyfriars on the Hog's Back, Surrey, has paired angels flanking a circular inscription. The angels are reminiscent of the figures of the four main chapel friezes. The most elaborate designs almost invariably pre-date the First World War. Perhaps their swansong is Compton's terracotta war memorial outside St Nicholas's church. Simpler designs with inscriptions on terracotta kerbs, slopes, scrolls and open books predominate in the interwar years. While the early, elaborate designs are scattered across Britain, probably reflecting personal links between the

Right: Mary Watts and Potter's Arts Guild, Pilgrim's Way cross, terracotta, private collection

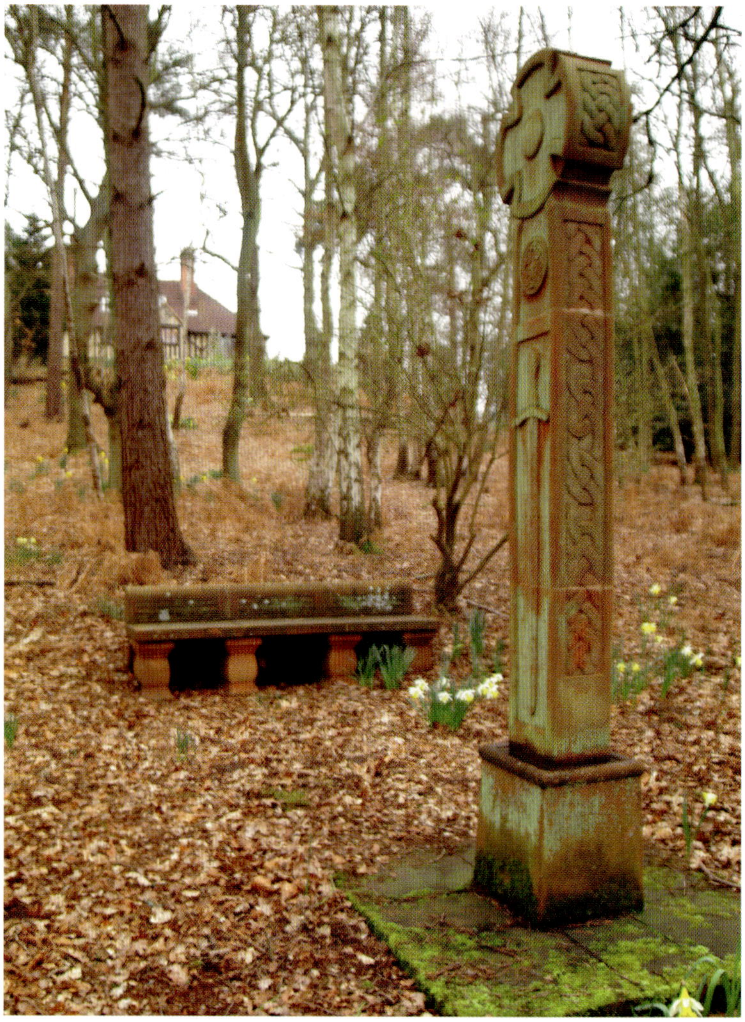

Below right: Potters' Arts Guild, gravestone of Margaret Gillett (d. 1907), terracotta, Compton Cemetery

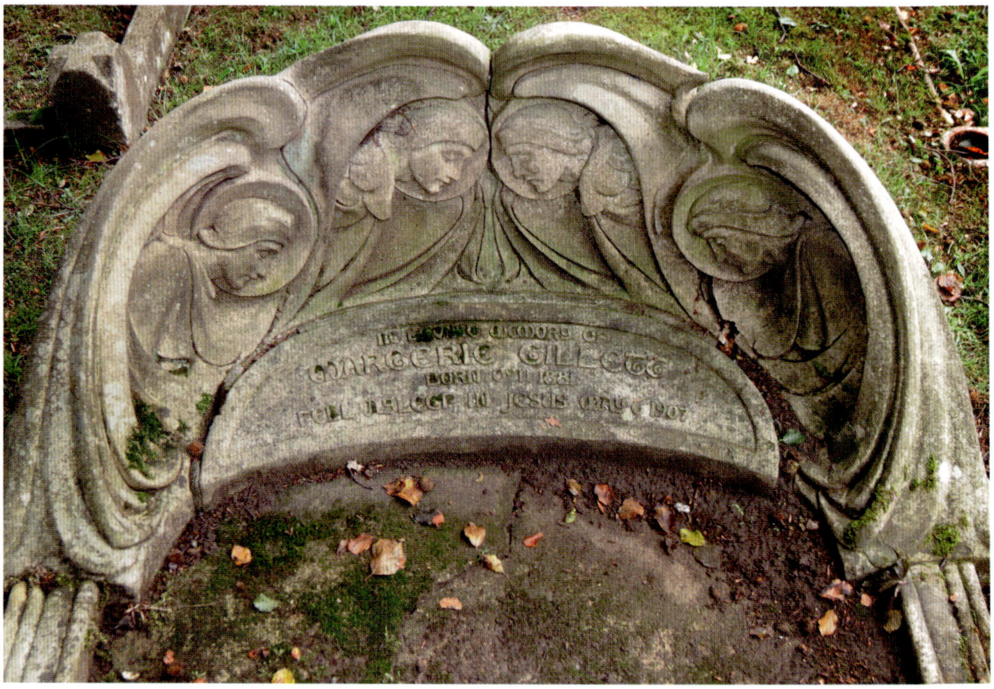

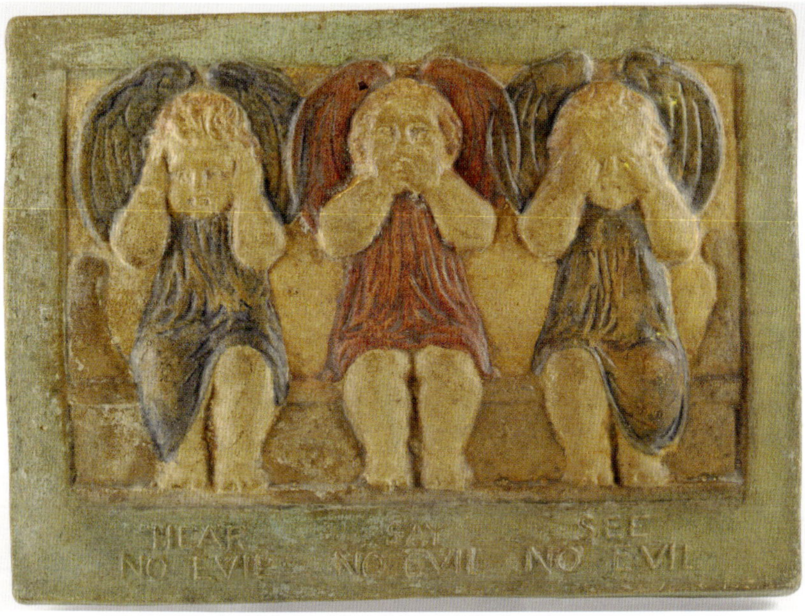

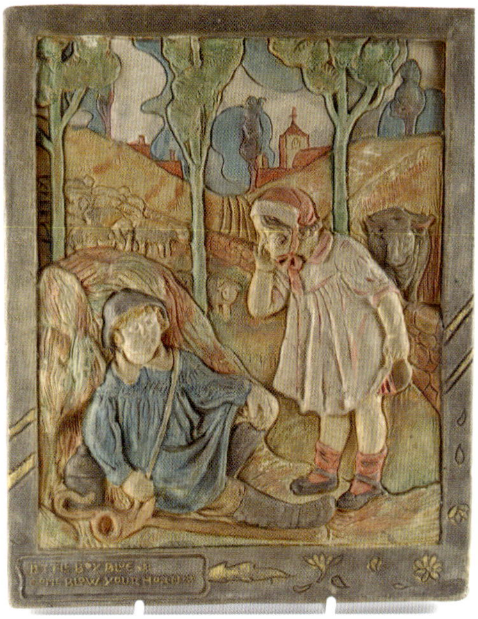

Above left: Compton Potter's Arts Guild, 'Hear no evil, say no evil, see no evil' book end, Watts Gallery

Above right: Compton Potters' Arts Guild, 'Little Boy Blue come blow your horn', c.*1920–29, painted ceramic, Watts Gallery*

commissioners and Mary Watts, the simpler designs are concentrated around Compton, Guildford and Godalming. Even in the inter-war period idiosyncratic designs were occasionally produced. The memorial to Ivy Johnson, who died in 1931 aged only twenty-seven, consists of a miniature grand piano (Mount Cemetery, Guildford). A common Compton gravestone is a mould-made cherub, used to commemorate infants or children. That in Peper Harow churchyard to Elizabeth Sheridan, who died shortly after her first birthday in 1914, is individually modelled and set in a unique, heart-shaped floral kerb. Poignantly, on the back of the figure is scratched 'made for my sweet ELIZABETH by her loving mother April 1914'.

The pottery also produced coloured ornamental ware, including statuettes, figurative plaques, bookends, lamp bases, bowls, vases, pendants and buttons.[34] These were made of white, friable commercial clay rather than the coarser local terracotta. Because the pottery's large, wood-fired kiln was not capable of heating this ware to glazing temperatures, it was painted, employing similar tempera recipes to those used for painting the chapel, and then waxed. This technique made it vulnerable. Many Compton pieces in good condition retain paper labels on their bases warning: 'Unfired colours. Do not Wash. Clean with a stiff brush.' Much must have been damaged and discarded. A glazed 1911 coronation mug for the Compton children and a similar Pilgrim mug, designed by George Aubertin of the pottery, would have been fired elsewhere and are exceptions in early Compton production.

No systematic documentation for the Compton ornamental ware remains. A single printed sales leaflet exists with illustrations and prices for twenty-eight designs probably dating from before the First World War.[35] A manuscript stock book, with illustrations (mainly line drawings) and prices for 128 designs and probably dating from the late 1920s or the 1930s, survives in a private collection but is not a complete stock listing.[36] It omits pendants, buttons and the plaques

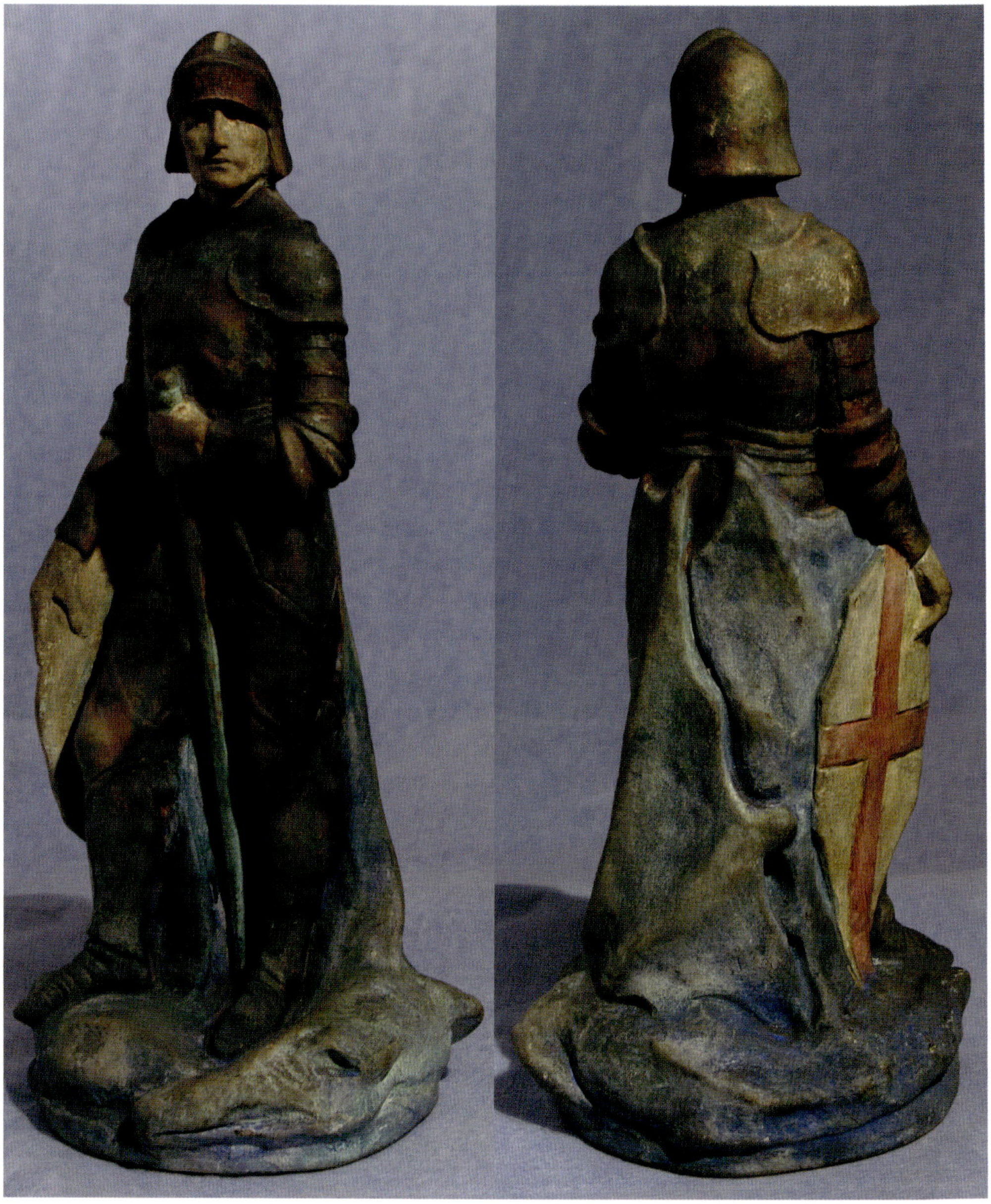

Compton Potters' Arts Guild, St Michael, c.1920–29, painted ceramic, Watts Gallery

that were still being produced and also featured in the earlier leaflet. Most of the ornamental ware was mould-made, but one-off pieces were created to special commission. In 1906 the ornamental ware, 'charming portable specimens of the Watts pottery',[37] was available from Compton village post office. It was also sold at Home Arts and Industries exhibitions,[38] and later from the pottery showroom on the drive to Watts Gallery (now used as the Watts Gallery tea shop). It was popular with gallery visitors and was distributed 'through agents all over the country'.[39]

The most distinctive of the Compton Pottery ornamental pieces are the early statuettes and plaques that share the decorative intensity of late Pre-Raphaelitism and the Watts Chapel. 'St Cecilia' is a close translation of a Burne-Jones stained-glass design into three dimensions, and the armoured figures of 'St Michael' and 'St George', which exist in many variants, derive their style from the elaborate

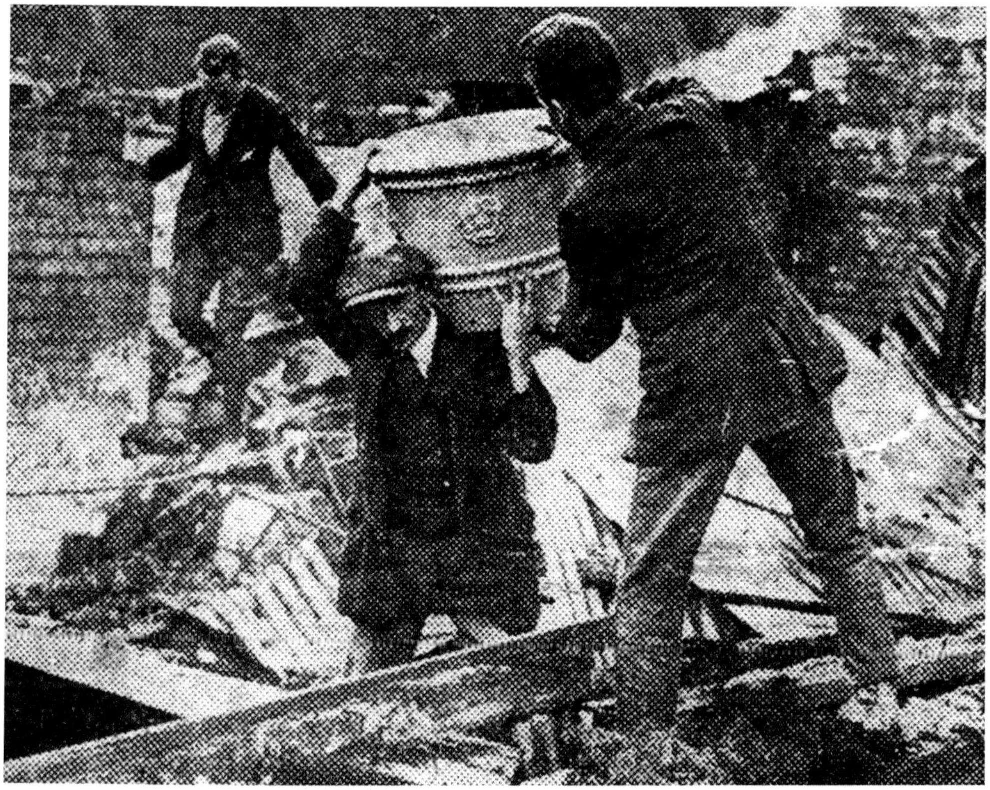

The aftermath of the fire at Compton Pottery, 1923, from an unidentified press cutting, Watts Gallery Archive

armour invented by Burne-Jones for the Perseus series of paintings and from the statuettes of Alfred Gilbert, an admirer of G.F. Watts. Some of the St Michael figures share the stylized wings of the angels in the Compton chapel. More ambitious pieces were produced to special commission, such as the figure for St Nicholas's church in Guildford.[40] For these the sensitive modelling skills of Tom Wren were called on, which also appear in his secular one-off pieces including the *Flower Girl* (private collection). The nursery plaques with their Edwardian and 1920s children also have a period charm. The pottery continued to respond to design trends in the 1920s and early 1930s, producing bright Art Deco bookends of stylized waves, trees and galleons. Mary Watts favoured the rich and subdued colours of her youth, and the pottery decorators would keep dark pieces to work on when she made her inspections.[41]

Many of the pottery workers, in their early twenties on the outbreak of war, served in the First World War. Five of seven known names of the seventeen early potters are on the Roll of Honour in Compton Parish Church recording all in the village who served.[42] The pottery resumed production after the serving soldiers had been demobilized. It continued successfully until the Wall Street crash of 1929 brought worldwide depression. It even survived a disastrous fire of 1923 when sparks from the kiln caught the thatched roof of the main building, destroying the upper floor and most of the stock. Queen Mary, who had visited some years earlier, sent a letter of sympathy, and the building was rapidly rebuilt in brick with a tiled roof.

The peak of prosperity for the pottery was in 1929 and its last twenty years were marked by struggle and decline in difficult economic circumstances. The

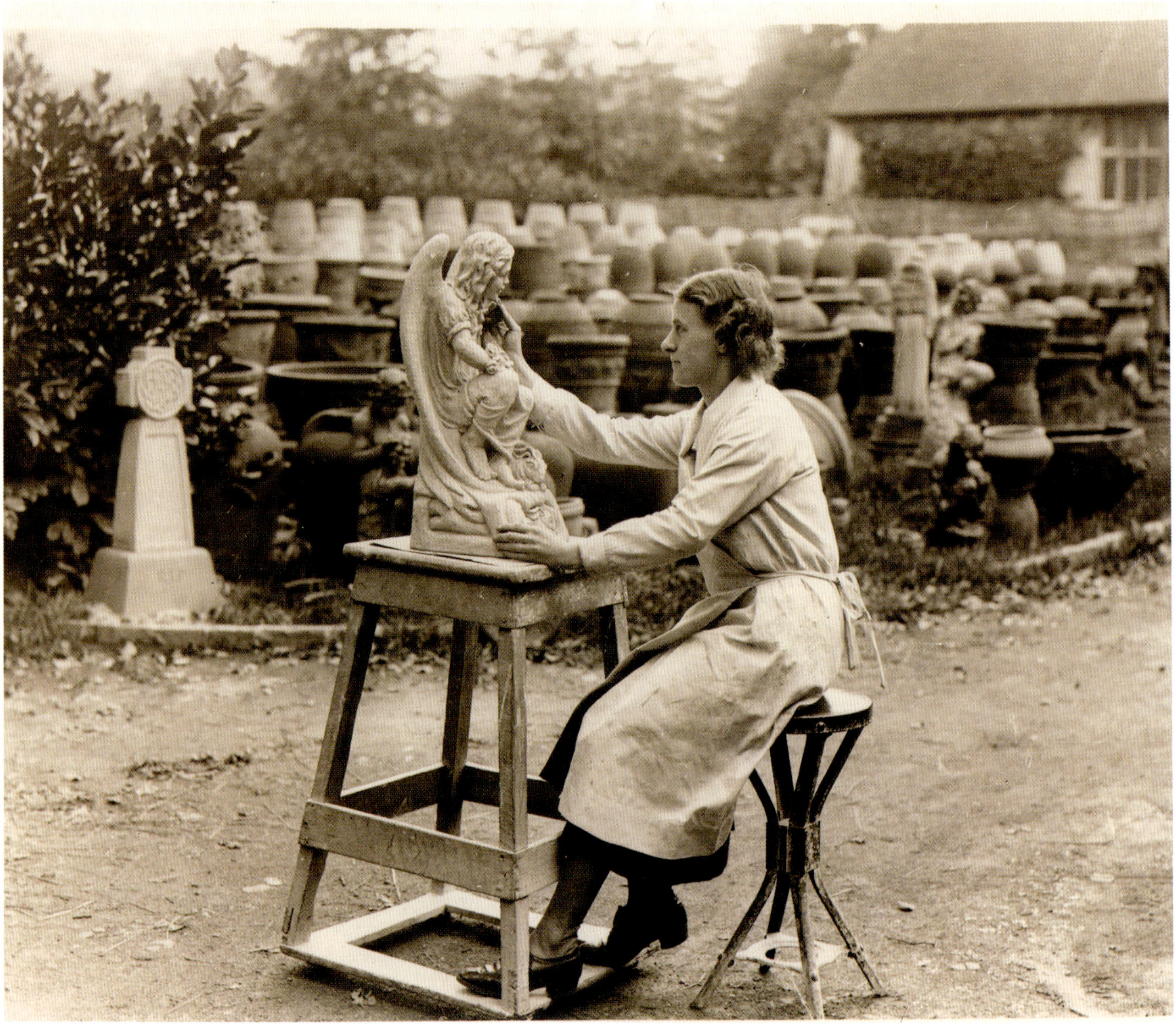

Modelling a figure of Molly Draper, 1939, from an original negative by D.W. Gardner

business had a small, ageing and shrinking workforce, elderly management (Mary Watts, the director, was eighty in the year of the Wall Street crash and James Nicol, the manager, around sixty-nine) and a tradition of sourcing design internally. Hence it was poorly placed to respond flexibly to changing markets and economic depression. Mary Watts supported the pottery, and the guild could use its accrued profits for maintenance. To an extent, this cushioned it from changes in the economy. However, dependence on these restricted sources of capital hampered growth and innovation; the business lacked sufficient funds and the guildsmen were unwilling to risk investing their own money in it. The market for terracotta garden ware was undercut by new cement products but, despite small-scale experiments with glazed ware in the early 1930s by Mr Candlin, the new manager, there was not the money or the will to build a new high-temperature kiln and introduce new ranges.

Business problems caused reorganizations in the 1930s. In 1929/30 the workers became discontented, leading James Nicol to retire in 1930. Mr Candlin

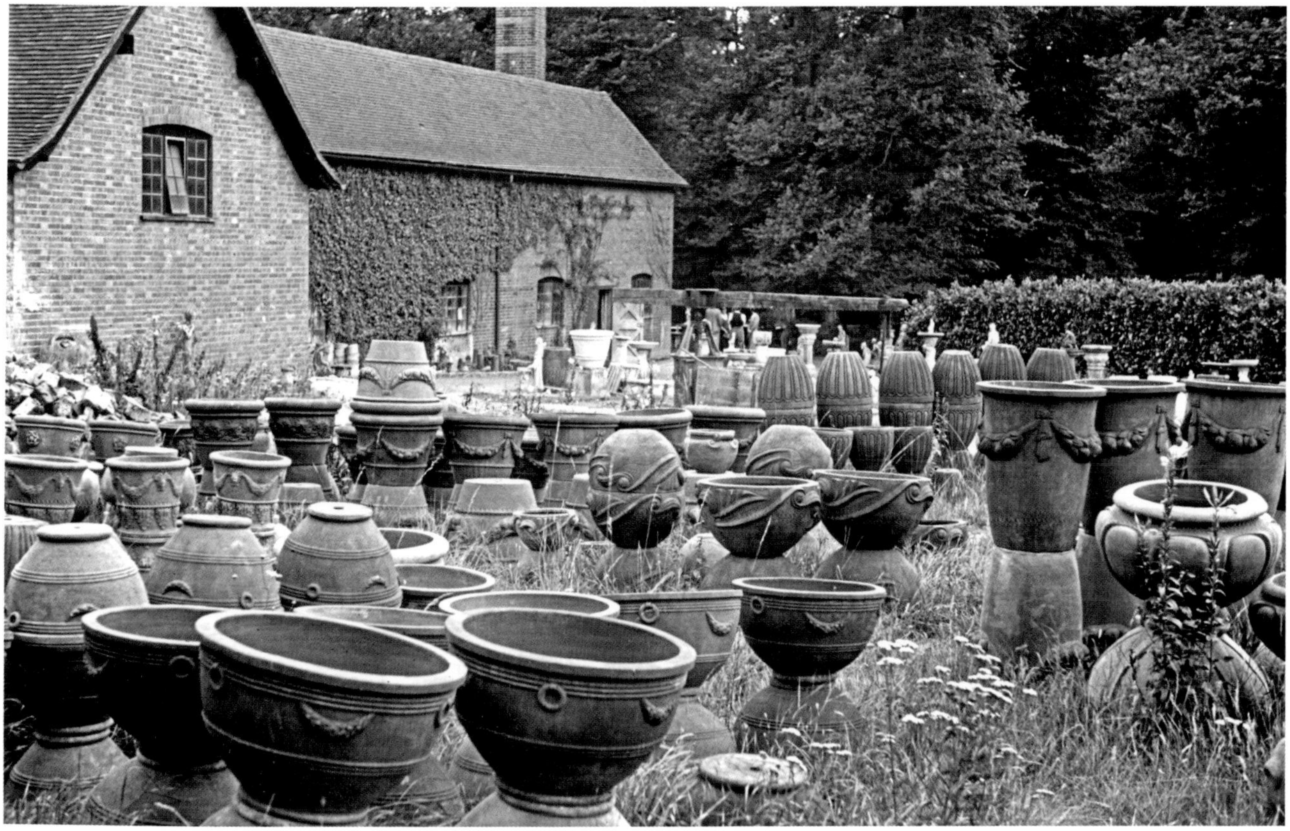

The pottery stockyard, 1939, from an original negative by D.W. Gardner

also proved unpopular. He was replaced by George Aubertin, one of the potters. In this period of tension seven potters left, including the talented Tom Wren and another key designer, reducing the workforce from seventeen to twelve. Each departure damaged the business because the men took their accrued capital with them. Mrs Watts resigned as director in around 1934, passing the directorship to the gallery curator, Rowland Alston (1895–1958).[43] In 1936 the profit-sharing guild was wound up and replaced by a limited company, Compton Pottery Ltd, later renamed Potters' Arts Guild Ltd.[44] The change gave it security of tenure as a lessee of Mary Watts but its survival now became dependent on its profitability. Although the change to a limited company allowed the pottery to seek outside capital, the workers were more concerned to preserve their employment than develop the business. Mary Watts accepted the change and charged only a nominal rent,[45] because of a sense of 'moral obligation' to the workforce.[46] In 1938 she died and in the following year war was declared.

During the war existing pottery stocks were sold from the showroom, but the pottery buildings were used by the Ardente company, which made listening devices for the Royal Navy and had requisitioned Limnerslease. The pottery experienced a brief and moderate prosperity after the war, because of bomb damage repair work and memorials,[47] but Board of Trade restrictions on non-essential production for the home market and 100 per cent purchase tax on purely decorative pottery products (such as the unglazed ornamental ware), along with increased overheads, made its final decline almost inevitable. With only six potters remaining, closure of the company was announced in 1951.

David Dunhill, a BBC announcer and local resident, decided to try to preserve the business.[48] Together with a Guildford solicitor, Mr P. Smith, who was the pottery's existing accountant and legal adviser, he bought a controlling interest in the company, which then traded as Compton Potteries Ltd. Dunhill and Charles Bone, who had been a ceramics consultant to the Rural Industries Board, researched current techniques and approaches at the potteries at Stoke-on-Trent. The Compton Potteries bought an electric kiln. Dunhill's wife, Barbara, who had trained as a textile designer, designed bowls, vases and tax-exempt household ware, such as plates, mugs and jugs. These were glazed with hand-painted decoration by female employees. Their bright colours and peasant-tinged designs appealed to early 1950s tastes, but the small kiln restricted output. The former guild potters fulfilled orders for terracotta work, including garden pots, architectural items and gravestones. However, because the old wood-fired kiln was no longer economic and its electric replacement was too small to fire them, these pieces were fired elsewhere, making them barely profitable. Meanwhile, the gallery trustees had acquired ownership of the pottery premises from the trustees of Mary Watts's will through money from the estate of W. Graham Robertson. This protracted transfer, completed around 1953, finally gave them control over the lease.[49] Their primary concern, quite properly, was for the future of the gallery: it was 'not to subsidise a pottery but to protect our amenities and benefit from a reasonable rent in a time of inflation'.[50] For all Dunhill's hard work, the pottery never made a profit under his directorship and debts mounted.[51] The renegotiation of the lease, the discovery of dry rot in the pottery roof and the expense of repair forced the closure of the business. The near continuous tradition of pottery on the site finally came to an end on 14 August 1956 after more than sixty years.[52] Two years later, the Town and Country Planning Acts were invoked by Surrey County Council, and the authorized 'light industrial' use of the pottery buildings was discontinued.[53]

NOTES

1 'From Diaries 1886–1895', MSW Diary Notes, 4 December 1891.
2 MSW Diaries, 3 and 13 August 1893. G.F. Watts was among those endorsing the Della Robbia Pottery in a printed circular of *c.* January 1896 (Watts Gallery Archive).
3 Wilson 2004, fig.38.
4 MSW Diaries, 1 October 1893; see also 4 September 1894.
5 MSW Diaries, 14 November 1895.
6 See, for instance, Webb 1911, p.102.
7 'Notes from the Workshop', Ffoulkes 1903, p.18.
8 Webb 1911, p.102.
9 Erskine *c.*1901.
10 M.S. Watts to James Nicol, 17 December 1900, Watts Gallery Archive.
11 Webb 1911, p.102.
12 M.S. Watts to James Nicol, 11 and 17 December 1901, Watts Gallery Archive. The second letter is quoted extensively in Blunt 1975, pp.231–32.
13 Calvert 2006, pp.9–10.
14 Louise Boreham, 'Louis Reid Deuchars and the Aldourie Pottery', *Journal of the Scottish Society for Art History*, vol.2, 1997, pp.1–9.
15 The kiln is absent in a postcard (private collection) that post-dates the construction of the main and sculpture galleries at the Watts Gallery (1905–6) and also the studio built for the printer Emery Walker to make reproductions after the works of G.F. Watts.
16 The couple are buried under one of the last Compton tombstones in Compton Cemetery.
17 'Indenture' and 'The Scheme of Constitution During the Life-time of Mrs. Watts', Watts Gallery Archive.
18 'Report on the Potters' Arts Guild'.
19 'Indenture' and 'The Scheme of Constitution During the Life-time of Mrs. Watts', Watts Gallery Archive. The indenture dated 15 March 1920 appears to transfer an existing scheme from the sole control of Mary Watts to a committee of four, which she headed.
20 Franklin Gould 1998, no.38, illustrated p.53 and no.40.
21 Franklin Gould 1998, pp.52–54, nos. 43 (design, Watts Gallery), 45 (letter of 20 December 1899, National Archive of Art and Design). Watts Gallery now possesses an exact modern re-weaving of this carpet.
22 Franklin Gould 1998, pp.60, 62, 74 (nos. 64–67).
23 'A labour of love. Beautifying the soldiers' mortuary chapel', *Aldershot News*, November 1929, quoted in Meg Botting, 'The Signor's Widow', *Hampshire*, January 1979, p. 36, cutting in Watts Gallery Archive.
24 Franklin Gould 1998, pp.63, 76.
25 Photographic documentation of the removal of the friezes is preserved in Watts Gallery Archive.
26 M.S. Watts to James Nicol, 17 December 1900, Watts Gallery Archive.
27 'Introduction', Liberty & Co. 1904.
28 See, for instance, Ffoulkes 1903 and Liberty & Co. 1904, which is also a catalogue of Liberty products. That the Germanic names are Liberty's rather than Mary Watts's original choices is suggested by a pre-war Compton Pottery price list of 1909 (William Morris Gallery, Walthamstow) where the normal Compton names appear.
29 Barbara Morris, 'Liberty's Pioneer Designer', in Franklin Gould 1998, pp.11–14.

30 Catalogue dated 1909, William Morris Gallery, Walthamstow, reproduced in Veronica Franklin Gould, *Archibald Knox and Mary Seton Watts*, privately published 2005, pp.38–41. Catalogue dated 1932, Watts Gallery Archive. At least two further catalogues of intermediate date are in Watts Gallery Archive.

31 For instance in *The Potters' Arts Guild*, an undated catalogue bequeathed by Winifred Harrison in 1975, Watts Gallery Archive.

32 Franklin Gould 1998, Chronology, p.16.

33 *The Potters' Arts Guild* (see n.31), front cover.

34 For a useful illustrated survey of this material, see Calvert 2006, especially pp.25–36.

35 Compton Pottery Ornamental Ware, Watts Gallery Archive.

36 Photocopy of manuscript stock book, Watts Gallery Archive.

37 Haking 1906, p.15.

38 The Home Arts and Industries Association exhibition at the Horticultural Hall, 1909, unsourced press cutting, Watts Gallery Archive.

39 'Report on the Potters' Arts Guild'.

40 I am indebted to Catherine Ferguson for this information.

41 Calvert 2006, p.26, and personal information, Richard Jefferies.

42 Thanks to Gail McNaughton for names of the potters. The Roll of Honour is printed in Boston 1987, pp.211–12.

43 The account of the business in the early 1930s is from 'Report on the Potters' Arts Guild'.

44 Calvert 2006, p.15.

45 'Private and Confidential: The Pottery Lease', undated [*c.*1955], Watts Gallery Archive. Mary Watts set a nominal rent of £20 per year.

46 'Report on the Potters' Arts Guild'.

47 For architectural work, see Calvert 2006, p.16; for memorials, see Watts Gallery Report, July 1949, Watts Gallery Archive.

48 A useful account of the pottery in the Dunhill years is found in Calvert 2006, pp.16–18. The gallery trustees' problems with the buildings and lease are in 'Trustees Meetings Agendas, Reports and Minutes, 1935–1957 misc.', Watts Gallery Archive.

49 Various papers, 'Trustees Meetings Agendas, Reports and Minutes, 1935–1957 misc.', Watts Gallery Archive. The pottery was held by a new charity, 'Graham Robertson for the Watts Gallery', whose trustees were the same as those for the gallery.

50 Rowland Alston, 'Private and Confidential: The Pottery', n.d. [*c.*1956], Watts Gallery Archive.

51 Rowland Alston to Brinsley Ford, 27 March 1956, in 'Pottery Dispute 1955–6', Watts Gallery Archive.

52 Minutes of Meeting of the Watts Gallery Executive Trustees Saturday 28 July [1956] at Compton, report of Mr. Woollcombe, Watts Gallery Archive.

53 W.W. Ruff of Surrey County Council to Brinsley Ford, 31 October 1958, Watts Gallery Archive.

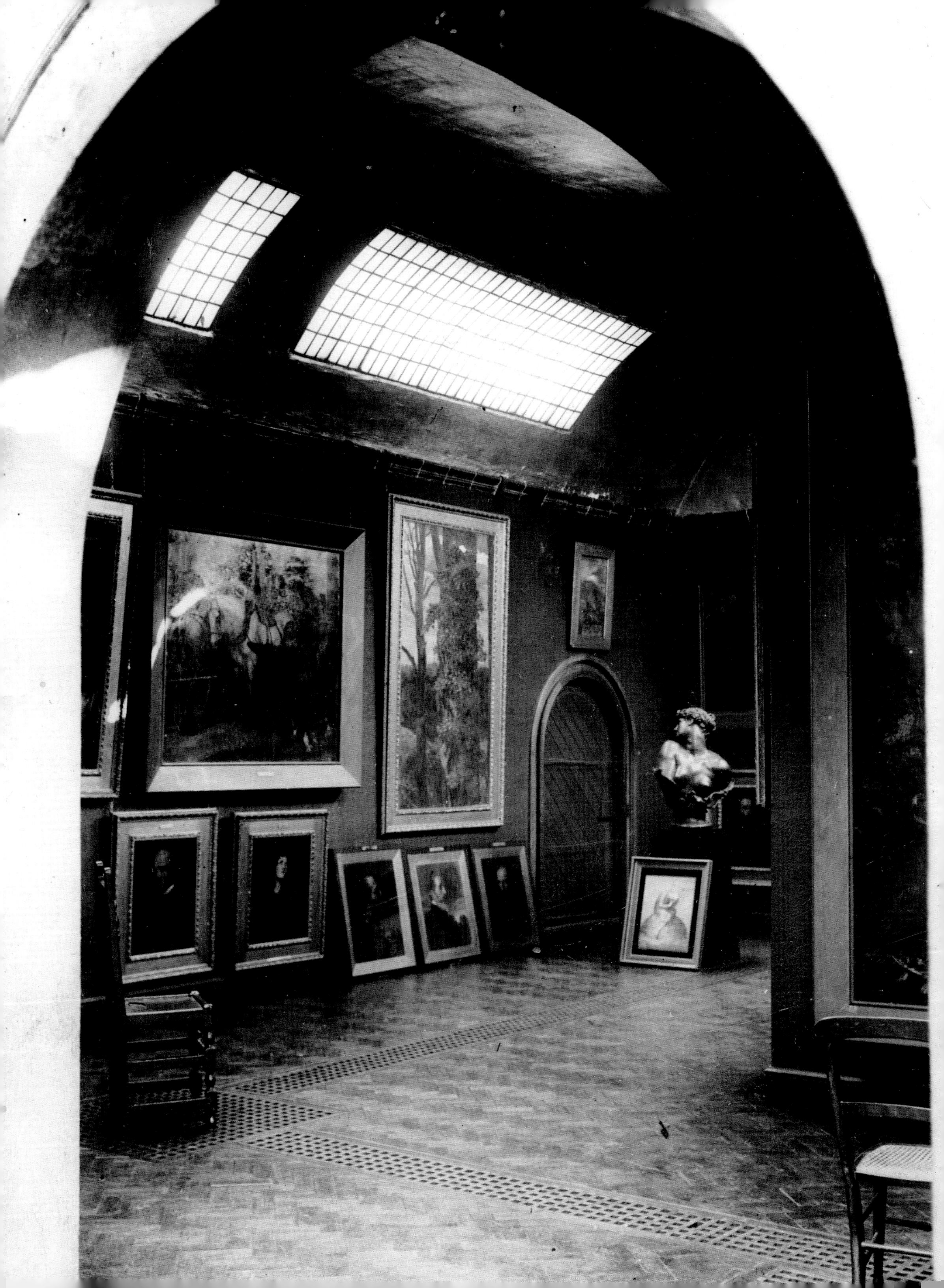

The Watts Picture Gallery

Mark Bills

> *Art since the beginning, and music from time immemorial, factors in the world's well-being, are more than ever valuable, and even necessary, in an age, like the present, of social surroundings devoid of outward beauty and nobility, where the workers have little leisure, and in a country where the uncertain climate precludes the general habits of outdoor recreation.* (G.F. Watts)[1]

The Watts Gallery was built to be at the centre of all that the Wattses had created in Compton. And art was always to be at the heart of the complex, art at it highest level. Watts made it clear that the artist had, as

> an interpreter of nature … revealed something more than had been previously perceived … This is the pleasant, instructive, and popular use of art, and this alone would be sufficient to place it in an important position; but in its higher manifestations it has a far greater reach and power, standing as it does on the same level with the greatest intellectual efforts of man.[2]

Watts's art aspired to this highest plane of art, embracing and expounding aesthetic concepts of beauty as well as ethical and spiritual truths. The Watts Gallery was built to show such art and within its walls were placed 'the collection of pictures in his private gallery'.[3] Watts wished this art to be seen by a wide audience, and he was commonly considered to be a servant of the nation, a role that he welcomed, painting for the inspiration of the many. He wished to show the immense vision of his entire output, even though, as some commentators noted, this was to the detriment of his fellow artists.[4] In order to do this, Watts gave many paintings to galleries throughout the land, but at its heart was a trinity of galleries that together reflected his grand vision: the Tate Gallery, the National Portrait Gallery and the Watts Gallery. As the influential art dealer and collector David Croal Thomson noted, 'the [Watts] gallery is so arranged as to give a comprehensive idea of the magnitude of the work the artist produced, and with the collections of his pictures in the Gallery of British Art [Tate], and in the National Portrait Gallery, to render this knowledge practically complete'.[5]

The Tate received the finished versions of his great allegorical masterpieces, interspersed with one or two other finished paintings. The National Portrait Gallery obtained his great portraits, particularly from the 'Hall of Fame' project, while the Watts Gallery held a body of work, personal to the artist, that, Mary noted, 'remains intact, and has been much augmented'.[6] Amassed from a lifetime's endeavour spanning over seventy years, it had remained in the artist's own hands and contained some of his earliest works from the 1830s, as well as others unfinished at his death in 1904. It included works that had remained unsold but in the main consisted of those consciously held onto by an artist who had no difficulty in finding buyers. The four social pictures, *The Irish Famine*,

Opposite: Part of the Red Gallery (now the Graham Robertson Gallery), c.1920s

Right: The Watts Gallery, 1906

Below: Little Holland House, Kensington (6 Melbury Road), with the additions designed by George Aitchison, drawn by Maurice B. Adams for the engraving published in the Building News, *7 October 1881, Watts Gallery Archive*

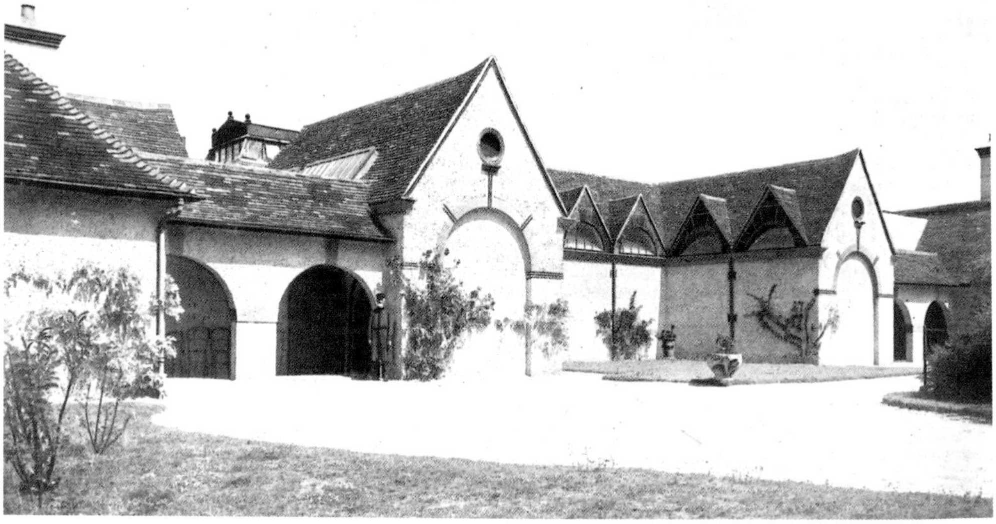

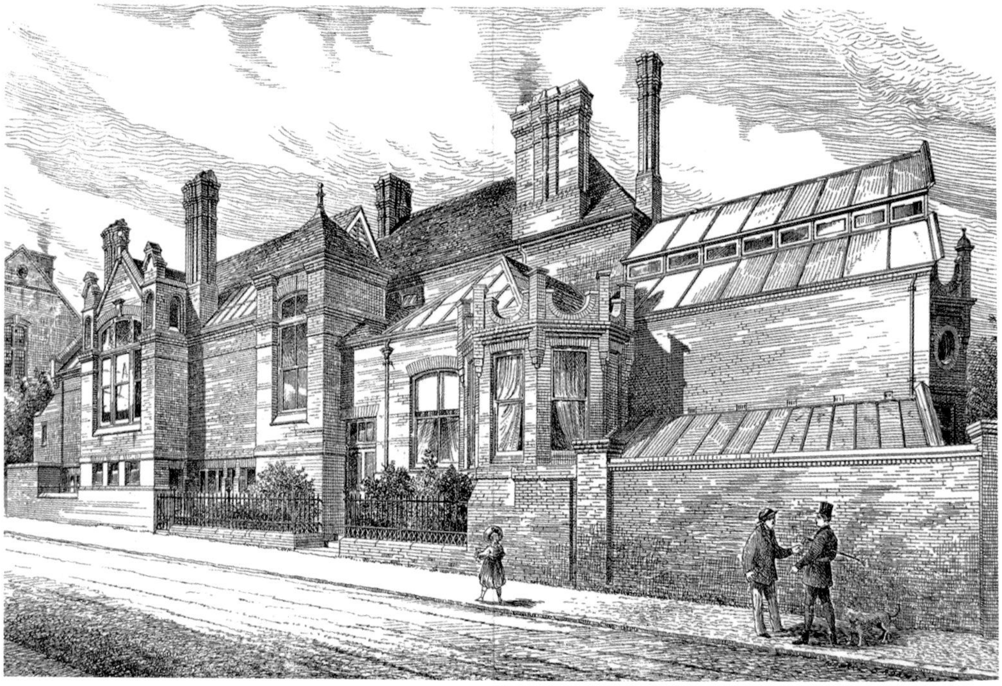

Found Drowned, *Song of a Shirt* and *Under a Dry Arch*, which were all painted in the last years of the 1840s and were significant in Watts's development and unique within his art, were kept in the collection.[7] Studies, too, formed part of the collection, as did various masterpieces and different versions of his other major works.

In 1881 he had had a purpose-built gallery created at Little Holland House to show this collection. It was opened at weekends, free to all, from two till six, 'a privilege largely taken advantage of by all sorts and conditions of people'.[8] After the building of Limnerslease, the site in Surrey had begun to expand with the addition of a kiln, chapel, barn studio and pottery, reflecting Little Holland House with its painting and sculpture studios but wider in its ambition. What

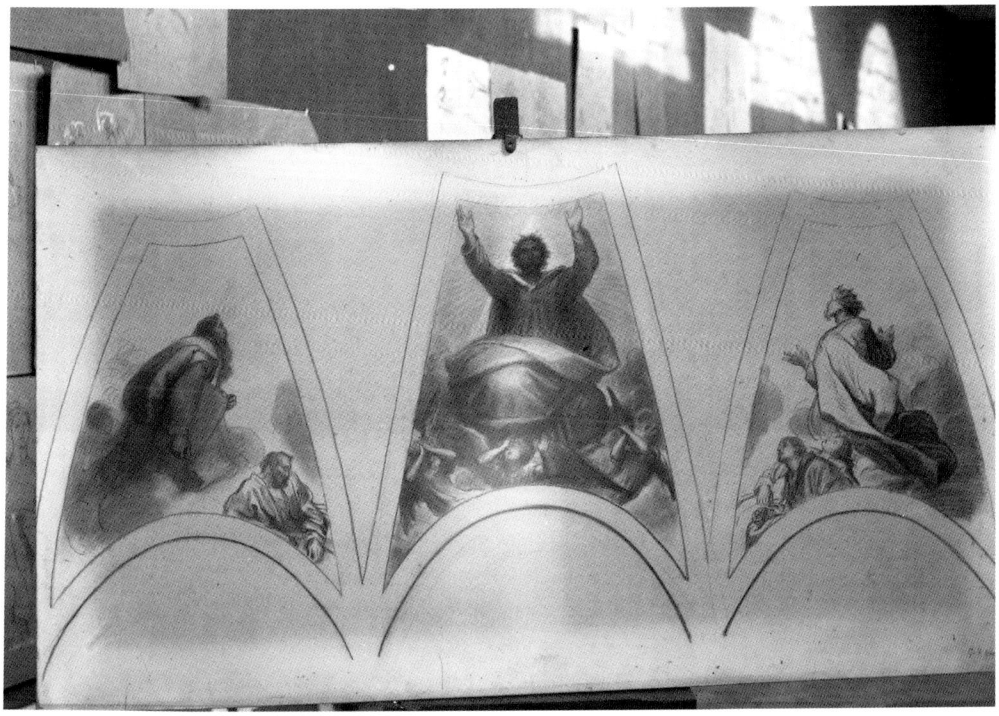

A rare photograph showing the interior of the Watts Gallery being used as a drawing studio, 1903

Compton did not have was a gallery. At Limnerslease he could show work within the context of a studio but not a gallery as he could in London. The decision was made to build a gallery in the heart of the Compton complex as a logical step in their art philosophy. Watts felt that he could not sustain two private galleries, one in London and one in Compton, so Little Holland House Gallery closed in 1903 when the paintings were moved to the newly built Watts Gallery in September.[9]

The Watts Gallery shared many similarities with the gallery at Little Holland House, not least its opening hours of two to six, which were retained at the Watts Gallery until 2008. The majority of the collection at Compton was from the Little Holland House Gallery, and the display of unfinished work and sketches cheek by jowl with finished works was a common element to both galleries. The rich red wall colouring as the background for his painting was adopted at both venues. If, in many ways, Little Holland House served as a model for the Watts Gallery, there were also significant differences. First and foremost was its rural rather than metropolitan location: the Watts Gallery was surrounded by nature. The London gallery, like many artist studio houses, was attached to the house, whereas the Watts Gallery was separated from the house by a road and landscape, even though both house and gallery were visible from the other. The Compton gallery had a more consciously public face, its opening hours were every day of the week rather than just weekends and the hostel element was entirely new and reflected the strong influence of Mary.

Stylistically, the Watts Gallery was a move away from Little Holland House and, rather than commissioning a fashionable architect like George Aitchison as he had for that gallery, Watts selected a local and relatively inexperienced architect in Christopher Hatton Turnor (1873–1940). Turnor was living in Compton with his parents in the first house he had designed, which was built

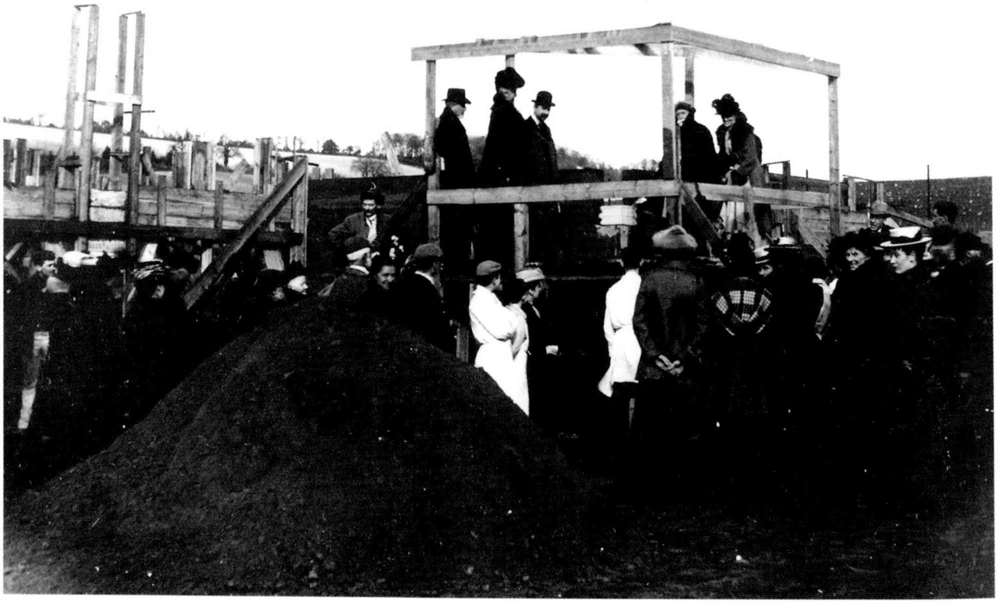

George and Mary Watts with Christopher Hatton Turnor laying the foundation stone of the Watts Gallery, on Watts's 86th birthday, 23 February 1903

in 1901 and named 'Berthorpe'.[10] He had worked for Sir Edwin Lutyens (1869–1944) and Robert Weir Shultz (1860–1951) in the late 1890s, and while he was resident in Compton, he struck up a strong relationship with Watts, whom the young man deeply admired. Turnor was later to recall:

> During those years at Compton, it was my privilege to see a good deal of G.F. Watts ('Signor') one of the greatest men I ever met, not only as a painter but as a thinker far in advance of his times on many subjects … Dear old Signor asked me to build the picture gallery at Compton, & to keep it a simple & rural type of building, my difficulty was that he would never tell me how many pictures it was to house, and I had to double it soon after completing it.[11]

Turnor's words reflect the simplicity of the Arts and Crafts design that was adopted, not the grand neoclassical style normally associated with a Victorian art gallery but a cottage-like exterior and relatively small scale, made more so by the accommodation on either end. It was built in rendered concrete and Surrey tiles, and its foundation stone, a beautiful terracotta block, was laid by Watts on his eighty-sixth birthday, marking the moment of 23 February 1903. Within the stone he buried a note, which showed that he was feeling his mortality and the belief that he was leaving something of value behind him:

> How much more potent are the evil works of man to produce effects while he lives, how much more potent to produce good effects are his good deeds after his death; his evil deeds while he lives may cause individual misery, family distress, disruption of states; his good deeds, in discoveries, in elevating poetry, in noble art, for ever after his death, go on accumulating benefits to humanity.[12]

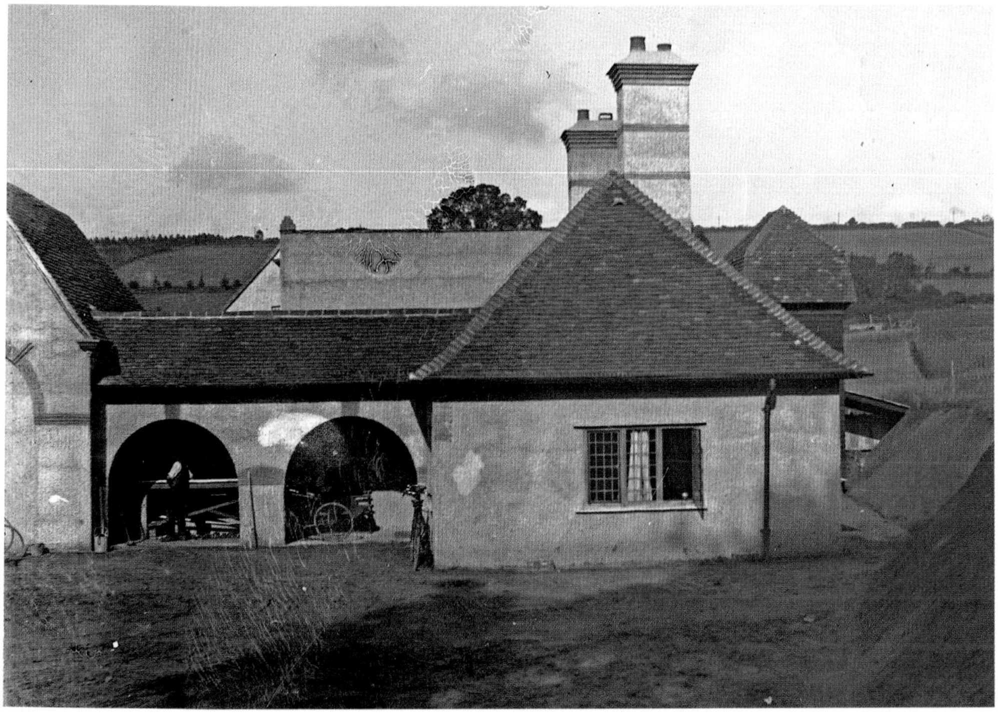

The Hostel at the Watts Gallery, 1904

The building was originally named the 'Hostel' referring to one of its functions, although the central section was consistently called the Watts Picture Gallery, which was adopted for the whole building when it reopened in 1906. When the gallery first opened its doors in 1904, the *Surrey Advertiser* wrote:

> A little building in Compton which has been given the name of The Hostel ... was designed to serve a double purpose: to provide a home for some of the young men and lads engaged in the terra-cotta pottery which Mrs Watts has successfully established at Compton ... At the two ends of the building are two homes for the young potters who come from a distance.[13]

It is difficult to be certain how many potters lived in the Watts Gallery when it first opened in 1904, although the large single drawer and cupboard allocated to each potter indicates that it was probably around a dozen. The 1911 census is useful in gauging the gallery's accommodation after Watts's death and the appointment of a curator in 1907. In 1911 the wings of the gallery accommodated Charles Thompson (curator from 1907 to 1937), his wife Annie Heather and their only child; six clay modellers, all single; three servants from the local area, a cook, a housemaid and a general servant; and guests, two of whom were staying when the census was taken. Of the clay modellers, Thomas Henry Wren was the oldest at twenty-six and most senior. Originally from the Monkshatch estate (see p.29), he had assisted Watts on his sculpture and modelled reduced replicas of both *Tennyson* and *Physical Energy* as well as the monument to Watts in Compton Cemetery. Four other modellers aged twenty-one were from Northants, Cheshire and Surrey and presumably came to the gallery at the age of fourteen as apprentices. The last, Hazelwood Beardsley Fitzgerald, aged eighteen and noted down as 'Art Assistant', came from London's Belgravia.[14]

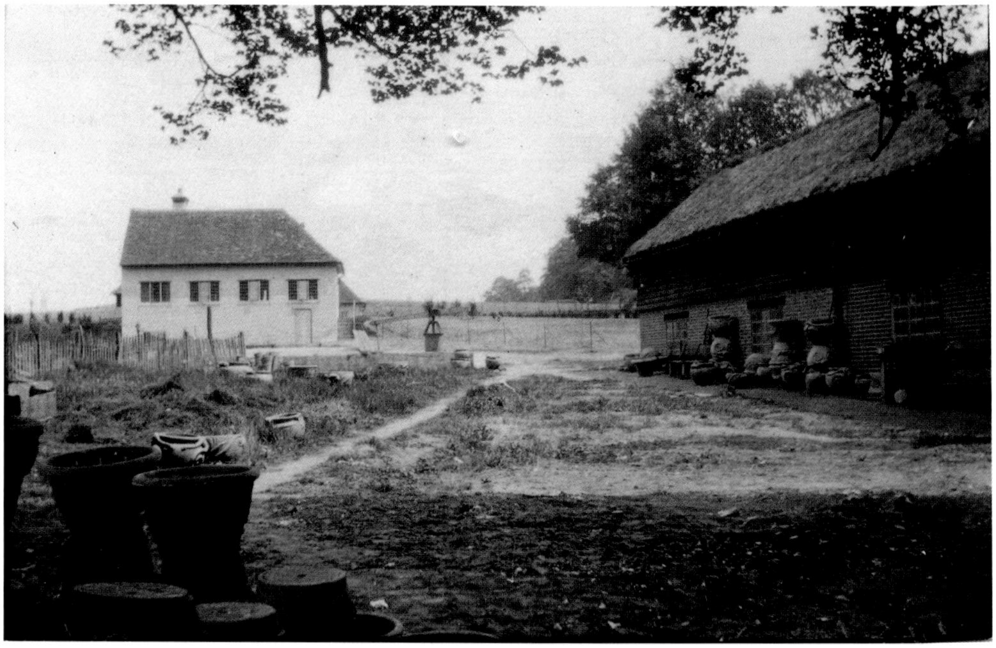

The Watts Gallery (left) and the pottery (right), 1904

The building had been completed sometime in the summer of 1903 and on 30 September that year Mary recalled in her diaries: 'Our pictures come from L.H.H. [Little Holland House] Gallery.' The closure of the London gallery did not mean that Watts was turning his back on his metropolitan audience, as the newly opened National Gallery of British Art (now Tate) had two rooms devoted exclusively to his work. The Watts Gallery opened its doors on Good Friday, 1 April 1904, and 'the privilege of inspecting the artist's work at first hand was taken advantage of by hundreds of visitors'.[15] Visitors entered through a loggia into a rectangular C-shaped corridor and out of another loggia at the other side. The gallery's walls (in a room later known as the Red Gallery) were decorated with a 'dark crimson hand-made linen in a raised design' produced by the Tynecastle company and named the 'Venetian Design'.[16] The ceiling was covered with silver leaf coated in a gold-coloured lacquer, which reflected the natural light that came in through semicircular and rectangular leaded windows. One hundred and five paintings were hung on the walls, a dense hang that had prompted Watts to write to Mrs Barrington some six months earlier that 'everything must be crowded here' and adding that 'I am sick of the whole thing!'[17] Watts had curated the space himself and Mary records that *The Good Samaritan* (1849–1904; Watts Gallery), 'was framed and hung in the then newly built gallery by his direction'.[18] Information was provided by Watts for visitors initially through slips of paper, as the *Surrey Advertiser* noted:

> There are altogether more than a hundred canvases in the gallery … A little plan has been adopted which should prove very helpful to those desirous of getting at the real meaning of the pictures … Below or by the side of many of the paintings is placed a slip of paper, upon which is written a short description of the theme, and in many cases a suggestion of the idea underlying them. These little helps to understanding must not be taken

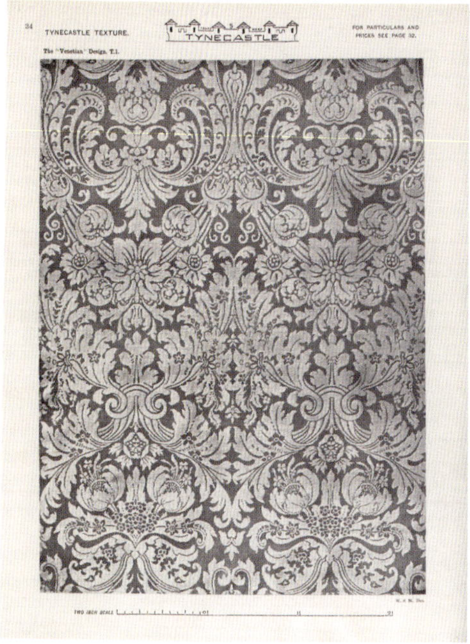

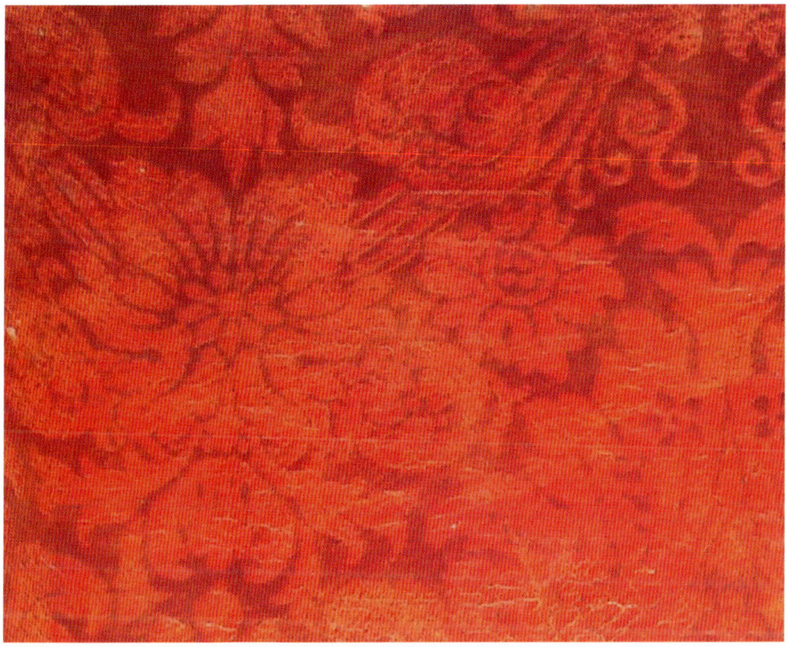

Above left: Tynecastle wallpaper, the 'Venetian Design T1', courtesy of the National Art Library, Victoria & Albert Museum

Above right: Surviving piece of Tynecastle wallpaper at Watts Gallery

> as a complete explanation of the pictures … But the suggestions are decidedly helpful.[19]

Later in the same year a gallery catalogue was produced, listing all 105 paintings on display, the bust of Clytie (presumably the bronze), and two plaster casts of the 'Elgin Marbles' from Little Holland House.

Watts lived to see the gallery open for only three months of his life, dying on 1 July 1904. His death sent ripples throughout the world as the lengthy and laudatory obituaries testify. The impact on the gallery was immense, with Mary closing it so that the collection could become the core of a large, travelling memorial exhibition.[20] This allowed her to expand the size of the gallery and display more works, something that Watts himself had wanted.[21] Mary also changed, in part through the High Court, the terms of Watts's original bequest to avoid the loss of many of the works in the collection. A trust of influential people was formed, including Mrs Watts, Lord Balcarres, Andrew Hichens, Sir Charles Holroyd and Mr Herbert Powell.

The extension was designed by Turnor and consisted of a large central gallery that ran the full-length of the Red Gallery with three arches cut for access. The overall effect was to open up the gallery, making it more spacious and providing room for viewing and contemplating works at a distance, which the corridor had not allowed. The design for the new gallery was much simpler, and green distemper on the concrete walls provided the background for the paintings, which were hung from a wooden picture rail. The sloping roof was gilded to reflect the light that came in through a large central lantern. The light was controlled by translucent blinds, which were operated by a manual pulley system. The extension was called the Green Gallery (now the Isabel Goldsmith Patino Gallery) in contrast to the original C-shaped Red Gallery (now the Livanos, Weston and Graham Robertson Galleries). Mary also added a sculpture gallery

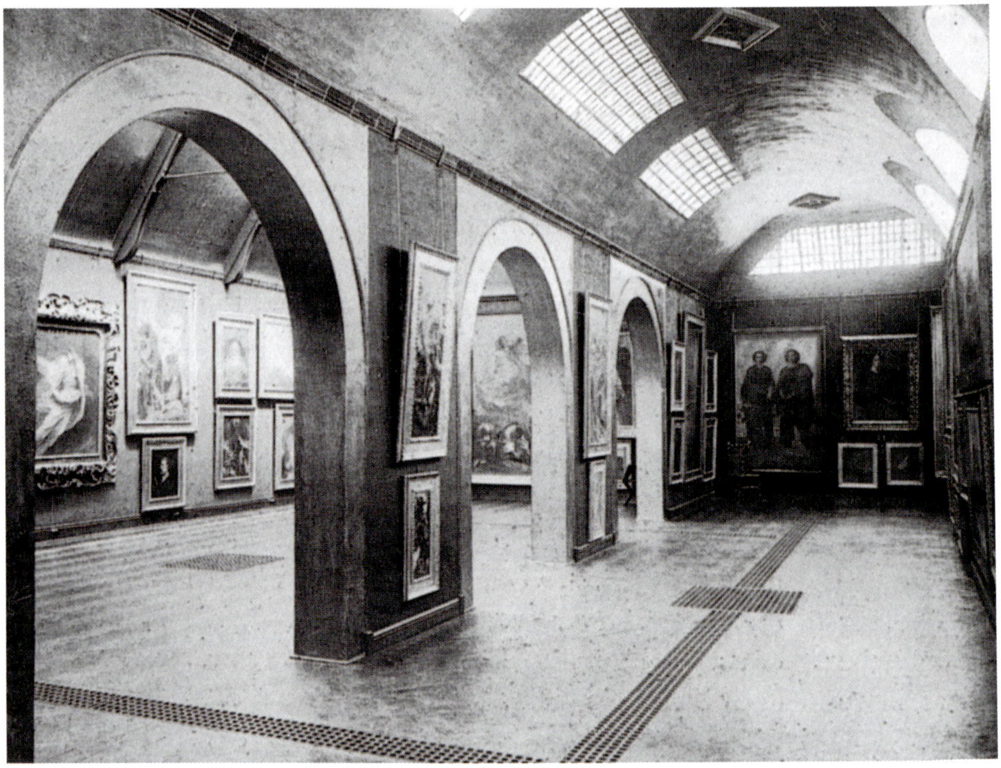

The Red Gallery (now the Weston Gallery), 1906

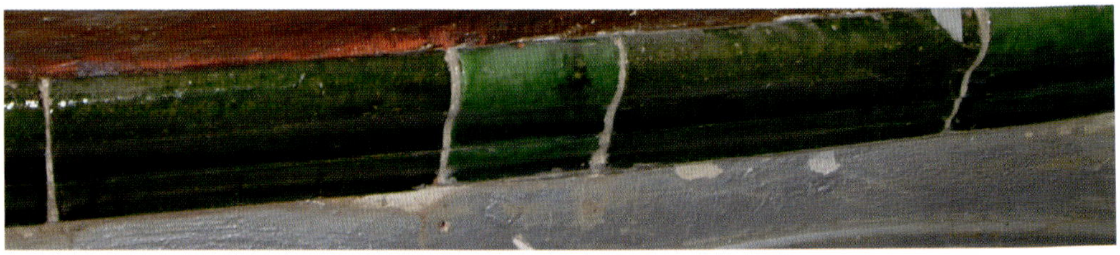

Green glazed ceramic hanging rail in the former Red Gallery, during restoration

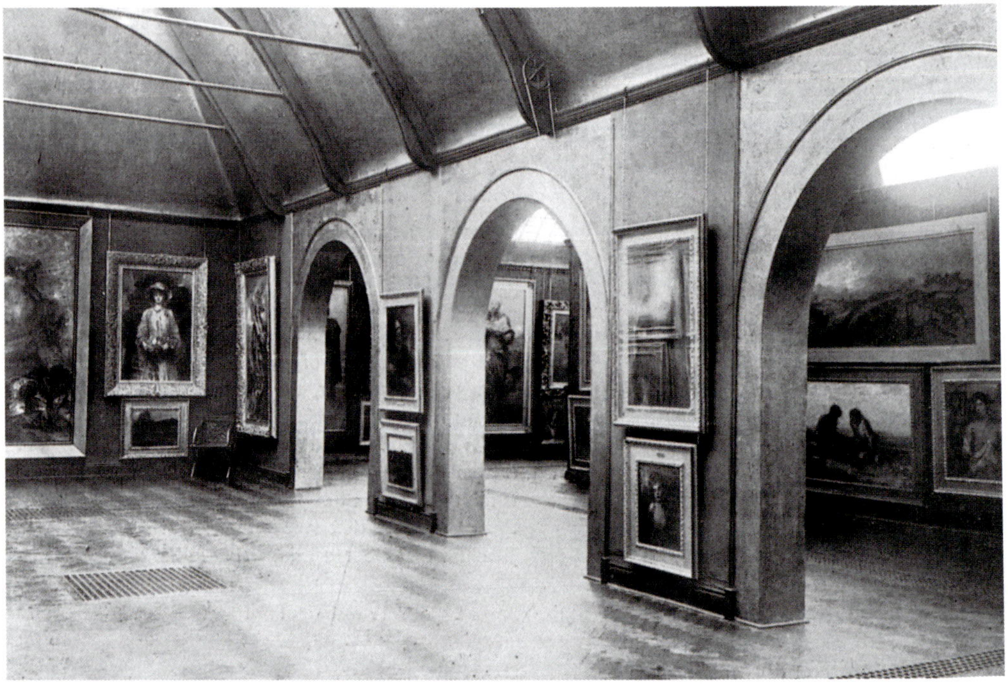

Right: The Green Gallery (now the Isabel Goldsmith Patino Gallery), 1906

Opposite: The Green Gallery, c.1922

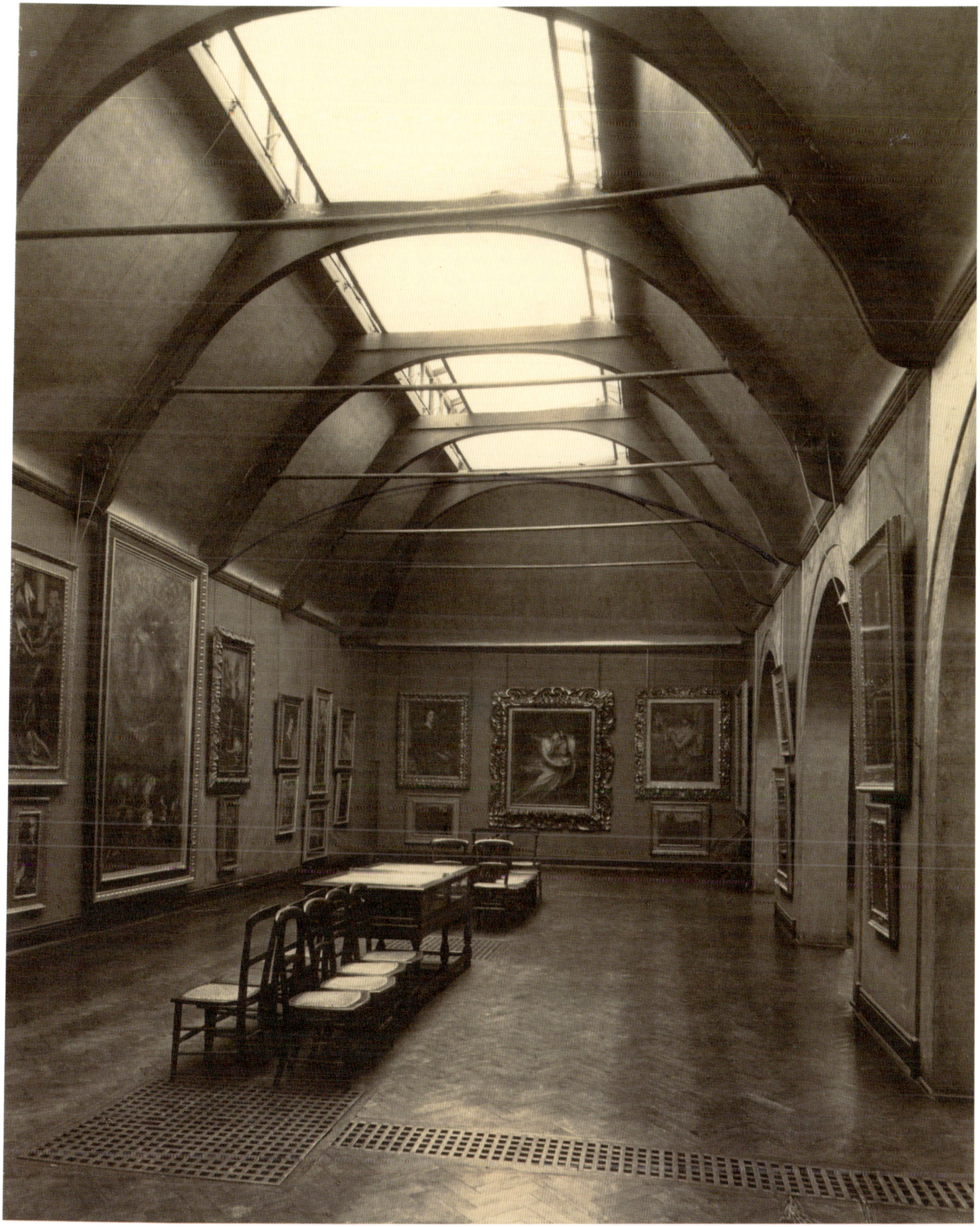

Opposite: The Sculpture Gallery with Physical Energy *and* Tennyson *(behind), 2004*

at this time to house Watts's great *gesso grosso* models of *Tennyson* and *Physical Energy*, which had been made at Little Holland House and the Barn Studio at Limnerslease. The hanging of the paintings was curated by Sir Charles Holroyd (1861–1917), director of the Tate and later from 1906 of the National Gallery, a reflection of the high regard in which Watts was held within the art world. Forty-five paintings were displayed in the new Green Gallery and ninety-two in the original Red Gallery, some thirty-two additional works.

The re-opening in 1906 was an unqualified success and newspapers and journals were ecstatic in their praise: the art press, in particular, produced prolonged and well-illustrated articles about the Compton Gallery.[22] The *Tribune* described the gallery and explained the success of the colour scheme and lighting:

> The gallery is a plain building, admirably designed for its purpose. The walls of one part of it are coloured red and of the other green, with an effect of quiet richness which enhances the rich colour of the pictures. The ceiling, where it slopes towards the top lights, is covered with soft gilding, so that the light reflected from it on to the pictures below is not harsh or glaring as it would be if reflected off a whitewashed ceiling, but warm and rich like sunlight, even on the most sunless days. This is a point that deserves notice of the directors of other picture galleries.[23]

The trustees met for the first formal meeting on 20 February 1907 'at the Gallery at Compton'; they had met prior to this, with the setting up of the trust, but it was not minuted. At the meeting Mary formally handed over the Green and Sculpture Galleries to the trust, and the gallery's first curator, Charles H. Thompson, was appointed. His first lengthy report written to the trustees in 1913 gives a wealth of information about the gallery's early years. A 'steadily growing interest in the collection on the part of the general public' was reported, as well as 'many artists and students … from Canada, Germany, Denmark, Japan, India, China … and very many visitors from the United States of America'. Specific visits included thirty-six Royal Academicians and Associate Royal Academicians, who were 'profuse in their expressions of admiration', and members of the International Art Congress of August 1908, who travelled to Limnerslease on 'a special train' that 'left Waterloo at 1 50pm'.[24] Thompson also notes that a corridor was built over 'the open-air path leading to the Sculpture Gallery into the Annexe' and filled with photographs of 'pictures and drawings [by G.F. Watts] which are not to be seen in the Collection'. The report ended with a statement about the gallery's purpose and the possibility of a further extension of the building, 'space for other works … and the exhibition, in glass cases, of some sketch books and other articles of value and interest connected with the Master whose message to his fellow men it is the aim of the collection to set forth'. The future expansion was not realized until about 1925 with the addition of the Sunken Gallery (now the Richard Jefferies Gallery) designed by Laurence Powell, a local architect.[25]

As the century progressed, Watts's reputation declined with the rise of modernism, and although Mary observed the changing attitudes, she was

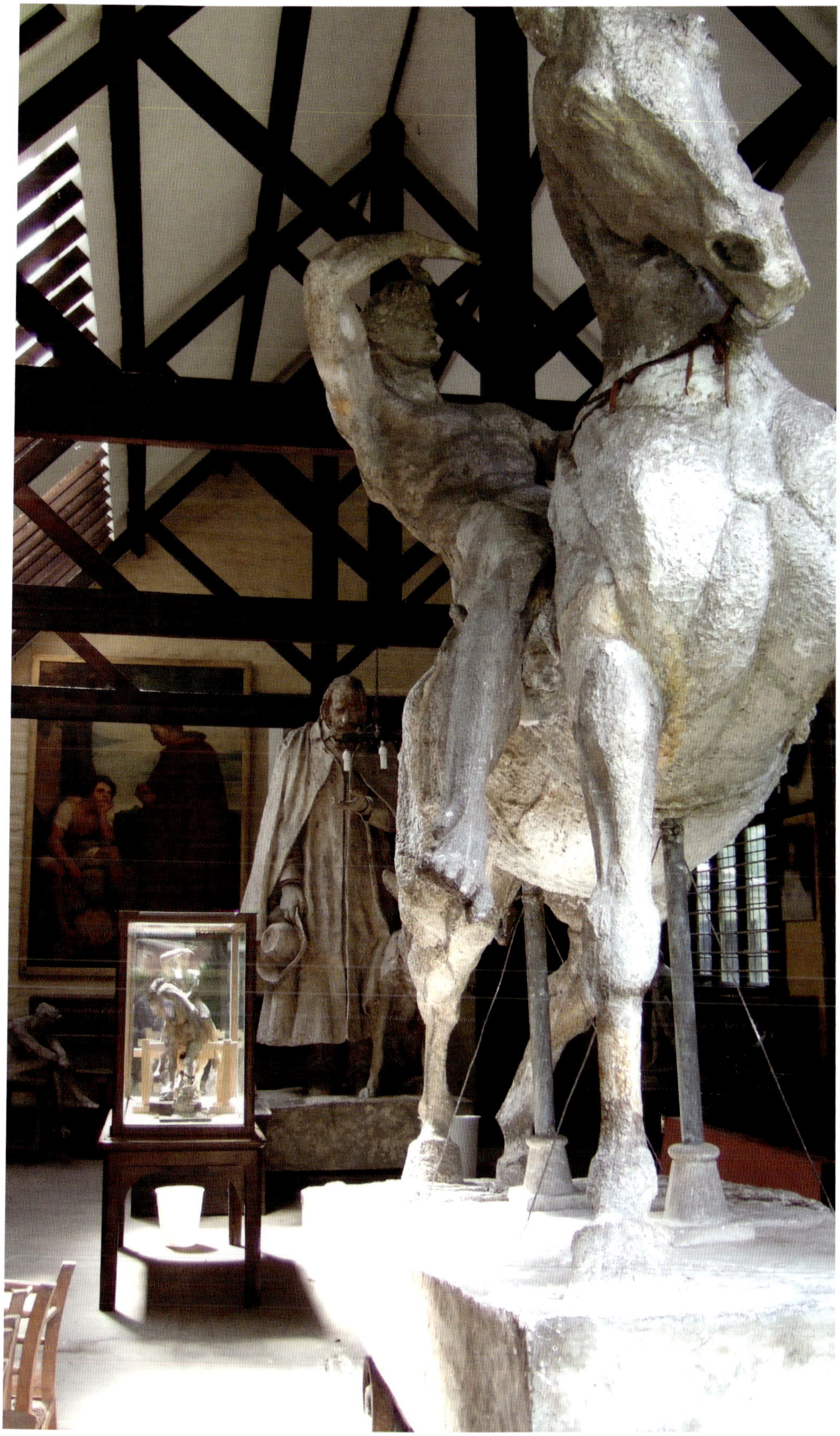

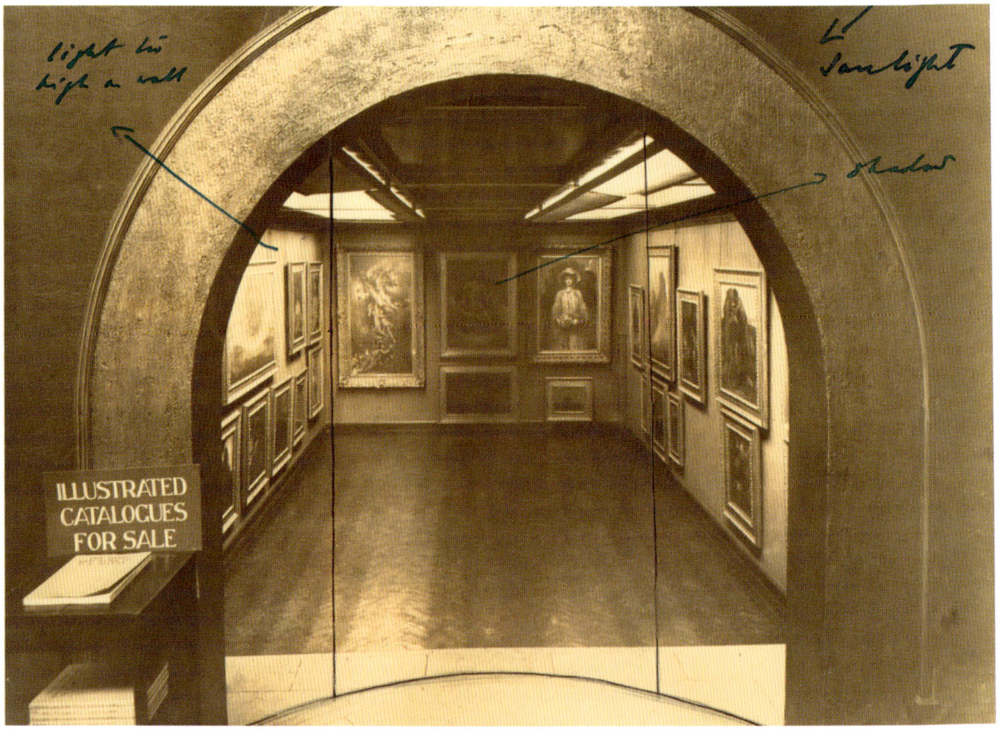

The Sunken Gallery (now the Richard Jefferies Gallery), in a 1930s photograph with Rowland Alston's notes on lighting

resolute in upholding the gallery's vision. When she died in 1938, it was the end of an age and everything was to change: a direct and personal link to the artist had gone. That year marked the lowest point in the gallery's history. Financial difficulties forced the trustees to take the radical step of putting Limnerslease on the market. The property was not sold at this time, but on 13 March 1939 the contents of the house were sold, which sadly included Watts's library and many of his smaller paintings valued at the derisory sums of between 5 shillings and 5 guineas.[26] The house remained in the possession of the Potters' Arts Guild, who rented it to the Ardente company during the 1939–45 war, and it was eventually sold in 1952. The supposedly permanent display of Watts's work in a special room at the Tate was brought to an end: 'The death of Mary Watts in 1938 effectively signaled the dismantling of the bequest.'[27] The room had been a significant London landmark and was visited by many who found an uplifting spirituality in its exhibition of Watts's large allegorical works.

Within the Watts Gallery itself radical changes took place with the trustees agreeing to the curator's plans for 'redecorating the Gallery and to put up partitions in the red gallery'. The whole gallery was 'modernized', wall colours changed to lighter tones, the picture rail lowered to avoid hanging too high on the wall, and walls built that reduced the large open space. The entry price went down from one shilling to sixpence, and the gallery was praised by *The Times* for its work:

> At that time [1904–6] the functional requirements of a picture gallery were imperfectly considered; it was looked upon as a place to house rather than display pictures; and beyond external seemliness, plenty of wall space and top lighting of a sort little else was attempted. What is being done resolves itself into the internal reorganization … the primary object of enabling the pictures

> to be better seen. This involves two principle factors: improved lighting and more suitable decorations for the walls … For the colouring of the walls, which, as originally applied, is rather 'fierce', a neutral tint has been adopted of a tone corresponding to the average middle-tone of the pictures, giving value to their light and darks.[28]

In retrospect, the attempt to homogenize the whole of the gallery went against the building's purpose and the vision of its founders. Yet Rowland Alston, who remained curator until his death in 1958, had modernized the gallery, not to oppose Watts, but in the belief that he was aiding Watts's reputation. Alston's admiration for and interest in Watts are revealed in his book on the Watts Gallery collection, *The Mind and Work of G.F. Watts*, published in 1929. Written when Mary was still alive, the work focuses on the artist's technique and reflects Mary's wish that curators of the Watts Gallery must be artists and gentlemen. The Arts Council exhibition of Watts held fifty years after his death in 1954 contained an essay by Alston that also focused on Watts's technique, and in this period his specialist knowledge led him to conserve some of the works at Compton.[29] Alston was an incredible character who had survived the Somme to take up art in a prisoner-of-war camp; deeply in awe of Watts, he researched gallery design to adapt the Watts Gallery to the contemporary world. For this he was praised by *The Times*:

> As curator Alston was conscientious and whole-hearted in his care for the fabric of the gallery and of its contents, and, not in the least, for the amenities of its delightful rural setting. From a somewhat ramshackle affair he developed it by degrees into a model little gallery, arranged with taste and admirably lighted on principles of which he made a special study in Holland.[30]

Despite controverting the original vision of the gallery, such changes gave a new lease of life to Watts.

After Alston's death the next curator to be appointed was Wilfrid Blunt, a debonair drawing master from Eton and brother of the eminent art historian Anthony Blunt. A gentleman artist and polymath, Blunt used the Watts Gallery as a place to study and write over twenty books on various subjects that interested him, most notably Islamic art, botany and music. He ran the gallery in an efficient and orderly way, although visitor numbers significantly deteriorated. His own admiration for Watts was expressed wryly in his biography of the artist, *England's Michelangelo*, and his defence of him against his critics, including in debates at the Oxford Union. His writing on Watts is among the most readable and entertaining on the subject, although at times, using witty exaggerations, he is scurrilous and detrimental about his achievements. In 1984 he began to suffer terminal ill health, and his assistant Richard Jefferies became curator.

Richard Jefferies had been an assistant to Blunt for a long period and his appointment as curator, very much as Blunt had wished, was with a deep knowledge of Watts. An almost permanent fixture in the gallery where he spoke engagingly to visitors, Richard provided a new theatricality. The cool stasis and order of Blunt's era were replaced by an eccentric charm. The addition of furniture, plants and the curator's idiosyncrasies imparted a rambling Victorian allure, creating the sense that nothing had ever changed. He railed against the modernization instigated by Alston and heroically kept the gallery going for over two decades. This meant preserving and amending it on a shoestring. Richard retired in 2006 after the 2004 centenary exhibition. All the curators have lived in the gallery itself and this relatively rare tradition still continues to this day.

The gallery's vision today looks back to its founders, G.F. and Mary Watts, in the way that it presents the gallery to its visitors. Research into the history of the gallery has been key to this development, along with appreciation of the great significance of G.F. Watts within nineteenth-century art. The aim is to preserve what is unique. As the Tate and National Portrait Galleries continue to show a selection of work by Watts, Watts Gallery maintains the vision of that great trinity of galleries and provides a national gallery in the heart of a village.

NOTES

1 Watts 1912, vol.III, p.259.

2 Watts 1912, vol.III, p.260.

3 Watts 1912, vol.III, p.xii.

4 'Without wishing to offend Mr. Watts, we must ask if it is judicious on his part, if it is just to his fellow artists, to propose to take up so much space in the National Gallery [now Tate], if that is where the pictures are to go, when such a course inevitably must mean the utter exclusion of the work of some of his fellows?' (*Chronicle*, 29 December 1896, clipping in Watts Gallery Archive.)

5 Thomson 1906, p.323.

6 Watts 1912, vol.III, p.xii.

7 See my entries on *Found Drowned, Irish Famine* and *Under a Dry Arch* in Bills and Bryant 2008, pp.112–21.

8 Bateman 1901, p.15.

9 On 30 September 1903 Mary recalls in her diaries: 'Our pictures come from L.H.H. [Little Holland House] Gallery.'

10 Berthorpe was named after his aunt Bertha Turnor: Turnor Memoirs.

11 Turnor Memoirs, p.221.

12 Christopher Hatton Turnor, photographic journal of his buildings with his own annotations, unnumbered, private archive.

13 *Surrey Advertiser*, 2 April 1904, clipping in Watts Gallery Archive.

14 Hazelwood Beardsley Fitzgerald became a known sculptor in the 1920s, and his time at the Watts Gallery served as an apprenticeship for him.

15 *The Times*, 2 April 1904, p.7.

16 Erskine 1906, p.190. The paper was produced by Tynecastle, a branch of the Morton and Co. furniture company begun in 1870 by William Scott Morton (1840–1903) with his brother John. In the 1870s the firm began to make wallpaper and became renowned for their invention of Tynecastle Tapestry, a canvas wall covering inspired by fifteenth- to sixteenth-century Spanish and Italian embossed-leather wall hangings. The three-dimensional nature of the canvas and the revolutionary way in which it was

made meant that it was a more economic, lighter, yet durable alternative to plasterwork.

17 Mrs Russell (Emilie) Barrington, *Reminiscences*, London 1905, p.148.

18 Watts *c.*1910, vol.1, p.65.

19 *Surrey Advertiser*, 2 April 1904, clipping in Watts Gallery Archive.

20 The exhibition opened at the Royal Academy early in 1905, and although it included a large number of loans, at its core were eighty paintings from the Watts Gallery. The vast exhibition, with minor changes at each of its venues, travelled to Edinburgh, Manchester and Newcastle, ending in Dublin in 1906.

21 'I would venture to suggest the advantages that would accrue if the Royal Academy could remove to the International buildings: there would be ample space for the schools, and a superb gallery, well lighted, in which no picture need be hung above the level of the eye, as no picture worth exhibiting ever should be. The public are familiarised with the locality, which is even more fashionable than Trafalgar Square.' (G.F. Watts in Watts 1912, vol.III, p.145.)

22 Thomson 1906; Erskine 1906; Brock 1906.

23 Brock 1906.

24 'The International Art Congress', *The Times*, 3 August 1908, p.11; Charles H. Thompson, Curator's Report, 15 November 1913 (reports from Feb. 1908 to 1913).

25 The 1957 Watts Gallery catalogue notes it being built in 1925 and Mary mentions it being built in her notebook dated 19 March 1925, Watts Gallery Archive.

26 Valuation of Limnerslease, 1938, Watts Gallery Archive.

27 Alison Smith, 'Watts and the National Gallery of British Art', in Colin Trodd and Stephanie Brown (eds), *Representations of G.F. Watts: Art Making in Victorian Culture,* Aldershot 2004, pp.153–68, esp. p. 165.

28 'Watts Picture Gallery, Improvements at Compton', from our art critic, *The Times*, 5 April 1938, p.14.

29 Arts Council of Great Britain, *George Frederic Watts O.M., R.A.*, exh. cat., Tate Gallery, London 1954.

30 *The Times*, 22 December 1958, p.11.

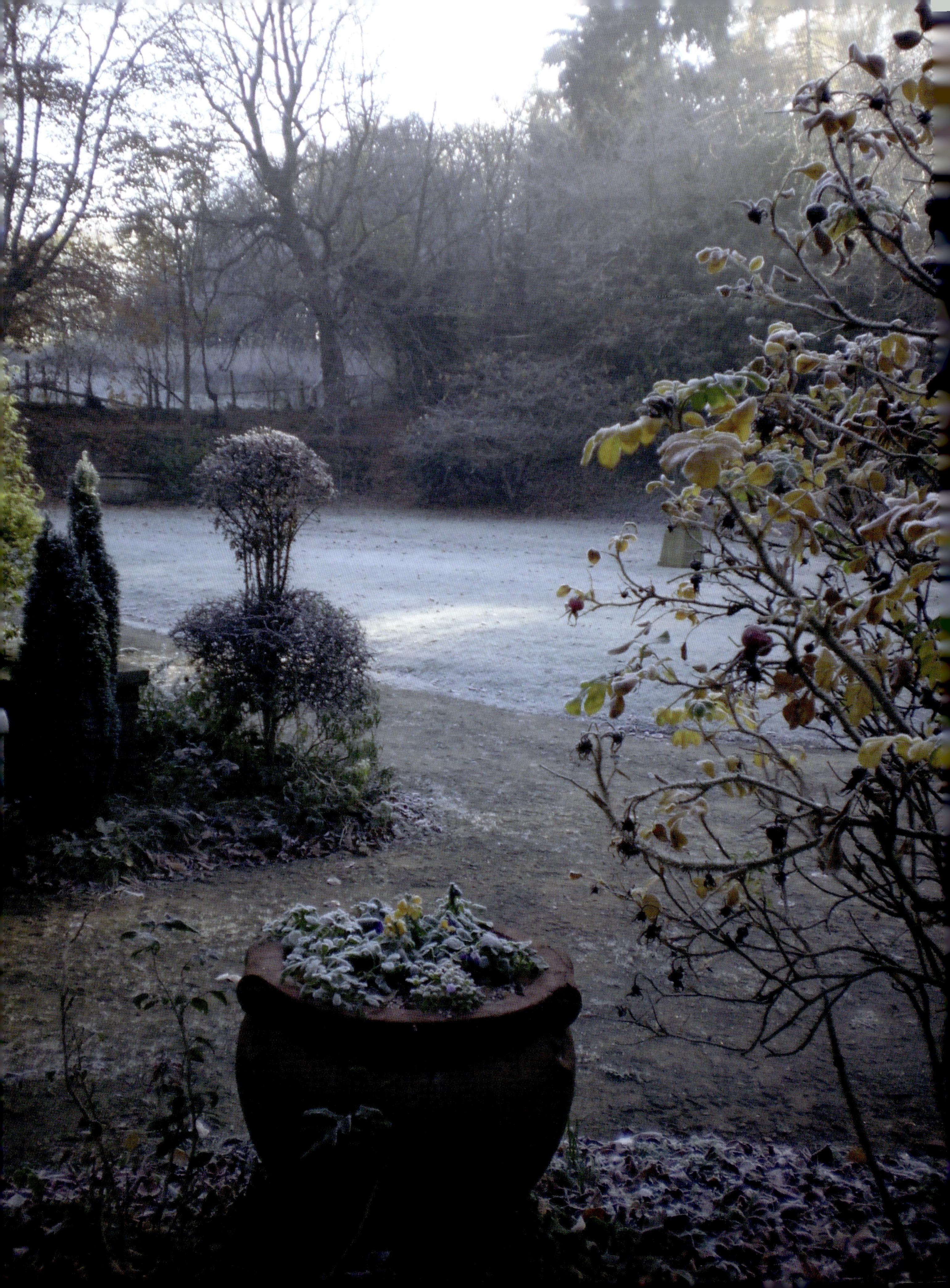

The Future of Watts Village in Compton

Perdita Hunt

The year 2004 marked a watershed in the history of Watts Gallery. It was the centenary of the artist's death and the centenary of the opening of the gallery. It was also a year in which the Watts Gallery Trustees had to make a choice between saving the gallery or losing it for ever.

The centenary of G.F. Watts was marked by exhibitions at the National Portrait Gallery, the Royal Academy, Tate Britain and Watts Gallery.[1] Such celebration of Watts's work was like a rainstorm in a desert. For too long the profile of the artist and his work had lain hidden in the stores of the national arts institutions and unseen, except by a few people, at Watts Gallery. Nevertheless, it was in meeting the challenge of mounting a serious retrospective of Watts's work at Watts Gallery that the urgency of the gallery's future became clear. To borrow *The Happy Warrior* (1884; Neue Pinakotek, Munich) from Germany required considerable persuasion and skill on the part of the exhibition's curator, Veronica Franklin Gould, as it was widely known that the conditions of the gallery were somewhat extreme – cold, damp and insecure. Despite this, the exhibition (and catalogue) *The Vision of G.F. Watts* was launched at Watts Gallery on 1 July 2004, a hundred years to the day since his death. The trustees who gathered on that day for the annual general meeting stood for a minute's silence to commemorate the founder and great master. At that same meeting they commenced their discussions on the future of the gallery. In 1998 Veronica Franklin Gould, who used to live in Compton and commenced our journey in reassessing G.F. and Mary Watts by writing a guide to Mary Watts's chapel, had also staged an exhibition to mark the sixtieth anniversary of Mary Watts's death. *Mary Watts: Unsung Heroine of the Art Nouveau* was attended by 15,000 visitors and as with any Watts exhibition it aroused both positive and negative responses.

These two exhibitions within a six-year period and the level of interest they generated were proof enough that there was an audience for G.F. and Mary Watts. The considerable amount of effort required to mount them and address the shortcomings of the building also showed that there was a need to repair the serious dilapidations if the Watts Gallery Trust was going to deliver its charitable purpose of promoting the understanding and appreciation of G.F. and Mary Watts in the context of the nineteenth century and preserve the gallery and its collection for future generations.

Apart from these two exhibitions, the gallery had been snoozing its way into oblivion. This was in no way due to the dedicated stewardship of Richard Jefferies, the then curator (only the fourth in one hundred years[2]), who was unstinting in his commitment to the gallery. He was also supported by an assistant curator – a trainee post that has provided much needed work experience to recent graduates from the Courtauld Institute of Art and other universities with courses in the history of art or museum management. But it was a fact that, given the lack of resources, the gallery could do little more than open and

Opposite: View from Watts Gallery entrance, winter 2006, photograph by Mark Bills

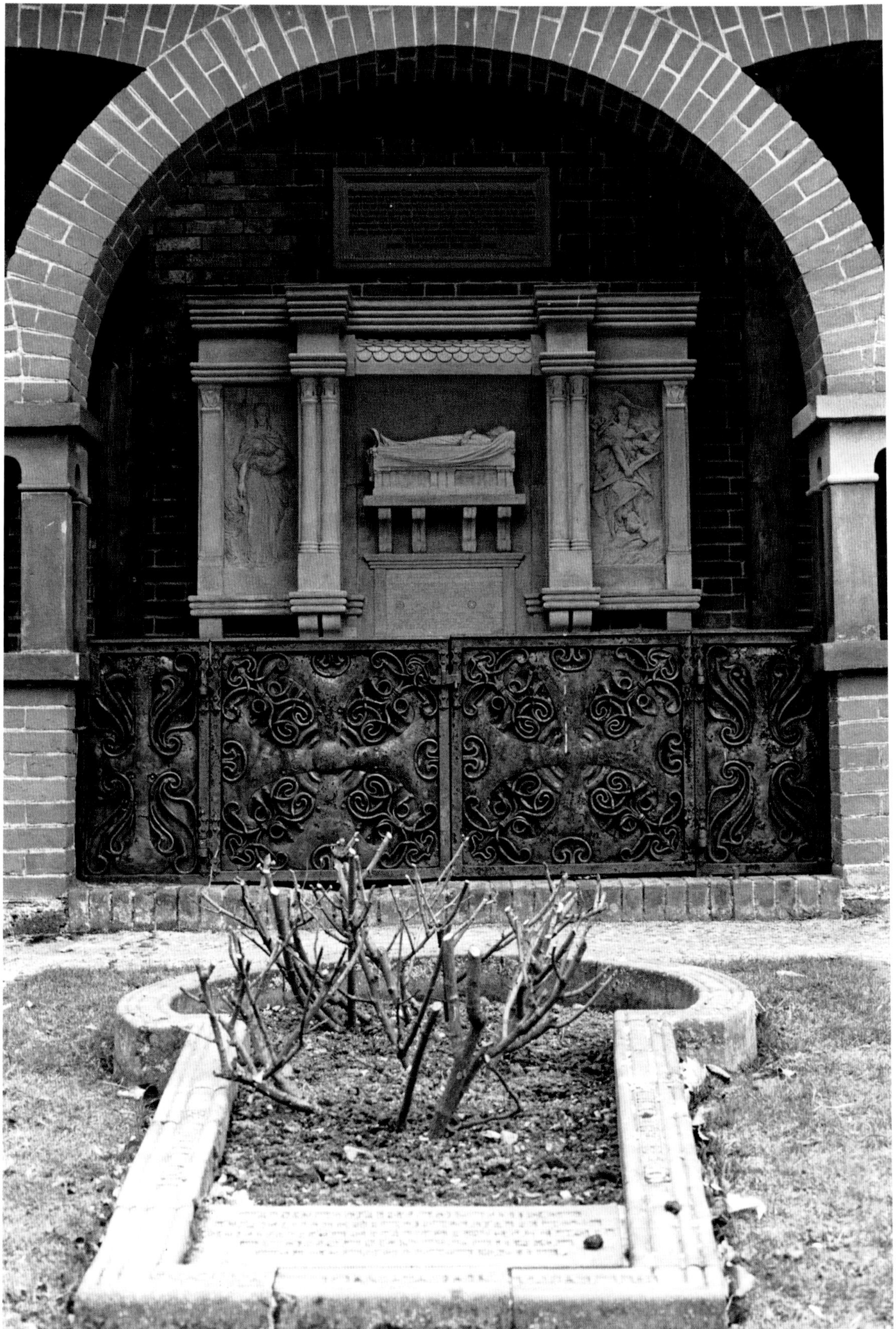

Opposite: Watts Memorial by Thomas Wren in the cloister at Watts Chapel, 1904, photograph by Frederic Hollyer

close its doors and the curator was rarely able to take holidays. At the time of the centenary there were seventeen Friends and five volunteers. The gallery attracted about 12,000 visitors. In winter the building felt the coldest place on earth, and there was mist on many occasions in the Sculpture Gallery, while in summer the heat was fierce. The paintings were subjected to very high lux levels and the damp was affecting the drawings. The trustees, a very honourable body lead by such chairmen as Sir Robert Witt, Sir Brinsley Ford and Richard Ormond, would visit the gallery once a year for the annual general meeting and tea on the lawn.

For those who knew the gallery, it was a much loved and hidden secret – the last bastion of old England, a hidden gem, an oasis. The wisteria creeping over the loggia at the front door, the passion flowers, so loved by Watts,[3] swarming over the curator's house (formerly the apprentice potters' accommodation), the vibrant fig tree in the sunken courtyard together created a scene from a nineteenth-century rural idyll. For those who knew Richard Jefferies, meeting the curator furthered the experience of travelling back in time, as this courteous bewhiskered gentleman took time to explain and show you round the collection. For many, this was how the gallery should remain. But, as with all such strategic dilemmas facing Watts Gallery, it was necessary to look back to its original aims before going forward. G.F. and Mary Watts believed passionately in 'art for all', and they built Watts Gallery to display permanently the art of G.F. Watts; the responsibility of the trustees is therefore to promote the work of G.F. and Mary Watts to their best advantage and to enable more people to enjoy more of the collection more of the time. The fact that the shell of the Wattses' ambitions, the gallery, had itself become a time capsule and a curiosity was an additional asset but could not become a barrier to achieving their vision. In short, the trustees and those who knew Watts either had the option to love the old gallery to death or revive its original purpose and give it new life.

HOPE

In October 2004 the *Hope* Project was conceived. The aim was to restore Watts Gallery in order to save the building and its collection for another hundred years. The trustees set out six aims: to save the building; to save the collection; to extend the education programme in order to establish Compton as a centre for exploring Victorian art, social history and craft; to increase audiences; to increase income; and to establish an organization that could deliver the vision of Watts.

Some generous trusts were incredibly magnanimous in providing funds to support the gallery for essential development right at the outset. The first, from the Pilgrim Trust, was to put in drainage for the gallery, which was succumbing to regular overflows of raw sewage, and the second from the Esmée Fairbairn Foundation was to support the appointment of a marketing manager. The Watts Gallery Trust will be forever grateful for this early support and for these trusts showing such faith.

One of the first tasks in any major fundraising campaign is to ensure that potential donors are aware of the cause. Here Watts Gallery had an uphill struggle. Many visitors had suggested that the gallery should be featured in the BBC TV *Restoration* series (2006) hosted by Griff Rhys Jones. The newly appointed marketing manager was asked as her first task to stay on the telephone

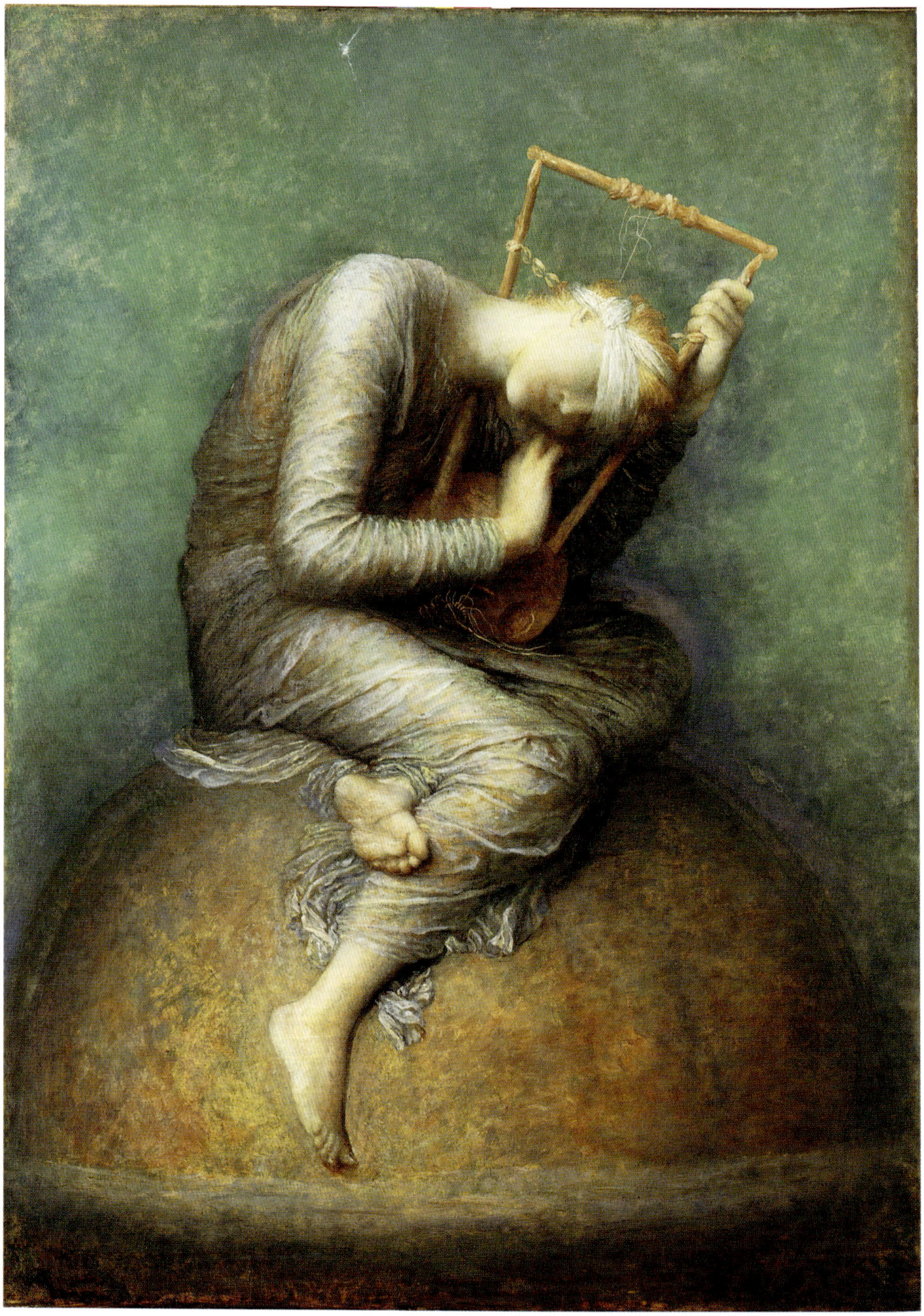

G.F. Watts, Hope, *c.1885–86, oil on canvas, 150 x 109 cm, private collection*

to the BBC until a positive response was received from the programme! It worked, and Watts Gallery was visited by the research group of *Restoration*. As a result of their enquiries the programme decided to feature Watts Gallery on *Restoration Village*. Ptolemy Dean and Marianne Suhr visited and commented: 'Indeed there is nothing quite like this complex gallery and chapel, a unique tribute to an artist who caught the mood of the late nineteenth century.'[4] The first programme was seen by over 1.5 million people. The volunteers at the gallery galvanized an

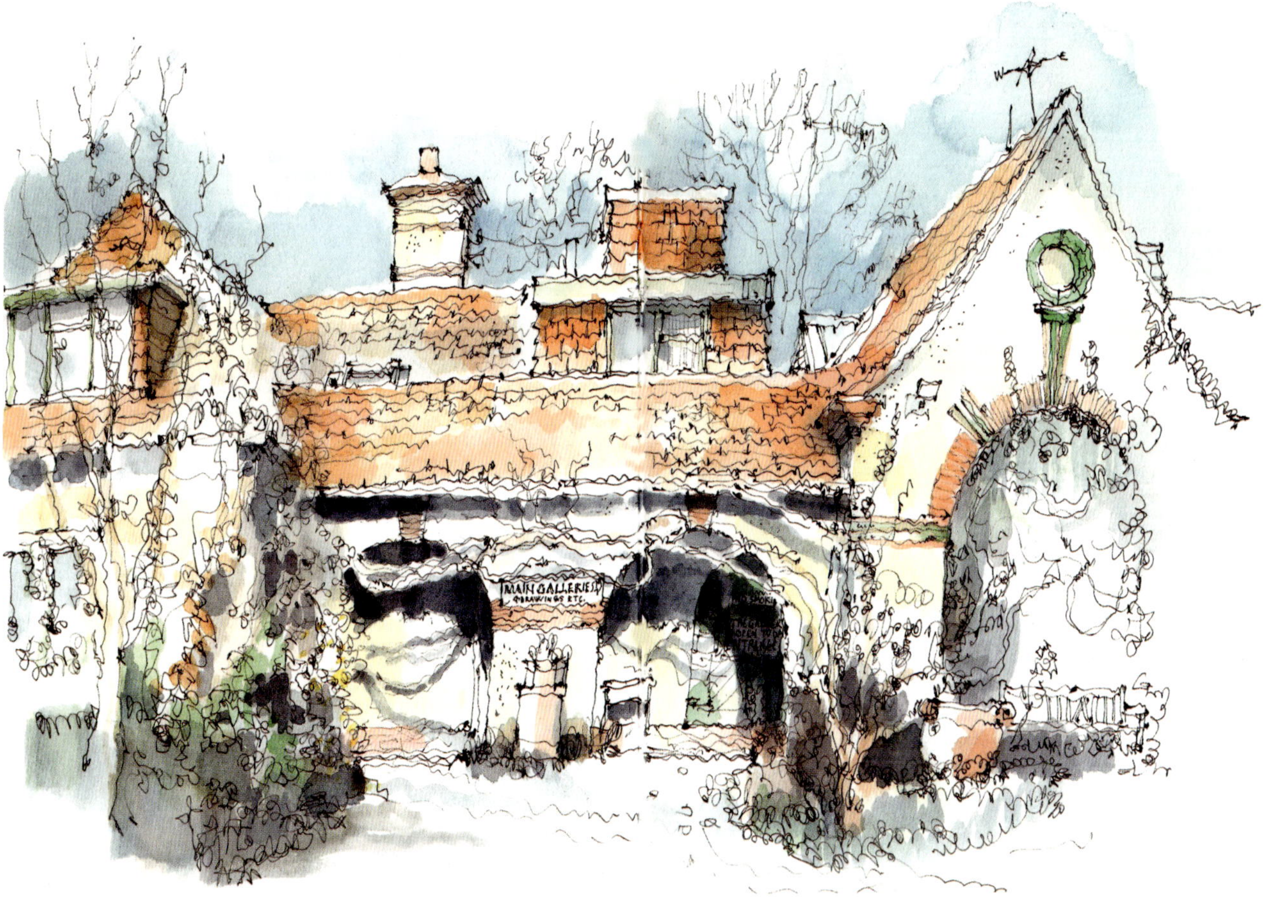

Ptolemy Dean,
Watts Gallery,
2006, watercolour,
Watts Gallery

amazing network of support, which resulted in Watts Gallery winning the south-east part of the competition. When it came to the final, which was staged live at the Weald and Downland Museum, Watts Gallery's fate was to be given the place of runner-up. Earlier, one of the administrators of a trust supporting Watts Gallery had said that the best possible place for the gallery to win was second. How true this proved to be. As a result, Watts Gallery secured the sympathy vote and went on to raise the £10 million that was needed to deliver the *Hope* Project. In the meantime, visitors to the gallery increased from 12,000 to 25,000.

The *Hope* Project was a remarkable journey for the passengers on the Watts Gallery ship over the six years from 2004 to 2010. In recognizing the need to secure support from the Heritage Lottery Fund, the ensuing work was informed by the exigencies set by distributors of public money. With initial support for project-planning work, the gallery commissioned a conservation management plan, an audience development and access plan, a training plan, an interpretation plan, a learning plan and many other key pieces of documentation and research. During this period the collection was inspected to assess its need for conservation. One of the greatest moments in the *Hope* journey was the gift from one of the best-known conservators in the country, Hamish Dewar. An owner of several Watts works himself and previously a resident of nearby Puttenham, Hamish

Conservation work at Hamish Dewar's studio, 2009

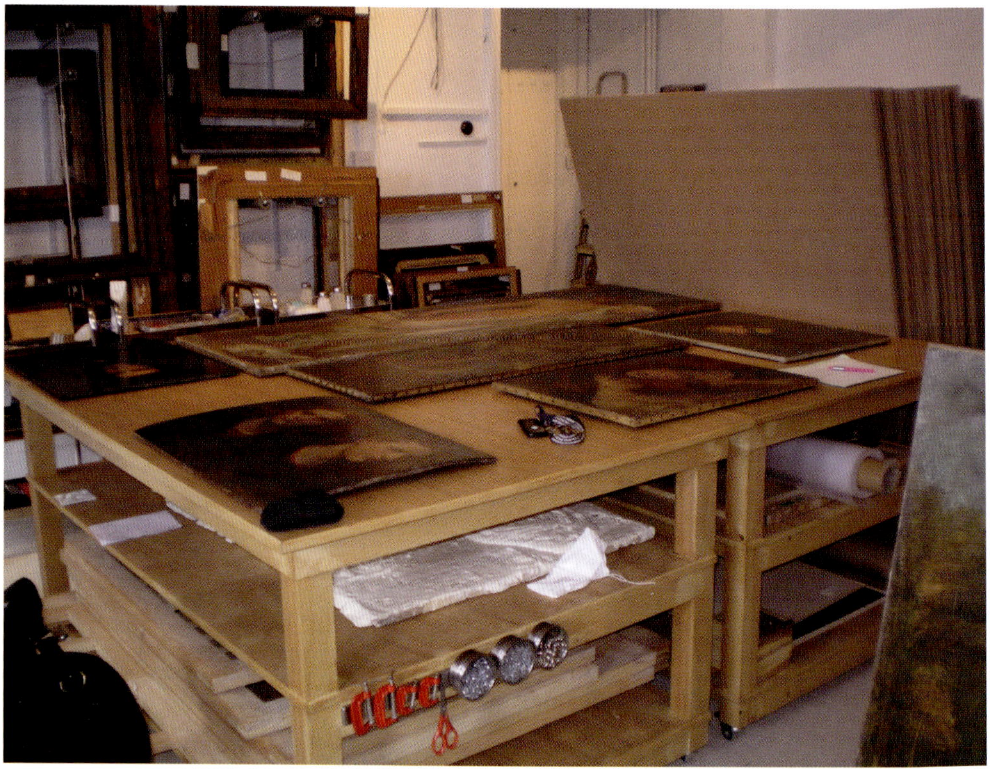

Dewar generously offered to conserve the oil paintings as a gift to the gallery. In addition to this, the gallery launched an innovative scheme, 'Adopt a Watts', which contributes to the costs of cleaning, conserving and reframing many works, boosted by a generous donation from Mr David Pike. The greatest concern was the viability of the monumental sculptural models. Although they needed cleaning, to the great relief of all they were found to be robust, and the only unexpected surprise was the discovery of a light bulb inside *Physical Energy*![5]

The name of the *Hope* Project was provided by a volunteer. Since the centenary exhibition in 2004, when the local Decorative and Fine Art Society generously offered to help steward, the gallery has recruited over 150 volunteers. The involvement of so many different people from all professions and all ages was a strong thread in the revival and resurgence of Watts Gallery during this period. Many volunteers were retired professionals, who lived within a twenty-mile radius of the gallery, but included some young mothers wishing to refresh their skills for a return to work, students of museum studies or art history, or art enthusiasts wishing to learn more about the collection. At one of the regular quarterly meetings with the volunteers the question was asked about what to call this major programme to save the gallery. '*Hope*, of course' came a shout from the back, from Marion May, great-niece of the builder of the Old Pottery. It was serendipity that the iconic painting of *Hope* was owned by one of the gallery's trustees, who then became Patron of the *Hope* Appeal and whose leading pledge of the *Hope* Appeal will be remembered through the naming of the main gallery: the Isabel Goldsmith Patino Gallery.

Many other positive associations transpired from using the image of *Hope*. Tate Britain chose the *Hope* in their collection as the centre of their refreshed, permanent display of Watts in the Victorian spectacle gallery throughout the *Hope* Project. Barack Obama cited *Hope* in his book, *Dreams from my Father*, as being the source of his inspiration for his later book, *The Audacity of Hope*;[6] and thanks to the generous owner of *Hope*, the painting was on show at the Guildhall Art Gallery during the presidential elections in November 2008, causing considerable interest among the media. When at a low point in the *Hope* Project the contractor restoring the building went into administration due to the economic climate, the image of a blindfolded girl astride the globe playing a broken instrument began to feel more like something from a work entitled *Despair*. However, as seen throughout this period of change, the bright star in the Watts sky always shone through.

It would not be appropriate to write of the *Hope* project without referring to the generosity of the benefactors, donors and supporters. On discovering the Watts story – and the fact that Watts himself gave so much to over thirty charities during his lifetime and selflessly left the legacy of a collection, a gallery, a pottery, a chapel, and a memorial to unsung heroes – many donors, trusts and foundations have felt moved and inspired to give to this effort to save the gallery. From paying to sign a roof tile to leaving a legacy, naming a gallery, giving challenge funding and giving in kind, the gallery was blessed by extraordinary philanthropy and friendship. The names of all those who have given in so many ways is acknowledged in a book, similar to one made by Compton village at the time of the creation of the chapel, and is on show in the gallery.

RESTORATION

One of the greatest concerns expressed by all visitors to the gallery was that the restoration should not remove or change the character of the building. The architects Zombory-Moldovan Moore felt the burden of this expectation in every decision they made. Their approach was helpfully informed by considerable research on the gallery undertaken by the recently appointed curator Mark Bills. In looking back, it became clear that the gallery had changed quite dramatically during different periods of curatorial stewardship. First, Mary added new galleries in 1906 as well as a print studio, and the Sunken Gallery (now the Richard Jefferies Gallery) was created in 1925. In the 1930s a new hanging system was introduced and stud walls were erected at either end of the Red Gallery. The apprentice potters' games room was used as a gallery in the 1980s.

The colour scheme of the gallery, about which there has been considerable discussion, has been revealed as originally rich red Tynecastle wallpaper with a silver gold ceiling and green ceramic picture rail. Pictures show the lantern created on the top of the Isabel Goldsmith Patino Gallery, which has rotted away over time. This will be re-featured in the restoration. The architects have taken advice from Purcell Miller Tritton, conservation architects, on areas like the roofs and windows. The typical character of an Arts and Crafts roof with its soffits and terracotta tiles will all be retained. The aim throughout is to have minimal interference with the original concepts. A measure of success would be for the visitor to the restored gallery to comment on the lack of change since it closed. Nevertheless, to achieve the required accessibility to all the galleries, lifts will need to be introduced. The guidance that came from a brainstorming session

Left: Idea for the Sculpture Gallery restoration by Zombory-Moldovan Moore architects, 2007

Right: G.F. Watts's model for Physical Energy *being moved to its temporary location during restoration, 2008*

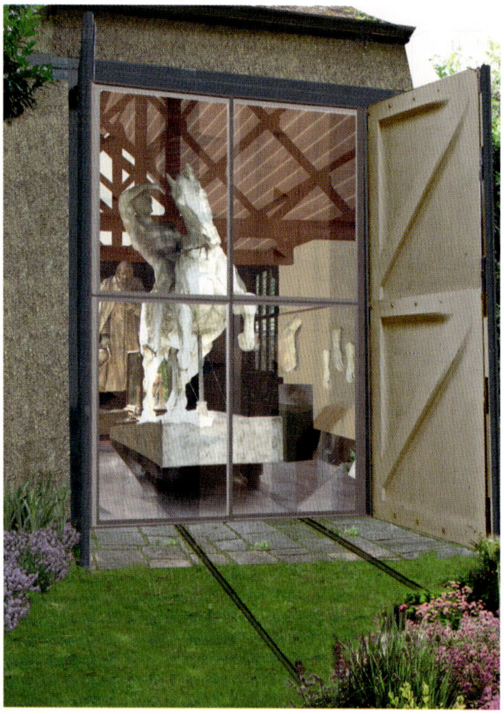

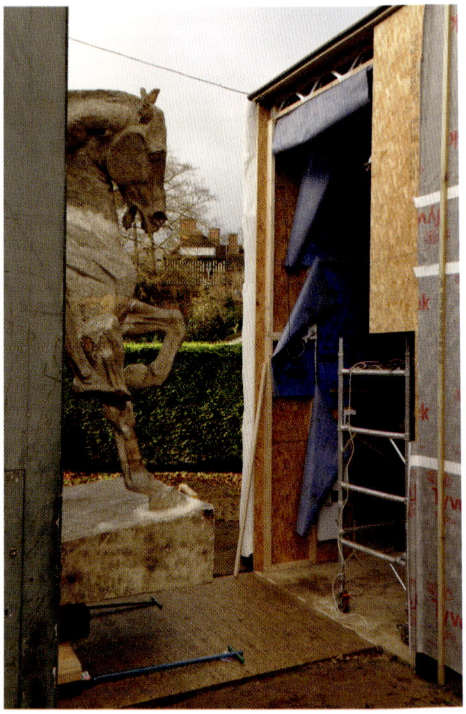

held at the Paul Mellon Centre, with leading representatives from the Tate, National Portrait Gallery and other institutions, was that Watts Gallery should have different approaches to the display of the collection in each gallery. Some galleries would feel more contemporary, while others, the original Red and Green Galleries, would be a replica of the original.

Another driver of the restoration has been the need to meet the national standards required for a Government Indemnity. This enables the gallery to borrow works from national institutions. The requirement is clear on security, safety and environmental controls. Watts Gallery was not equipped to meet these standards. This has involved introducing a considerable amount of machinery without damaging the look and feel of the gallery. The architects and design consultants have worked with the existing elements of the building, subtly introducing heating and cooling systems, for instance, that use the original central heating vents in the floor. The other challenge has been to address the level of lighting in the gallery. A model of the gallery was placed in a sky dome at the Bartlett School of Architecture, University College London, where the effect of the sun's rays at different times of day was monitored. This provided guidance on the thickness of glass and the placing of sensitive work in the collection. Artificial lighting also proved a challenge. Watts had always envisaged Watts Gallery as a daylight gallery. As an artist, Watts only liked to work by daylight. However, the gallery requires the capability to host events in the evenings and allow a visitor on a late winter's afternoon to enjoy the collection at its best. Finding the appropriate recesses for installing a lighting system that was functional but not obtrusive has taken many late evenings of demonstrations. The visitor will judge whether we have succeeded.

On a more pragmatic note, the restoration has enabled Watts Gallery to welcome more visitors in comfort. The area that used to be the kitchen garden to

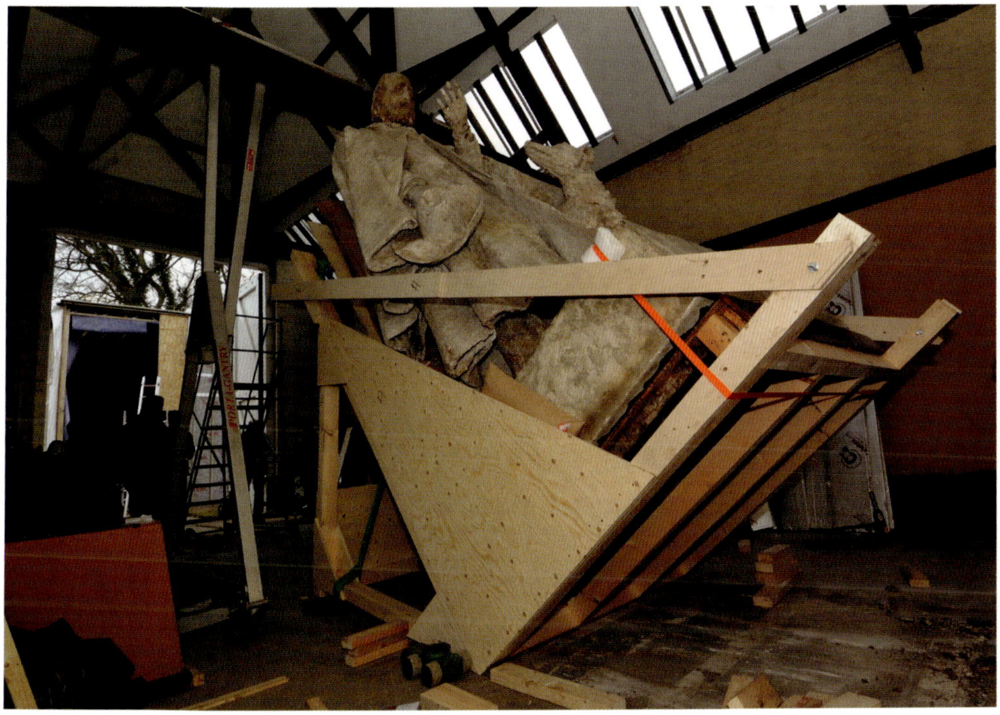

G.F. Watts's model for Tennyson *being moved to its temporary location during restoration, 2008*

the rear of the gallery has become the orchard car park, enabling thirty-eight more cars to be parked. Where there was just one public convenience, there are now five!

Finally, the restoration was intended to promote the vision of G.F. and Mary Watts. In the gallery there are now two rooms dedicated to study and research: the John George Study Room and the Seminar Room. Both these rooms house some of the library and archive, The Rob Dickins Collection and the Christopher Wood Library and Archive, and enable the curatorial fellow and interns to research the collection in proximity to the actual works of art. The studio has become the Foyle Art for All Learning Studio and is equipped with a kiln. Situated in the embrace of the gallery, it offers groups of all ages the opportunity to prepare for a visit to the gallery and then return to undertake artwork or ceramic work. The building is also accessible for community use.

One of the most exciting aspects of the restoration and the plans was rediscovering the gallery as Watts originally saw it. New vistas have opened up with the removal of the stud walls. The green ceramic picture rail glows, and with the restored red wallpaper, the warmth of the setting for Watts's freshly conserved works of art is a sight to behold.

A gallery without walls

To prepare for the work required on the gallery was a momentous task. The collection had to be fully inventoried and then stored or taken out on show. It was also important to estimate the fragility of some of the collection and stabilize these before moving them. The most dramatic process was shifting *Physical Energy* and *Tennyson* into their temporary stable. One day from 9am to 9pm, after meticulous planning on the part of Oxford Exhibitions Services, *Physical Energy* was rolled out, the first time

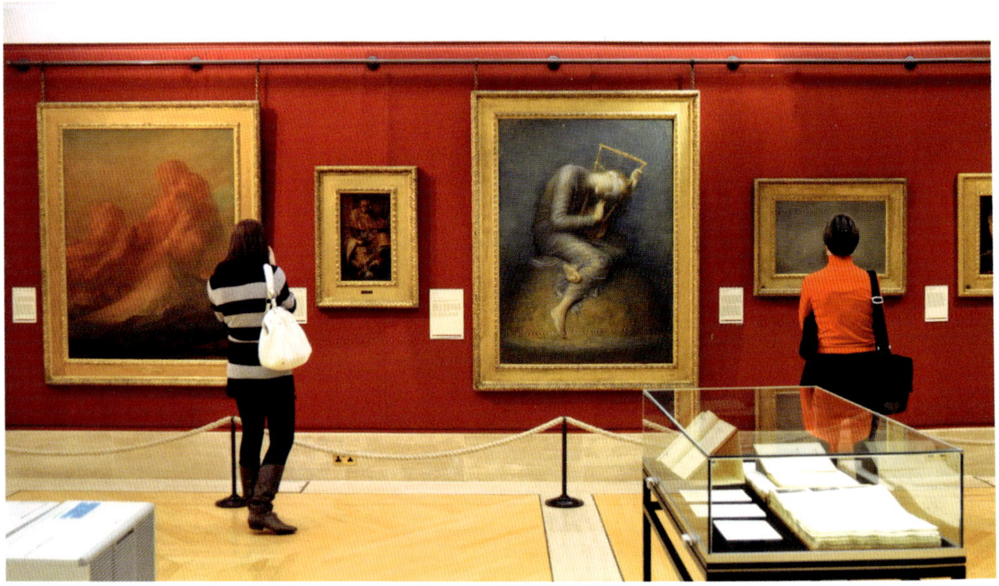

Watts in the City: Victorian Visionary *exhibition at the Guildhall Art Gallery, London, 2008*

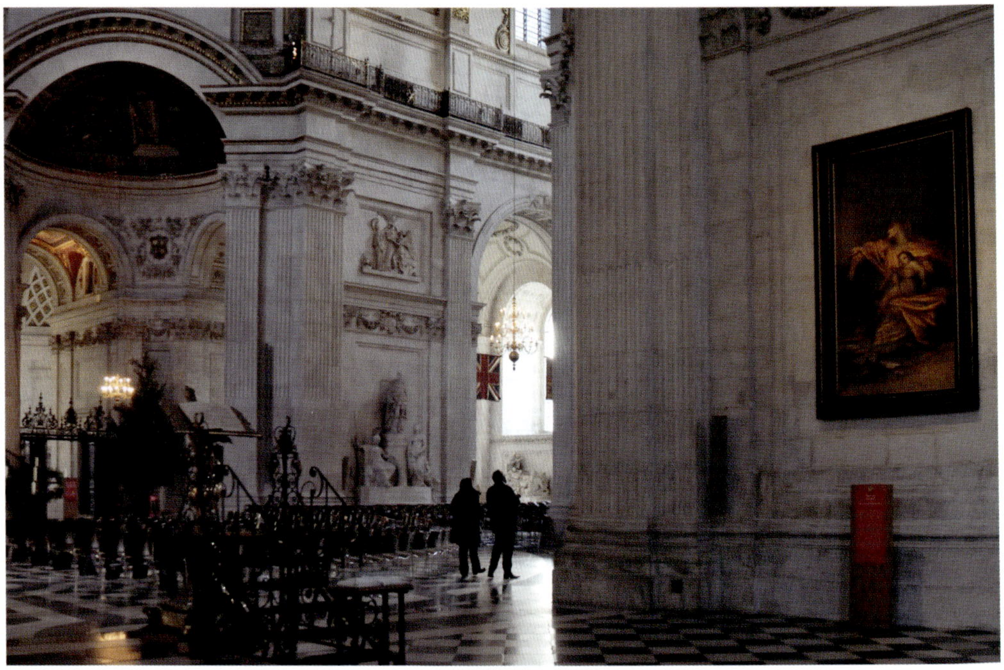

*Watts in the City: installation of G.F. Watts's paintings (*Peace and Goodwill *visible) in the nave of St Paul's Cathedral, 2008*

since the Queen's coronation, to take up residence in its temporary setting. *Tennyson* had to be laid on his back and then put upright in the temporary shelter.

The opportunity to house the curator and his family, together with some of the collection and the library and archives, in Watts's home, Limnerslease, during the restoration of the gallery was a stroke of luck and generosity on the part of the owners. Instead of selling their property, Richard Conway and Julia Kemp agreed to lease the Great Studio, the end part of Limnerslease, to the gallery. As well as meeting the urgent practical needs of housing the collection and people, this space where Watts worked and where Mary Watts held her evening pottery classes opened up new possibilities of developing Watts's vision of art for all, and achieving the concept of Compton becoming a centre for exploring Victorian art, social history and craft.

Watts in the City

The plan to tour the collection mirrored that made by Mary Watts in 1905 when, in preparing to build the main gallery, she also toured the collection. The curator Mark Bills developed a major programme to raise the profile of Watts called the 'Watts in the City' season. The exhibition of sixty key pieces from the collection, entitled *G.F. Watts: Victorian Visionary*, with an excellent accompanying catalogue that included new research prepared by Mark Bills and Barbara Bryant, was opened at Guildhall Art Gallery on 11 November 2008. On 1 December 2008 Jeremy Hunt MP, then Shadow Secretary of State for the Arts, opened *Parables in Paint*, an exhibition of Watts's spiritual paintings at St Paul's Cathedral.

In addition to these two major exhibitions, the Watts in the City season gave the gallery the opportunity to draw attention to one of Watts's least known legacies: Postman's Park in the City of London. Watts's 'art for all' beliefs encompassed the idea of acknowledging the brave deeds of ordinary citizens through specially commissioned memorials to be shown in a public place. Postman's Park is the only such memorial, and during the Watts in the City season a celebration was held at Postman's Park to highlight its unique contribution to our heritage and to unveil a plaque that links the memorial to Watts's own gallery in Compton. This celebration, coinciding as it did with the first new memorial since 1938 to be added to Postman's Park, created considerable interest in the idea of honouring self-sacrifice and providing a memorial for unsung heroes.

A CENTRE FOR EXPLORING VICTORIAN ART, SOCIAL HISTORY AND CRAFT

Watts Gallery owns a library and archive of unique value. It contains papers, diaries and photographs that provide an insight into the society and work of G.F. and Mary Watts. As explored in previous essays, they shared a vision of providing education and learning through art, and the Compton legacy enshrines the aims of its founders to provide art for all with a collection and archive that are of international importance.

With the growing interest in Watts Gallery created by the *Hope* Project and the BBC's *Restoration Village*, the gallery has attracted further gifts of archives and libraries to take forward its ambition of becoming a centre for exploring Victorian art, social history and craft. The most notable gift was The Rob Dickins Collection – over 4,500 photographs of Victorian artists and statesmen – given to the gallery for use and reproduction by researchers and publishers. Part of the collection toured throughout the UK and to New York, providing a new insight into the society in which Watts moved. Christopher Wood, a major collector of nineteenth-century art and one of the most distinguished dealers in the field, bequeathed his library of books, catalogues and archives. Allen Staley, an expert in nineteenth-century art based in New York, has also pledged his considerable library on the subject. These gifts are already acting as a honeypot for scholars who regularly visit from University College London, Cambridge, the Courtauld Institute, Royal Holloway College and others.

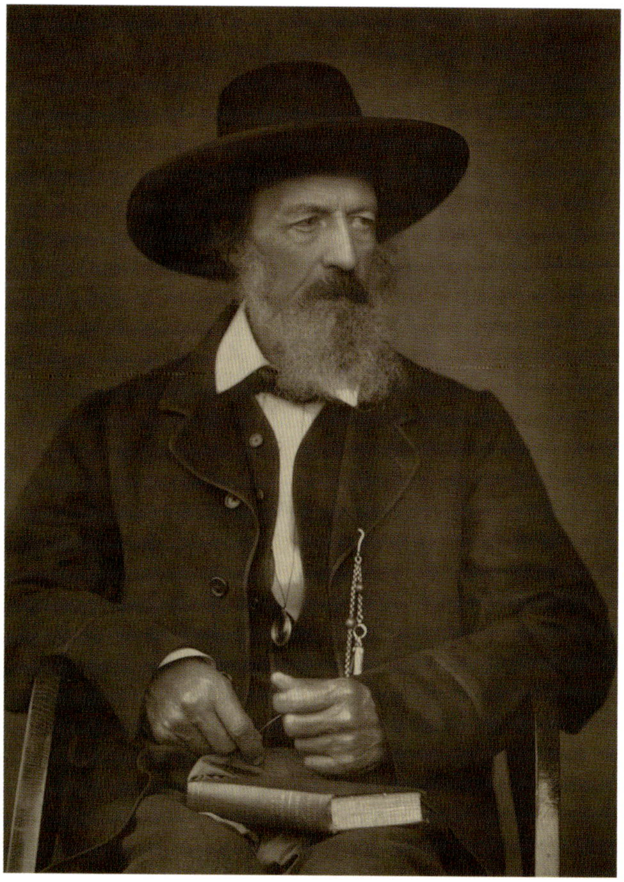

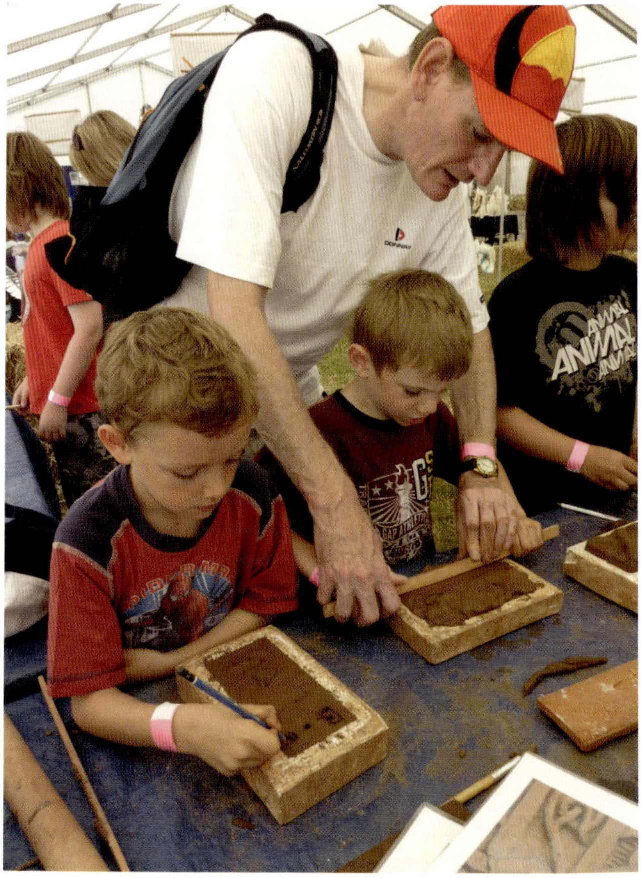

Above left: Alfred, Lord Tennyson, photograph by Barraud

Above right: A Hope Wall *workshop at* Celebrating Surrey *festival, 2010*

Real progress has been made in attracting new scholarship and research on Watts and his contribution to artistic development and thought. An annual symposium focuses on a different aspect of Watts and has been held in association with the Courtauld and the University for Creative Arts. Funded scholarships and a trainee curator, as well as a series of publications on the art of Watts, are all resulting in a new understanding of Watts and an increased interest in the influence of his work. Recent publications have included a book on *Physical Energy*, Postman's Park and Little Holland House.

ART FOR ALL

Watts's vision of art for all has underpinned the *Hope* Project. An important part of the case made to the Heritage Lottery Fund for support for the restoration centred on the need for Watts Gallery and on the outreach that the gallery would undertake to engage with more people and different communities. The consultation with stakeholders – local authorities, funders, visitors, volunteers – revealed in part a lack of awareness of the value of the collection housed by Watts Gallery and its potential impact on visitors, researchers and new audiences. To commence the engagement with audiences for learning at Watts Gallery, the Trustees of Watts Gallery were grateful to receive the support of the Peter Harrison Foundation to appoint a Head of Learning. The role started at the gallery in 2008 and the post-holder produced some innovative work involving women inmates at HM Prison Send, Surrey, and young offenders. From this work it was clear that the Watts collection and Watts's ideas and paintings still resonate a hundred years on.

Starting in its centenary year, Watts Gallery has appointed each year an artist in residence chosen from the final graduates in fine art at the University for the Creative Arts. Each year the artist chosen has been offered an exhibition of their work, while invited to give workshops to learning groups and special needs groups. The exercise has been mutually beneficial and resulted in continuing work for the artists in, for example, the residency at HMP Send. Part of the restoration of Watts Gallery encompassed a space for the artist in residence, providing visual evidence of the gallery's role of looking forward as well as back.

THE FUTURE OF THE WATTS VILLAGE

It is clear from the previous chapters that the Wattses' impact on Compton is important. Although restoration has begun with Watts Gallery, the pottery, the chapel and Limnerslease all form an integral part of our heritage and therefore need to be secured for the future and made available to the public. G.F. and Mary Watts painted their ideals and the social developments of the time onto this Compton canvas. Bringing the whole picture back to life is our current task.

As with the evolution of Watts Gallery, it is important to look back before looking forwards. The basic tenets of the Wattses' belief in art for all involved creating beautiful and lasting objects; attracting debate and the society of creative people to push the boundaries of artistic pursuits; providing open access to art as well as teaching and self-improvement through art; having a good business sense; and being part of the local community. Remarkably, G.F. and Mary Watts achieved all this in Compton. Together they commissioned Limnerslease from Ernest George, and Mary decorated the ceilings and fireplaces to capture different spiritual dimensions and thought. They designed the cemetery chapel, a lasting memorial of Mary's fascination in the symbolism of spirituality and a testament to working with the community to produce aesthetic public art. Limnerslease was a hub of artistic activity. It was visited by Tennyson, William and Evelyn De Morgan, Edward Burne-Jones, Val Prinsep, Joseph Joachim, Donald Tovey and many others. Here Watts painted, read, talked, wrote and sculpted.

G.F. and Mary Watts created Watts Gallery – a gallery offering not only art for all but also accommodation for apprentice potters who could be nurtured during their professional development in the pottery. Watts had no inherited income: all that he spent he earned. It is remarkable to think that this artistic couple also succeeded in founding a business in the middle of feudal Compton that survived for over fifty years. At its height the Compton Potters' Art Guild was employing a large number of potters producing ceramics for a national market. It was a sustainable business that trained and involved local people. The long-term future of the chapel was safeguarded through the provision of a custodian's house alongside to maintain the site. Similar forward-thinking was used with the gallery when the apprentices left and a 'gentleman curator', a custodian and five attendants were employed, with some living on site to maintain the gallery. They opened the gallery on certain days with a charge of one shilling using a turnstile. This approach is typical of the practical, business-

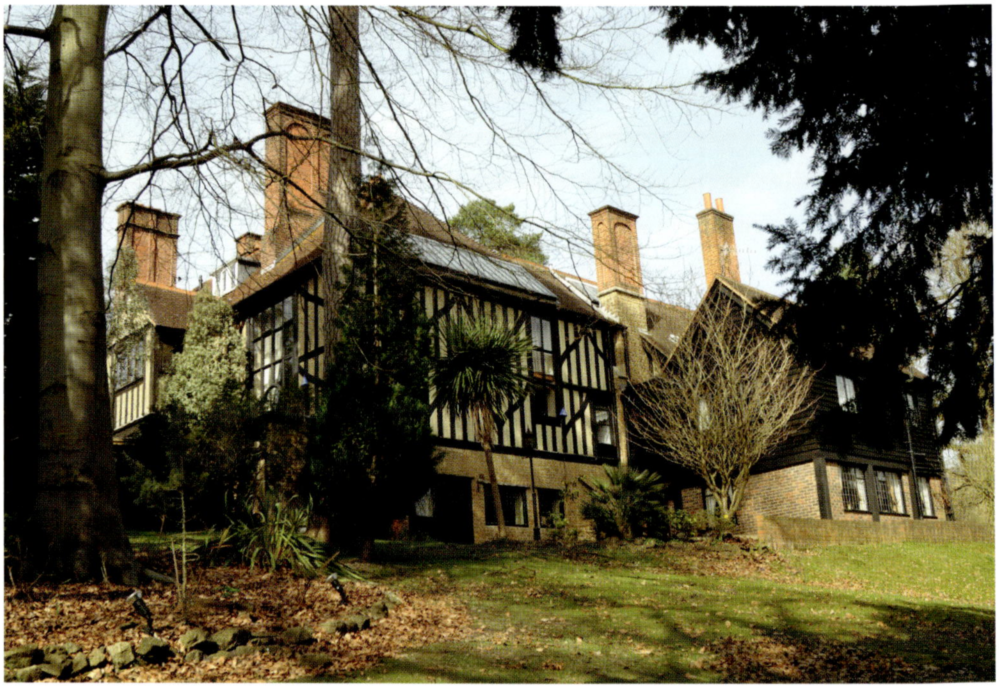

Limnerslease, showing G.F. Watts's studio (centre)

like thinking that informed so much of what G.F. and Mary Watts did to ensure that their legacy survived. The chapel, gallery, pottery, Limnerslease, the crosses on an A3 slip road, a memorial in the garden at Limnerslease, the De Morgan kiln, Compton village hall and Quakers' Acre in Guildford – all demonstrate the Wattses' investment in this small hollow in the Surrey hills called Compton.

How does this vision develop from here? How does one interact with such a complete canvas? First is the desire to bring it back to life to show the creativity and the vision of the period. It is hoped that every visitor to the gallery will want to continue their journey and see the chapel. Every person who falls upon the chapel wants to visit the gallery. Surely, their exploration of Watts should be completed by visiting his home and studio to understand the artist as a man?

The opportunity to secure Limnerslease for the benefit of future generations of visitors, students and the local community would achieve a further step in reviving the Watts village canvas. Visitors could witness the exact place where many of Watts's works were painted, they could enjoy Watts's painting table, easel and paint brushes, and see the views of pines that he painted in his landscapes. Students could stay a while and enjoy the richness of the archive and library while visiting the real buildings and places in which so many of the thoughts and ideas of the nineteenth century have been expressed. Young apprentices could work with master craftsmen or artists in Mary Watts's original craft studios and learn a craft and technical skills sadly lacking in today's school curriculum. Limnerslease could once again become the hub of thinking and creativity by hosting an annual summer school for artists, experts and amateurs to learn the traditional skills of the period, at the same time as feeding from the inspiration of the collection and using the models and écorchés from which Watts himself drew. In this way we shall be able to take the values of the past into the future.

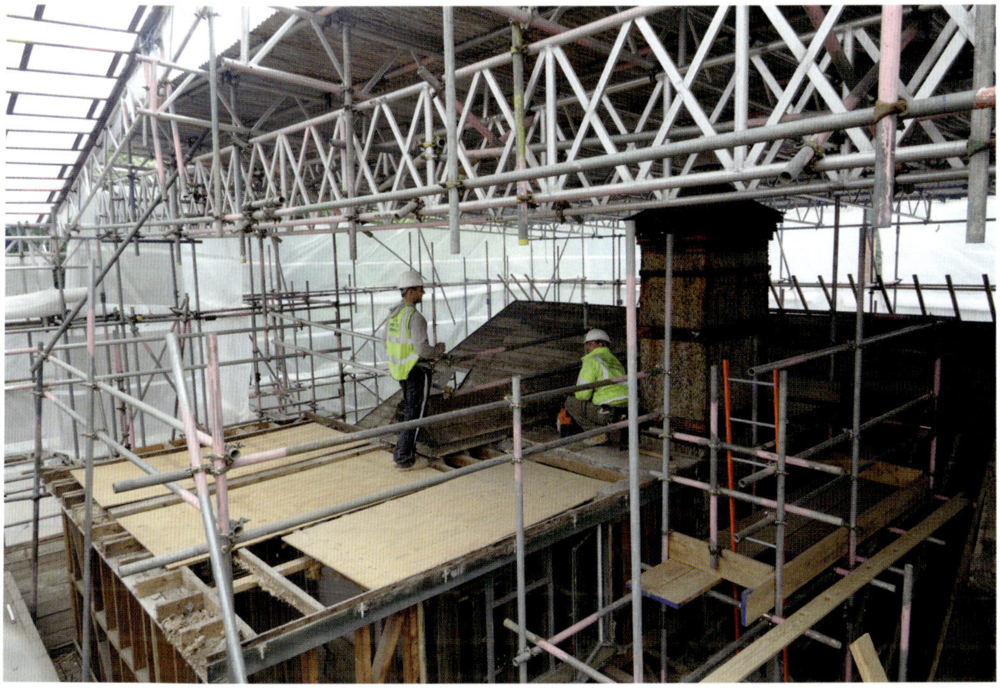

Left: Restoration of Watts Gallery exterior, 2009

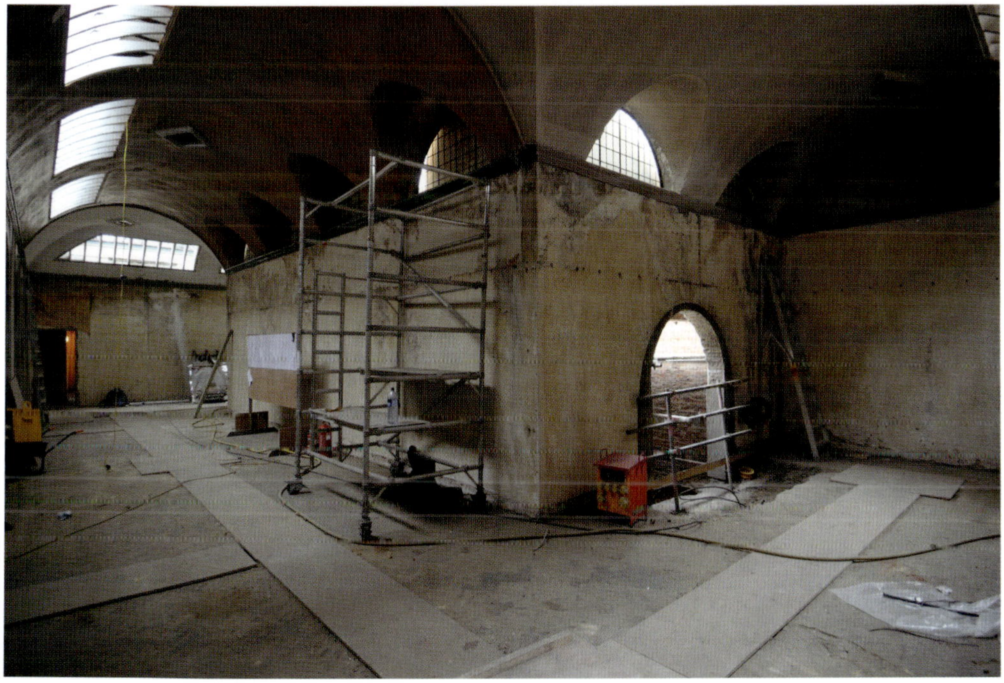

Below left: Restoration of Watts Gallery interior, 2010

Apprenticeship is still highly regarded as the approach to long-term successful learning. The gallery offers the post of assistant curator to trainees, which has resulted in successful careers for every post-holder to date, while the annual artist-in-residence scheme is a further form of apprenticeship for the artist to work with learners, who can be mentored and supported in developing their art. Given the richness of the Watts collection and the tradition of apprenticeships on site, the trustees share a vision of returning the Watts Gallery estate to an active centre for pottery, arts and learning.

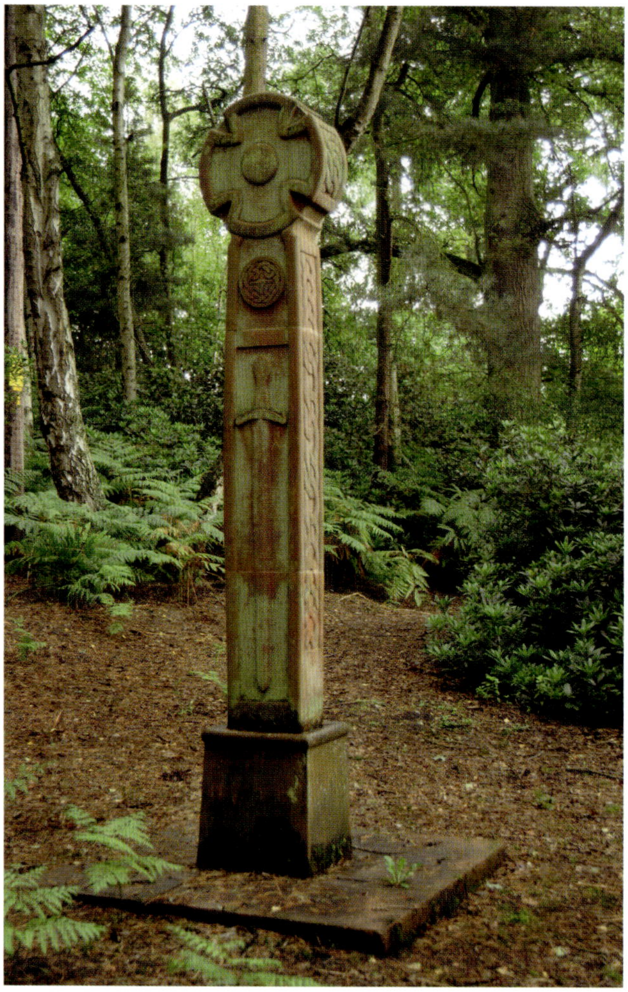

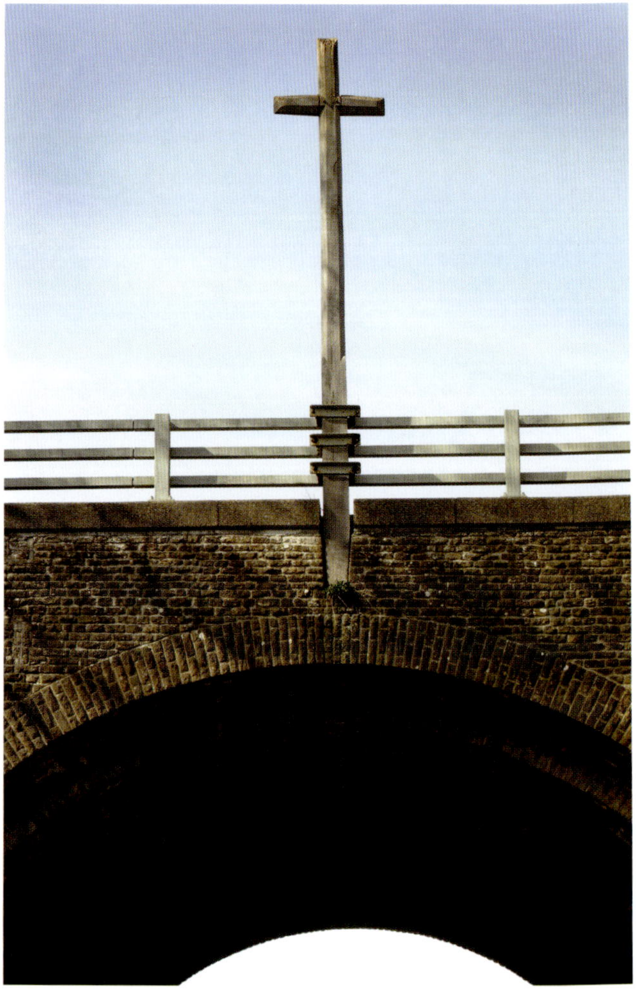

Above left: Pilgrim's Way memorial in the grounds of Limnerslease

Above right: Mary Watts's cross on a Lutyens road bridge over the Pilgrim's Way

Unique is an overused word, but in the case of Compton it earns its place. Where else can one find an artist's home, his gallery, a chapel and pottery founded by him and his wife, as well as memorials a plenty and all within a quarter-of-a-mile area? Wilfrid Blunt mentions that Compton was described by a Berlin newspaper as England's Bayreuth.[7] The village boasts the only purpose-built art gallery for a single professional artist's collection that exists in the UK, and indeed the Bayreuth Festspielhaus, an opera house specially constructed for and exclusively devoted to the performance of Wagner's operas, provides an interesting parallel. In particular, some feel this is true in terms of each artist's widow, who presided so ferociously over their spouse's artistic legacy. Another musical parallel could be Britten's Snape Maltings, which has the composer's home, The Red House, and the library and music room where he wrote nearby.

When Mary Watts died in 1938, Limnerslease was handed over to the Potters' Arts Guild, the contents were dispersed, and the Watts gallery at Tate Britain was closed. Watts's name and Compton's significance as the home of one of Britain's greatest artists went into free-fall and were lost from view. With the return of interest in Victorian art and the tremendous generosity of trustees, donors, benefactors, volunteers and the local community who have supported

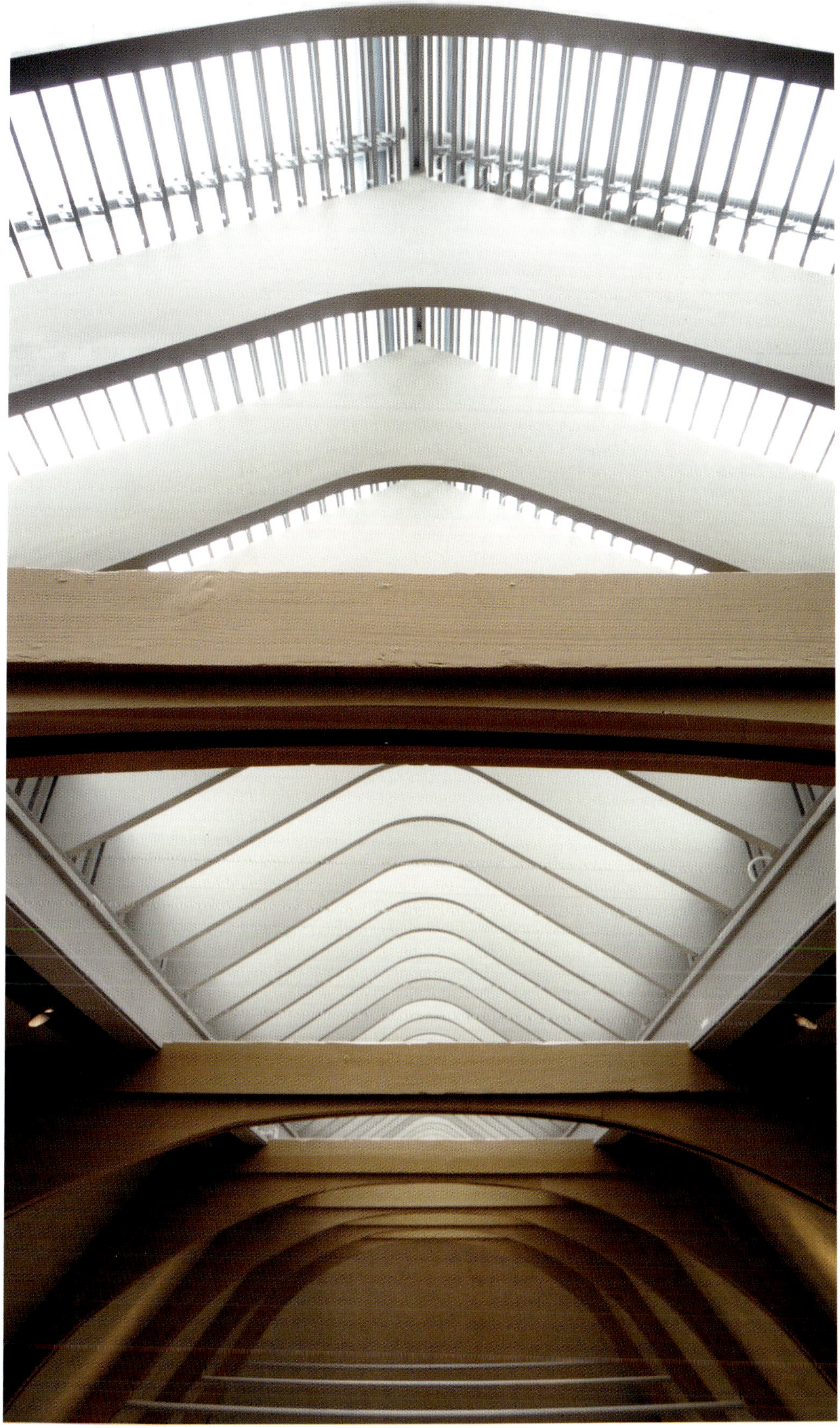

Watts Gallery
after restoration, 2010

the resurgence of Watts in Compton, the Watts village is now a real possibility, and every step in returning Compton to its former glory will be a step along the path originally laid by G.F and Mary Watts in the 1890s.

Watts Gallery lies on the Pilgrim's Way, as do memorials to Watts in the form of a ceramic cross placed there by Mary and wooden crosses on either side of a Lutyens road bridge, which now forms part of a slip road off the A3. On the ceramic cross Mary has written: 'George Frederic Watts OM RA. His Pilgrim's Way. 1891–1904. By his wish this cross placed here.' Originally, pilgrims would have travelled from Canterbury to Winchester to pray for St Swithun, who was buried at Winchester cathedral. The route was then used in reverse as pilgrims journeyed from Winchester to Canterbury cathedral to pray at the shrine of Thomas Becket. At this small intersection, where the Pilgrim's Way meets the North Downs Way, there is another reason for a pilgrimage: an opportunity to experience and view the legacy of one of Britain's most important artists from the nineteenth century and that of his wife Mary Seton Watts, a talented ceramic artist, presented in a visionary cluster of unique buildings with a collection of international importance dedicated to study and learning in the heart of the countryside.

NOTES

1 *G.F. Watts Portraits: Fame and Beauty in Victorian Society*, National Portrait Gallery, London (2004); *The Vision of G.F. Watts*, Compton (2004); *England's Michelangelo: Drawings by G.F. Watts RA, from the Royal Academy Collection*, Royal Academy (2004); *The Symbolic Paintings of G.F. Watts*, Tate Britain (2004).

2 There have only been five curators in the Watts Gallery's 105-year history: Charles H. Thompson (1907–31), Rowland Wright Alston (1931–58), Wilfrid Blunt (1959–85), Richard Jefferies (1985–2006) and Mark Stephen Bills (2006–).

3 Cartwright 1896, p.30.

4 P. Wilkinson, *Restoration Village*, Swindon 2006.

5 The light bulb was placed there when casting in 1957. For more information about Watts's sculpture *Physical Energy*, see S. Brown, *G.F. Watts,* Physical Energy*: Sculpture and Site*, Compton 2007.

6 B. Obama, *Dreams from my Father: A Story of Race and Inheritance*, Edinburgh 2007, ch.14.

7 Blunt 1975, p.230.

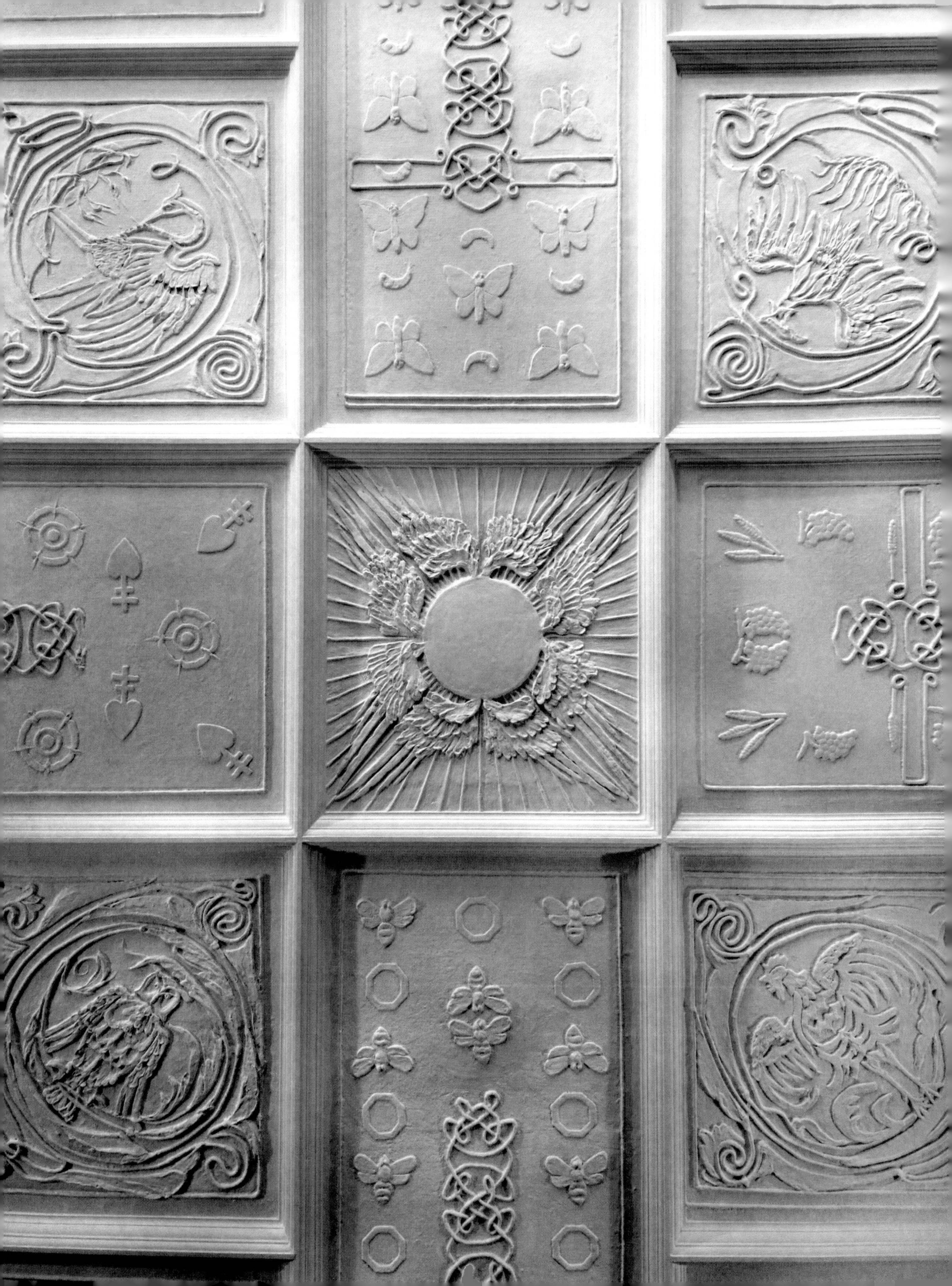

Appendix: Mary Watts's Ceiling Decoration at Limnerslease

Catherine Hilary

During the years 1890 to 1896 Mary Watts designed, created and installed three decorated ceilings in her new home, Limnerslease. These ceilings have survived in a remarkable condition due to the durability of gesso, which Mary used to build up her reliefs. Valuable insight into her interests and research into ancient religions and symbolism, which inspired much of the decoration, is provided in her Chapel Notebook and diaries. The development of, and alterations to, the designs can be found in plans she made of each ceiling.[1]

There are effectively three sections of ceiling decoration, divided up by the architectural structure of the house. The ceiling in the Red Room (sitting room) was the first to be completed in 1891 and was intended as a tribute to G.F. Watts's life and work.[2] The second section is located in the entrance hall at Limnerslease and represents ancient civilizations and religions.[3] The last ceiling decoration, which was added in 1896, was the smallest and was placed next to the bay window at the far side of the Red Room.[4] Mary referred to it as the 'Signor' window ceiling,[5] and it functions as an annexe to the Red Room ceiling since it, too, is clearly dedicated to G.F. Watts. In terms of its timing and the development of her imagery, Mary's ceiling decoration can be seen as a prelude to the creation of her masterpiece, the Watts Chapel.

RED ROOM (SITTING ROOM) CEILING

This ceiling has twenty-one panels: seventeen measure *c.*75 x 80 cm each and four are *c.*79 x 159 cm each. The relief on the central panel is a winged sun. Mary notes that due to its circular shape it is both a symbol of the universe and an ancient symbol of eternity without beginning or end.[6] Since it provides light, the sun is life-giving and has been associated with gladness and strength. The wings of the sun symbolize motion, vitality and goodness as well as providing 'loving shelter'.[7]

From the central panel four large rectangular panels representing different kinds of joy extend to the edges. The joy of work is denoted by bees and cells. The joy of the senses is represented by vines and ears of wheat (for wine and bread). The joy of the soul, which comes from having faith in the life beyond this life, is symbolized by butterflies and chrysalises. And the joy of the heart is shown by Egyptian hieroglyphs depicting hearts with double crosses above them. Each heart is flanked by a rose, which Mary notes is the Christian symbol of compatibility and the Greek or Roman symbol of faithfulness to a friend.[8]

Opposite: The Red Room ceiling

Between each of the panels of joy are four square panels, in which Mary combines trees and birds within swirling circles. An owl, signifying wisdom, is modelled with the tree of knowledge. A phoenix, representing hope, is placed close to an oak, symbolic of strength and durability. An olive tree and a pelican are juxtaposed, indicating peace and love. Watchfulness and patience are represented by a cock and a mulberry tree.

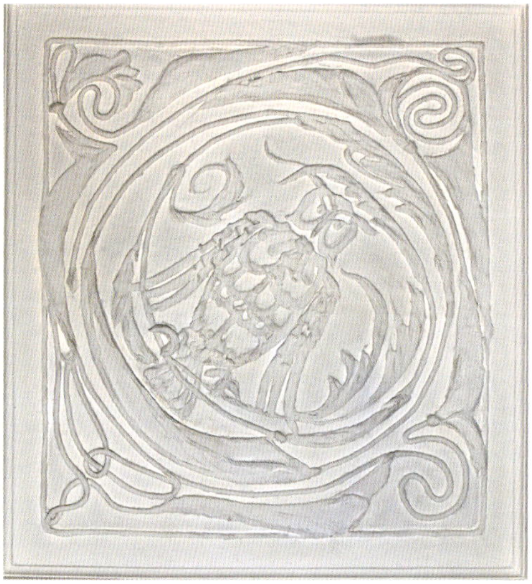

Owl symbolizing wisdom on the Red Room ceiling

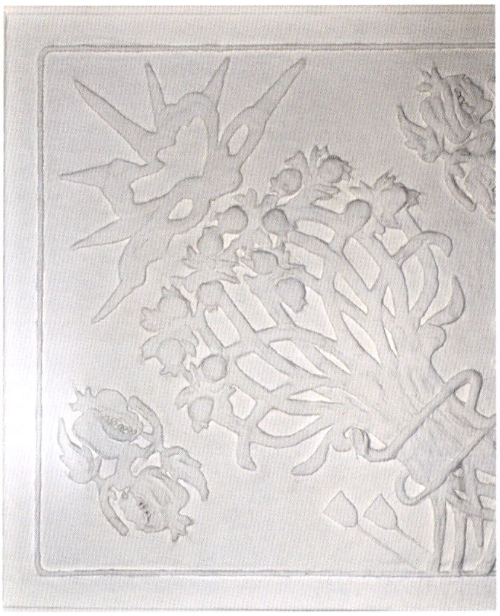

Tree of Knowledge on the Red Room ceiling

Interspersed within this rich symbolism are eight identical panels displaying the hand of blessing with a pattern of a crowned heart entwined with palms. Of the three ceiling decorations, that in the Red Room has the greatest number of parallels with Mary's designs in the Watts chapel.

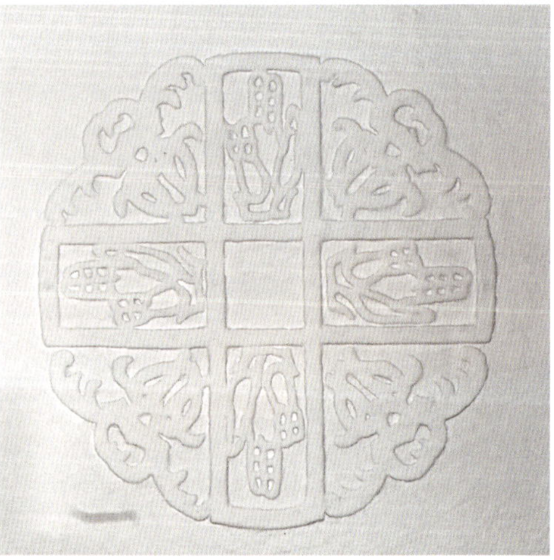

Crowned heart entwined with palms on the Red Room ceiling

HALLWAY CEILING

Mary's design for the second ceiling originally included twenty-two panels, nineteen of which were assigned to specific ancient civilizations and religions. The rest were recorded as, simply, 'symbols'.[9] This design was significantly altered and simplified, as the ceiling now possesses only five of the original nineteen civilization and religion panels. These five panels (each *c.*114 x 89 cm) are all symmetrical in layout and intricately detailed. The first decorated row of the ceiling, parallel to the main entrance and the window, is made up of two large rectangular panels, which depict, respectively, Buddhist and Brahman themes. The next row on this ceiling has three much simpler symbolic panels (each *c.*72 x 66 cm) depicting variations of crosses and suns.

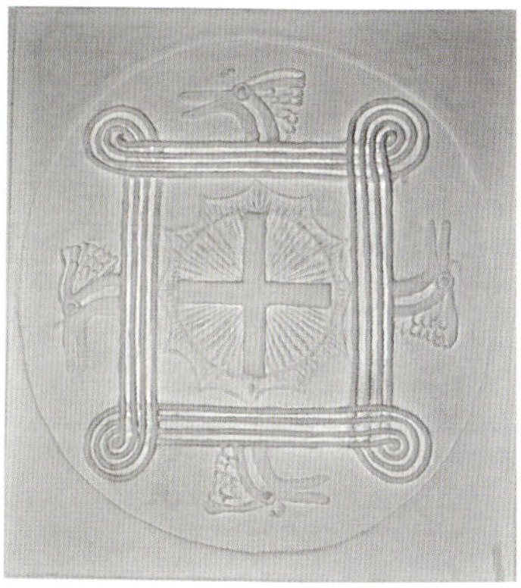

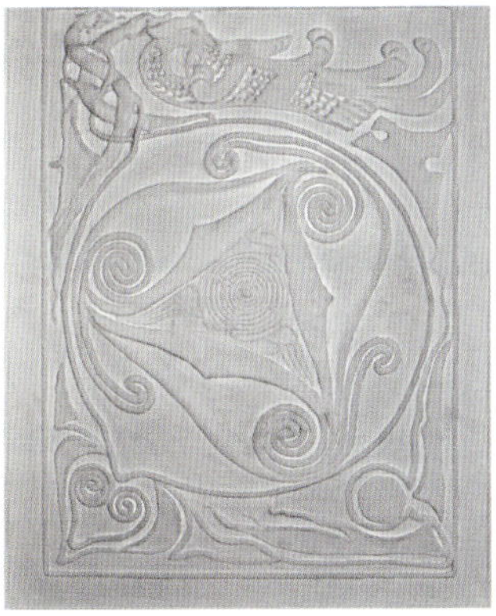

Left: One of the three symbolic panels on the hallway ceiling depicting crosses and suns

Right: One of the seven symbolic panels on the hallway ceiling depicting spirals, a heart, a peacock and a maze

The following larger row includes a Hebrew or Jewish panel, a Chaldean or Assyrian panel, and an Egyptian panel. Alongside the doorway to the Red Room a row of seven symbolic panels (each *c.*73 x 98 cm except the corner panel) depict spirals, hearts, knots and bird imagery. Although each symbolic panel differs, they are typical of the direction in which Mary's style developed as she began to work on the chapel decorations.

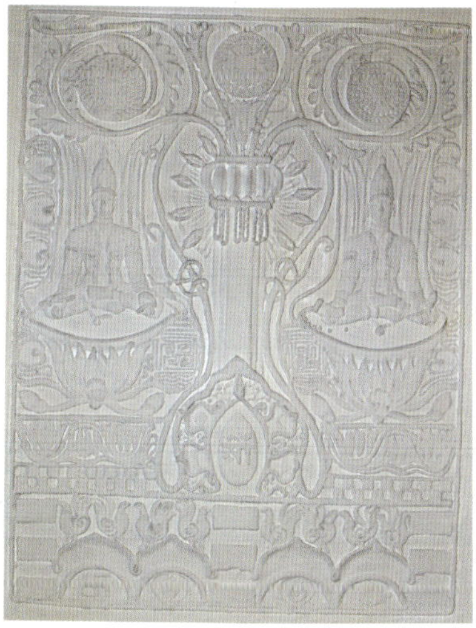

Buddhism panel

The Buddhism panel has two enlightened Narayana figures resting on lotus flowers on water. They are separated by the Bodhi tree, or tree of knowledge. Along the bottom are symbols such as the tortoise, an emblem of Kasyapa, the protector, and a swastika, a prominent symbol on the famous footprints of Buddha.

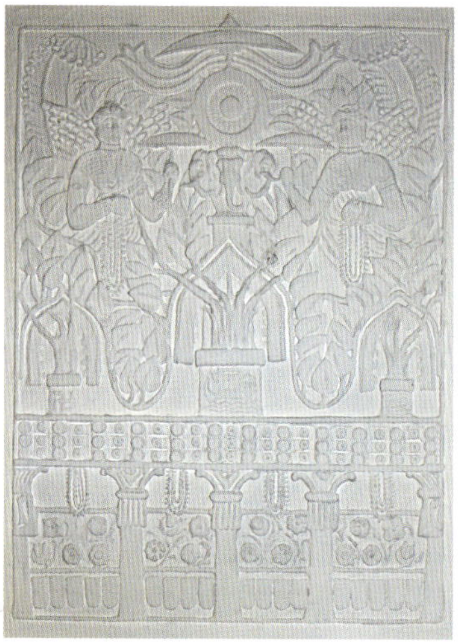

Brahman panel

Brahma, the Hindu god of creation, is represented in the Brahman panel. Some believe that Brahma was self-born in the lotus flower; others believe he was born in water. Mary incorporates both ideas and includes the god's *japa mala* (rosary beads) that he uses to keep track of time. The central motif of the elephant and wheel is Mary's interpretation of a pillar at the northern entrance of Sanchi in India.[10]

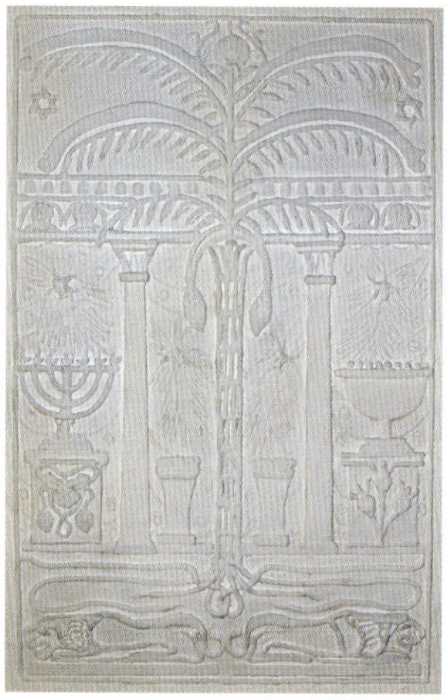

Hebrew panel

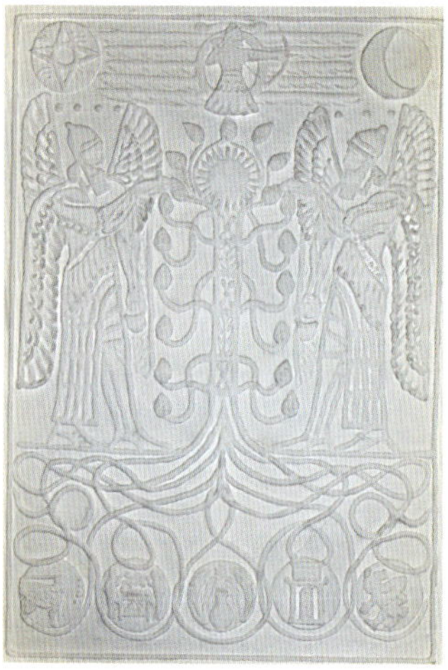

Chaldean panel

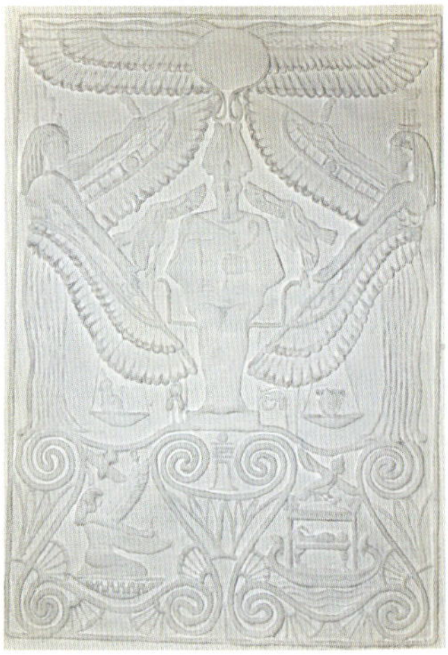

Egyptian panel

The Hebrew or Jewish panel contains symbols such as the Lion of Judah, the Menorah and the Star of David.

The Chaldean or Assyrian panel is almost a direct copy of a *c.*865 BC panel from Nimrud in Assyria brought back to the British Museum by Henry Layard in the mid-nineteenth century.

On the Egyptian panel Mary depicts a typical funeral scene and includes symbols such as scrolls to represent the Book of the Dead, the ankh as the key of life and the lotus flower for rebirth and creation.

THE SIGNOR WINDOW CEILING

The third section of Mary's ceiling decoration has Celtic influences and lettering and is the most autobiographical. It occupies a small space between the Red Room and the bay window and acts as an extension to the 1891 ceiling. It is made up of one rectangular panel (*c.*155 x 148 cm) in the centre, two rectangular

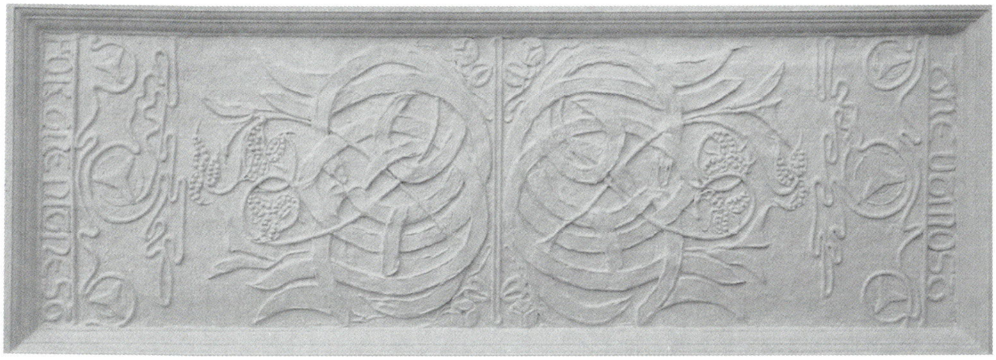

The Signor window ceiling

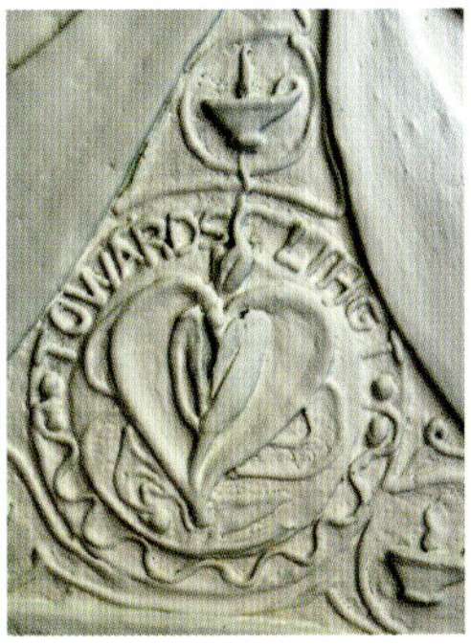

Detail of the square end panel in the Signor window ceiling with the text 'Towards Lihgt [sic]'.

panels (each *c.*24 x 77 cm) on either side and two panels (each *c.*58 x 52 cm) at each end. It was designed and begun at the same time as the ceiling in the Red Room but not installed until 1896. The central panel depicts a starry sky with spiralling plants reflected in a pool. G.F. Watts's motto, 'The Utmost for the Highest', is divided across the top and bottom. The four rectangles on either side are each different and are decorated with the image of the pelican, symbolizing love, interwoven with wings, knots and hearts. The squares at each end are made up of triangular shapes with swirling scrolls at the joins. Inside these Mary has inserted the words, 'Towards lihgt [light]', 'A Little Child', 'To lease among the sheaves', and 'With the sun', and added corresponding imagery. The Latin words in the small semicircles extending across two square panels at each end read 'Lux' (Light) and 'Pax' (Peace). In the semicircles opposite, Mary adds at one end her husband's birthday, 'February 23 1817', and at the other, 'Limnerslease 1891'.

NOTES

1 All in Watts Gallery Archive.

2 MSW Diaries, 25 January 1891. Mary shows her ceiling design to her husband and writes that it 'is the concrete expression of the spiritual atmosphere that Signor has around him – the aroma of his thought put into the silent language of my symbols'.

3 Mary notes that she and George are reading books on Chaldean and Buddhist religions in her 1893 diary (2, 9 and 15 January). On 13 March 1893 she records making her design: 'I have thought out too a sort of scheme of design which I think will be decorative and carry the meaning to be crowded into it well.'

4 Mary's diary entry on Wednesday, 21 October 1896, reads: 'The window panels are all up. I am glad they are but I think I should like to do them all over again.'

5 Mary refers to this ceiling as the 'Signor' window ceiling on her design on a loose sheet of paper, Watts Gallery Archive.

6 Ibid.

7 Ibid.

8 Ibid.

9 Design for hallway ceiling, MSW Chapel Notebook. At one time Mary's plan also included panels representing 'Seanti [?]', 'Greek', 'Hebrew', 'Central America', 'Persia', 'Scandinavia', 'Nomad', 'China' and 'Christian'.

10 Drawing and notes, MSW Chapel Notebook.

CHRONOLOGY

1817
23 February: George Frederic Watts is born in Queen Street, Bryanston Square, London.

1849
25 November: Mary Seton Fraser Tytler is born in Ahmednagar, India.

1870–73
Mary receives professional art training at the South Kensington Schools and the Slade.

1881
G.F. Watts has a gallery built at Little Holland House for the display of his collection.
Winter: Watts has a full-scale retrospective exhibition of over 200 of his paintings at the Grosvenor Gallery, London.

1884–85
Watts exhibits fifty works at the Metropolitan Museum of Art in New York.

1886
20 November: G.F. Watts marries Mary Seton Fraser Tytler in Epsom, Surrey.
Mary is elected to the Council of the Home Arts.

1886–87
George and Mary honeymoon in Egypt, Constantinople, Athens and Messina.

1889–90
The Wattses spend the winter with Andrew and May Hichens at Monkshatch in Compton.

1890
24 March: Mr More Molyneux of the Loseley estate accepts an offer from Hichens for £200 per acre for the site at Compton. The Wattses employ the architect Ernest George to design Limnerslease, and building work begins on 20 June.

1891
18 July: The Wattses take possession of Limnerslease.

1891–96
Mary creates the ceiling relief decoration at Limnerslease.

1894
25 May: Compton Parish Council resolves to purchase grassland on Budborough (now Budburrow) Hill on which to build a cemetery.

1895
A cardboard model of the cemetery chapel is made.
9 August: Mary finishes the design and discusses it with the architect George Redmayne, FRIBA.
2 October: Compton Parish Council pays William More Molyneux of Loseley £74 7s for three-quarters of an acre on Budburrow Hill.
November: Mary turns the billiard room at Limnerslease into a studio for her Thursday-evening Terra Cotta Home Arts classes for the local villagers.

1896
March: Mary is granted permission to sink a well at the cemetery's northern edge.

1897
Decorations for the chapel are exhibited at the annual Home Arts and Industries exhibition held in the circular upper gallery of the Albert Hall. Tate Gallery devotes two rooms to Watts's work.

1898
The building and exterior decoration of the chapel are completed. The chapel doors are exhibited at the annual Home Arts and Industries exhibition held at the Albert Hall.
1 July: The chapel is consecrated by the Bishop of Winchester, Randall Davidson.
13 December: Watts begins to use the gallery's Barn Studio for sculpting *Tennyson*.

1899
The altar design of the chapel is exhibited at the annual Home Arts and Industries exhibition held at the Albert Hall. The Wattses complete payment to the Hichenses for Limnerslease estate.

1901
A census is taken for Limnerslease estate. Plans for the pottery buildings are drawn up. James Nicol arrives from Scotland to manage the pottery industry.

1902
Watts is awarded the Order of Merit by King Edward VII.

1903
23 February: The foundation stone of the Watts Gallery is laid on G.F. Watts's eighty-sixth birthday.
September: The art gallery at Compton is completed and paintings arrive from Little Holland House.

1904
1 April: The Watts Gallery opens and includes a hostel for up to twelve apprentice potters.
15 April: A small version of G.F. Watts's *All-Pervading* is hung over the altar, completing the decoration of the interior of the Watts Chapel.
1 July: G.F. Watts dies, aged eighty-seven. His ashes are placed in the chapel in a casket designed by Thomas Wren.

*c.*1904
The Watts Gallery closes, and an extension is designed by the gallery's architect Christopher Hatton Turnor.

1905–6
A memorial exhibition of Watts's collection is held in London, Manchester, Newcastle, Edinburgh and Dublin.

1906
The Watts Gallery reopens after the addition of an extension including the Sculpture Gallery.

*c.*1906
Little Holland House in Kensington is sold by Mary Watts.

1911
The cloister above the chapel to the east is completed.

1915
Mary extends a kitchen garden at the Barn Studio and a Roman villa is discovered.

1916–21
Mary produces gesso decoration for a second chapel at the Cambridge Military Hospital in Aldershot.

1923
A fire at the pottery causes the destruction of the upper floor and most of the stock.

*c.*1925
The Sunken Gallery, designed by Laurence Powell, is added to the Watts Gallery.

1930
James Nicol retires as manager of Compton Pottery.

1934
Mary resigns as director of the pottery. The Watts Gallery curator, Rowland Alston, replaces her.

1938
Mary Watts dies. Trustees organize a redecoration and re-hang in the Watts Gallery. Final Watts room at the Tate closes and is used for special exhibitions. Limnerslease is made over to the Potters' Arts Guild; many contents are sold.

1938–45
Limnerslease is used by Ardente, which produces radar and sonar for the navy.

1951
Announcement of the closure of the pottery company.

1952
Limnerslease sale.

1956
David Dunhill tries to save the business but it finally closes on 14 August.

1959–85
Wilfrid Blunt is Curator of Watts Gallery.

2008
Watts Gallery closes for *Hope*, a major restoration project.

2011
Watts Gallery reopens.

BIBLIOGRAPHY

BATEMAN 1901
Charles T. Bateman, 'Mr. G F Watts and his art', *Windsor Magazine,* June 1901

BILLS 2010
Mark Bills, *Watts Chapel: A Guide to the Symbols of Mary Watts's Arts and Crafts Masterpiece*, London 2010

BILLS AND BRYANT 2008
Mark Bills and Barbara Bryant, *G F Watts: Victorian Visionary,* London 2008

BLUNT 1975
Wilfrid Blunt, *England's Michelangelo: A Biography of George Frederic Watts*, London 1975

BORZELLO 1987
Frances Borzello, *Civilizing Caliban: The Misuse of Art 1875–1980,* London 1987

BOSTON 1987
Cecilia Lady Boston, *The History of Compton in Surrey* (1933), reprinted Compton 1987

BROCK 1906
A. Clutton Brock, 'A Surrey Shrine', *Tribune*, 4 June 1906

CALVERT 2006
Hilary Calvert, *Compton Pottery,* Watts Gallery 2006

CARTWRIGHT 1896
Julia Cartwright, 'George Frederic Watts, R.A.', *Art Journal: Easter Annual*, 1896

CHAPMAN 1945
Ronald Chapman, *The Laurel and the Thorn: A Study of G F Watts,* London 1945

CHAPMAN 1969
Ronald Chapman, *The Education of Davey Porteous*, London 1969

ERSKINE *c.*1901
Mrs Steuart Erskine, 'Mrs G.F. Watts' terra-cotta Industry', unsourced magazine article, Watts Gallery Archive, n.d. [*c.*1898–1904, probably *c.*1901]

ERSKINE 1906
Mrs Steuart Erskine, 'The Watts Memorial Gallery at Limnerslease', *Studio*, August 1906

FFOULKES 1903
Charles John Ffoulkes, *An Exhibition of Modern Celtic Ornament* …, exh. cat., Grafton Galleries, London, n.d. [1903?]

FRANKLIN GOULD 1993
Veronica Franklin Gould, *The Watts Chapel: An Arts and Crafts Memorial*, Compton, 1993

FRANKLIN GOULD 1998
Veronica Franklin Gould, *Mary Seton Watts (1849–1938): Unsung Heroine of the Art Nouveau*, exh. cat., Watts Gallery, Compton 1998

FRANKLIN GOULD 2004
Veronica Franklin Gould, *G.F. Watts: The Last Great Victorian*, New Haven and London 2004

FRIEDERICHS 1895
Hulda Friederichs, 'An Interview with Mr. G. F. Watts, R.A.', *The Young Woman,* December 1895

HAKING 1906
Hilda Haking, *The Shrine of G.F. Watts, R.A., in his Surrey Home*, London 1906, p.5, first published in the *Girl's Realm,* September 1905

*HOME ARTS AND INDUSTRIES ASSOCIATION c.*1895
A Notice of the Work and Objects of the Home Arts and Industries Association, pamphlet, Watts Gallery Archive, n.d. [*c.*1895].

LETHABY 2004
W.R. Lethaby, *Architecture, Mysticism and Myth* (1892), Mineola, NY, 2004

LIBERTY & CO. 1904
Liberty & Co., *Book of Garden Ornaments*, sales catalogue, London 1904

MARSH 1982
Jan Marsh, *Back to the Land: The Pastoral Impulse in Victorian England from 1880 to 1914*, London 1982

MSW CHAPEL NOTEBOOK
M.S. Watts, Chapel Notebook (no page numbers), *c.*1886–1904, Watts Gallery Archive

MSW DAY BOOK
M.S. Watts, Day Book, 1870–86, Watts Gallery Archive

MSW DIARIES
M.S. Watts, Diaries, 9 vols, 1887–1908 (incomplete run with pages missing), Watts Gallery Archive

MSW DIARY NOTES
M.S. Watts, Diary Notes, 1886–1904 (made by Mary Watts for her biography of G.F. Watts from diaries many of which are no longer in existence), Watts Gallery Archive

'REPORT ON THE POTTERS' ARTS GUILD'
'Report on the Potters' Arts Guild', undated typescript [*c.*1936], Watts Gallery Archive

RUSKIN 1903–12
John Ruskin, *The Works of John Ruskin*, ed. E.T. Cook and Alexander Wedderburn, 39 vols, London 1903–12

THOMSON 1906
David Croal Thomson, 'The New Watts Gallery at Compton', *Art Journal*, November 1906

TURNOR MEMOIRS
Christopher Hatton Turnor, handwritten memoirs, private archive, n.d.

WATTS 1905
M.S. Watts, *The Word in the Pattern: A Key to the Symbols on the Walls of the Chapel at Compton by Mrs George Frederic Watts*, London 1905

WATTS *c.*1910
'Catalogue of the Works of G.F. Watts, compiled by his widow', three unpublished manuscript volumes of paintings compiled by M.S. Watts, begun *c.*1910 and continued thereafter, Watts Gallery Archive. The first volume contains 'Subject' pictures (which includes every painting except portraits) and the other two, his portraits.

WATTS 1912
M.S. Watts, *George Frederic Watts: The Annals of an Artist's Life*, 3 vols, London 1912

WATTS 2000
M.S. Watts, *The Word in the Pattern: A Key to the Symbols on the Walls of the Chapel at Compton by Mrs George Frederic Watts*, Compton 2000 (first published 1905)

WEBB 1911
Wilfred Mark Webb, 'The Potters' Art Guild at Compton', *Country Homes*, November 1911

WILSON 2004
Shelagh Wilson, 'Watts, women, philanthropy and the home arts', in Colin Trodd and Stephanie Brown, eds, *Representations of G.F. Watts: Art Making in Victorian Culture*, Aldershot 2004, pp.169–83

WOOD 1902
Esther Wood, 'The Home Arts and Industries Association', *Studio*, vol. 26, July 1902

INDEX

Aitchison, George 33, 122–33
Aldourie Pottery 13, 105, 117
Alexander Morton & Co. 106, 134
Alexandra, Queen 106
Alston, Rowland 115, 118, 132–34, 155, 163
Andrew, Eve 77
Andrews, George 29, 34
Ardente Company 43, 115, 132, 163
Arnold, Matthew 53
Art Workers' Guild 57, 60
Arts and Crafts 9, 16–18, 33, 40, 47, 52–53, 56–57, 60, 63–68, 71, 79, 95, 98, 106, 108, 124, 143, 164
Ashbee, Charles Robert 56–57, 68, 79
Aubertin, George 111, 115

Baden-Powell, General Robert 36
Balcarres, Lord 127
Barnett, Rev. Samuel 49, 53, 67
Barnsley, Sidney 57
Barrington, Mrs Russell 16, 22, 25, 49, 126, 135
Barrow, George 71, 75
Bartlett School of Architecture 144
Bayreuth Festspielhaus 152
Restoration (BBC TV series, 2006) 139–40, 147, 155
Becket, St Thomas 154
Bell, Vanessa 29
Benson, Edward (Archbishop of Canterbury) 70
Bills, Mark 44–45, 98, 134, 137, 143, 147, 155, 164
Blow, Detmar 57
Blunt, Anthony 133
Blunt, Wilfrid 15, 19, 22–23, 63, 88, 117, 133–4, 152, 155, 163–4
Bone, Charles 116
Boxall, Albert 71, 75
British Museum 68, 88, 160
Britten, Benjamin 152
Brownlow, Lord Adelbert 47–48, 54, 63–64
Brunt-Nye, Thomas 105
Bryant, Barbara 22, 44–45, 134, 147, 164
Budburrow Hill 87, 162
Burne-Jones, Edward 67, 73, 98, 112–3, 149
Butler, Josephine 36, 45

Cambridge 11, 106–7, 147, 163
Cameron, Julia Margaret 12–13, 22
Candlin, Mr 114
Canterbury Cathedral 154
Carlyle, Thomas 68, 83
Cartwright, Julia 16, 22, 29–30, 33, 36, 44–45, 155, 164
Century Guild 57, 68
Chapman, Ronald 22, 42, 44–45, 164
Clack, Estcourt James 43
Columba, St 90
Compton Potters' Arts Guild 79, 104, 111–2
Conway, Richard 146
Cottage Arts Association 47, 56
Council of the Home Arts 54, 162
Courtauld Institute of Art 137, 147–8
Cummins, Harvey 75
Cumnock Pottery 105

Dalou, Aimé-Jules 13, 22, 67, 103
Davidson, Randall 77, 162
Dean, Ptolemy 140–1
Della Robbia Pottery 33–34, 45, 56, 68, 103, 117
De Morgan, William Frend 67, 70, 75, 103, 149
Deuchars, Louis 59, 73, 75, 77, 105, 117
Devey, George 56
Dewar, Hamish 142
Dressler, Conrad 68, 103
Duckworth, George 29
Duncan, John 98
Dunhill, David 116, 118, 163

Elgin Marbles 37, 127
Ellice, Arabella 109
Erskine, Mrs Steuart 17, 23, 117, 134–5, 164

Farnham 56
Farran, E. Gertrude 106
Fisher, Alexander 79
Fitzgerald, Hazelwood Beardsley 125, 134
Ford, Sir Brinsley 118, 139
Friederichs, Hulda 22, 34, 44–45, 164

George, Sir Ernest 9, 26, 31, 75, 105, 149, 162
Gilbert, Alfred 113
Gillet, Hugh 70, 77, 83
Gillet, Margaret 109–10
Gladstone, William 36
Glasgow School of Art 105
Godalming 27–28, 111
Grafton Gallery 65, 106, 108, 164
Greene, Plunket 34
Greenfield, Harriet 109
Grey, Earl (Governor General of Canada) 106
Grey, Hon. Mabel de 56
Grosvenor Gallery 9-10, 48, 162
Guild of Handicraft 17, 56–57, 68
Guild of St George 57
Guild of Women Binders 57, 106
Guildford 48–49, 56, 83, 111, 113, 116, 150
Guildhall Art Gallery 143, 146–7

Haking, Hilda 22–23, 41–42, 45, 118, 164
Head, Mary A. 29
Helmstead 105
Heritage Lottery Fund 141, 148
Hichens, Andrew 17, 19, 25–26, 28–29, 40, 127, 162
Hichens, May 17, 19, 25–26, 28–29, 40, 127, 162

Hill, Miranda 49
Hog's Back 56, 109
Holland, Lincoln 56
Holroyd, Sir Charles 127, 130
Home Arts and Industries Association 16, 47–8, 51–55, 59–60, 63–65, 67, 78, 103, 118, 164–5
Home Arts Exhibition 60, 73, 75, 79
Hope Project 139, 141–3, 147–8
Horsfall, T.C. 49
Horticultural Hall 61, 63, 65, 118
Hunt, Jeremy 147

Illustrated London News 37–8, 45
International Art Congress (1908) 130, 135
Iona 90

Jebb, Eglantyne Louisa 47, 63, 75
Jefferies, Richard 64, 118, 130, 132, 137, 139, 143, 155
Jekyll, Gertrude 57, 64, 108
Joachim, Joseph 34, 36, 149
Johnson, Ivy 111
Jones, Griff Rhys 139

Kelmscott Manor 52, 56–57
Kemp, Julia 146
Kyrle Society 49

Lake, John 70
Layard, Henry 160
Leighton, Sir Frederic 15, 25, 29–30, 52
Leland, Charles 47
Lethaby, W.R. 95, 98, 100, 164
Liberty & Co. 59, 65, 79, 81, 106, 108–9, 117, 164
Limnerslease 9, 14, 17, 19–20, 25–6, 28–34, 36–45, 51, 53–54, 56, 61, 63, 67–8, 70–71, 73, 75, 79, 87, 93, 100, 103, 105–6, 115, 122–3, 130, 132, 135, 146, 149–50, 152, 157, 161–4
Lincoln Cathedral 40
Little Holland House 11–13, 16–18, 22, 25–26, 29–30, 40–41, 45, 67, 100, 122–3, 126–7, 130, 134, 148, 162–3
Loseley Estate 26, 70–71, 105, 162
Lutyens, Edwin 57, 108, 124, 152, 154

McGill University, Montreal 106
Mackintosh, Lilian 29
Mackmurdo, A.H. 57, 60, 65, 68
Macmillan, Hugh 11, 22
Manchester City Art Gallery 49
Martin, John 75
Mary, Queen 108, 113
May, Marion 142
Melbury Road 25, 29, 87, 122
Metropolitan Museum of Art, New York 11, 162
Michelangelo 33, 133, 155, 164
Mitchell, Frank 75
Molyneux, William More 26, 70, 162
Monkshatch17, 20–21, 25–30, 34, 77, 125, 162
Montefiore, Claude 93
Morris, William 52, 56–57, 65, 71, 98, 117–8

National Association for the Advancement of Art and its Application to Industry 17, 22, 64
National Gallery 126, 130, 134–5
National Portrait Gallery 22, 41, 45, 83, 121, 137, 144, 155
New Gallery, Regent Street 60, 63, 93
Nicol, James 79, 105, 114, 117, 162–3
Northern Art Workers' Guild 57

Obama, Barack 22, 143, 155
Ormond, Richard 139
Oxford 11, 33, 77, 133, 145

Parthenon 36, 45
Pike, David 142
Pilgrim's Way 110, 152, 154
Postman's Park 147–8
Potters' Arts Guild 57, 59–60, 79, 81, 83, 104–5, 107–12, 115, 117–8, 132, 149, 152, 163, 165
Powell, Herbert 127
Powell, Laurence 130, 163
Prince Albert 98
Prinsep, Val 25, 149
Prior, E.S. 57

Quaker's Acre 159

Rathbone, Harold 68
Redmayne, George 59, 70, 87, 162
Riccardo, Halsey Ralph 75
Riviere, Briton 17
Rossetti, Dante Gabriel 73
Royal Academy 135, 137, 155
Royal Albert Hall 54, 59, 65
Royal Botanic Society 109
Royal Holloway College 147
Royal Horticultural Society 109
Royal Hospital for Sick Children 68, 70, 98
Royal Navy 115
Rural Industries Board 116
Ruskin, John 16, 51–53, 56–57, 60, 63–64, 67, 71, 93, 100, 165

St Paul's Cathedral 146–7
Sayce, Archibald 93, 100
Saywell, Ray 108
Sex, Clarence 75, 82–3
Shaw, Norman 56
Sheridan, Elizabeth 111
Shultz, Robert Weir 124
Slade School of Art 13, 47, 67, 162
Smith, James 54, 63–64
Smith, Mr P. 116
Snape Maltings 154
Society for the Protection of Ancient Buildings 56
South Kensington Art Training Schools 13, 47, 162
South London Gallery 22, 51, 63
Staley, Allen 147
Steadman, Thomas 75
Sturgis, Julian Russell 109
Suhr, Marianne 140
Surrey Advertiser 84, 125–6, 134–5
Surrey County Council 116, 118

Tate Britain 11, 20, 22, 37–38, 41, 45, 121, 126, 130, 132, 134–5, 137, 142, 144, 152, 154, 162–3
Tennyson, Alfred Lord 40, 98, 101, 148–9
Terry, Ellen 12
Thompson, Charles 125, 130, 135, 155
Thompson, George 38, 45
Thomson, David Croal 121, 134–5, 165
Times, The 22, 83, 132–5
Tovey, Donald 34, 45, 149
Traquair, Phoebe Anna 68, 70, 83, 95, 98

Turnor, Christopher Hatton 33–34, 36, 44–45, 123–4, 127, 134, 163, 165
Tytler, Charles Edward Fraser 12

University College London 144, 147
University for the Creative Arts 148–9

Vernon, Gertrude 109
Victoria & Albert Museum 65, 106–7, 127
Voysey, C.F.A. 108–9
Vesci, Countess de 69

Wagner, Richard 108, 152
Waterford, Lady 84, 103
Watts, G.F., works of:
—All-Pervading, The 79–80, 98
—Can These Bones Live? 39
—Court of Death, The 37, 45
—End of the Day 39, 45
—Good Samaritan, The 126
—Green Summer 39, 45
—Hope 11, 22, 140, 142–3
—Mammon 11
—Physical Energy 29, 40, 44, 125, 130, 142, 144–5, 148, 155
—Tennyson 29, 39–41, 44, 125, 130, 145–6, 162
— Time, Death and Judgement 48
— Sea Ghost, A 14–15
— Surrey Landscape 39
Watts, Mary Seton, works of:
—Epsom Beggar, The 54–55
—Mother and Child 13, 68
— Word in the Pattern, The 59, 75, 77, 79, 81, 87, 93–94, 98, 100, 106, 165
Weald and Downland Museum 141
Webb, Philip 57, 64–65, 71, 112
Weeks, Osmund 67
White, Maud Valerie 34, 45
Whitechapel Art Gallery 22, 49
Wilde, Oscar 11, 22
Williams-Ellis, Clough 105
Wilson, Shelagh 17, 23, 63–64, 117, 165
Witt, Sir Robert 139
Wonham, Martha 'Cis' 105
Wood, Christopher 145, 147
World, The (magazine) 13
World War, First 41, 60, 106, 109, 111, 113
World War, Second 43
Wren, Thomas H. 29, 59, 79, 83, 106–7, 113, 115, 125, 139, 163
Yeats, W.B. 95

Zombory-Moldovan Moore Architects 143–44